THE JOURNAL OF
JOHN WESLEY

The
Journal of John Wesley

A SELECTION

Edited with an Introduction

by

ELISABETH JAY

Oxford   New York

OXFORD UNIVERSITY PRESS

1987

Oxford University Press, Walton Street, Oxford OX2 6DP

Oxford New York Toronto
Delhi Bombay Calcutta Madras Karachi
Petaling Jaya Singapore Hong Kong Tokyo
Nairobi Dar es Salaam Cape Town
Melbourne Auckland
and associated companies in
Beirut Berlin Ibadan Nicosia

Oxford is a trade mark of Oxford University Press

British Library Cataloguing in Publication Data
Wesley, John
The journal of John Wesley: a selection.
1. Wesley, John 2. Methodist Church—
Clergy—Biography. 3. Clergy—England—
Biography
I. Title II. Jay, Elisabeth
287'.092'4   BX8495.W5
ISBN 0-19-212268-1
ISBN 0-19-281859-7 Pbk

Library of Congress Cataloging in Publication Data
Wesley, John, 1703-1791.
The journal of John Wesley.
Bibliography: p.
Includes index.
1. Wesley, John, 1703-1791—Diaries. 2. Methodist
Church—Clergy—Biography. I. Jay, Elisabeth.
II. Title.
BX8495.W5A3   1987   287'.092'4   [B]   87-1563
ISBN 0-19-212268-1
ISBN 0-19-281859-7 (pbk.)

Set by Latimer Trend & Company Ltd.
Printed in Great Britain by
The Guernsey Press Co. Ltd.
Guernsey, Channel Islands

Contents

CHRONOLOGY

1703   17 June, John Wesley born, fifteenth child and second surviving son of Samuel Wesley (Rector of Epworth, Lincolnshire) and Susanna (née Annesley).

1707   Charles Wesley born.

1709   John Wesley last of the children to be rescued from the fire which devastated Epworth Rectory. The providential sense of being 'a brand plucked from out of the burning' made a lasting impression on Wesley (see the epigraph to the Hopkey Journal, Appendix A and planned epitaph: *Journal* entry for 26 November 1753).

1714   Admitted as 'poor scholar' to Charterhouse.

1720   Entered Christ Church, Oxford.

1725   Ordained deacon. April to September assisted father in parochial duties. (Also August 1727–September 1728 and October 1728–November 1729.)

1726   March, elected Fellow of Lincoln College, Oxford.

1728   Ordained to the priesthood.

1729   November, returned to Oxford to undertake teaching and supervision of undergraduates; joined and became leader of an informal study group whose members attempted to rule their lives in accordance with Anglican pietistic tradition (e.g. frequent attendance at Holy Communion). Group variously designated 'the Sacramentarians', the 'Godly' or 'Holy Club', or 'the Methodists'. Charles Wesley had been a founder member of this group.

1735   October, three members of the Holy Club, Benjamin Ingham, John and Charles Wesley, together with Charles Delamotte sailed for the new American colony of Georgia, founded by James Oglethorpe (soldier and philanthropist) partly as a settlement for debtors discharged from prison. John Wesley was particularly drawn by the opportunity for a mission to the heathen. Detailed daily *Journal* begun on the sea voyage. On board began his first close acquaintance with German Moravians from Herrnhut.

1736   February, arrived in Savannah.

1737   December, left for England, depressed by the Sophia Hopkey affair (see Appendix A) and the apparent failure of his ministry.

1738   February, back in England Wesley met Peter Böhler, a Moravian pastor preparing to work in America. Böhler was emphatic on the need for personal faith and assurance of salvation. Wesley joined a religious society in London, comprised of Böhler's friends, which met for study, prayer, and mutual confession. At such a meeting in Aldersgate St. on 24 May Wesley experienced conversion. (Charles Wesley had had a similar experience three days earlier.)

14 June, Wesley set out with Benjamin Ingham for Germany to strengthen his faith and seek fellowship with the Moravian Brethren.

16 September, returned to England and immediately 'began again to declare in my own country the glad tidings of salvation'.

1739   2 April, responded to George Whitefield's call and preached his first open-air sermon at Bristol. (Whitefield, a one-time member of the Holy Club, was now a popular preacher, but banned from many Anglican pulpits. He wished to return to his ministry in America and asked Wesley to continue his work in Bristol, preaching wherever opportunity arose. See *Journal* entry for 31 March 1739.)

May, ground purchased for the first Methodist meeting-house at Bristol.

June, foundation of the school at Kingswood, for poor children and older people.

Later that year Wesley acquired the Foundery at London as a Methodist meeting-house, school, home for his preachers, and ultimately for his own family.

End of the year, witnessed a six-month dispute which ended in the Methodists breaking with the Moravians over their belief in the need for an absolute faith and an abstention from the means of grace (church attendance, Holy Communion, prayer, and fasting) whilst waiting for this faith.

1741   In the early part of this year a dispute began over Predestination, a doctrine espoused by some Calvinistic Methodists, and in particular by George Whitefield, which was to lead to a division between those who, like the Wesley brothers, espoused Universal Redemption and those, such as Whitefield, Lady Huntingdon, and the Calvinistic Methodists in Wales, who clung to the doctrine of Particular Election.

Wesley refuses to discountenance preaching by lay helpers.

October, Wesley embarked on a preaching tour of south Wales, preaching in the churches where this was possible, but in private houses or the open air where it was not.

1742   May, began his first preaching tour in the north of England.

June, not being permitted the use of the church, Wesley stood upon his father's tomb-stone to preach at Epworth.

23 July, Wesley's mother died.

1743 October, Staffordshire riots provide the most dramatic example of violent opposition to the growing force of Methodism.

1744 June, the first Conference was held at the Foundery in London.

1745 September, Wesley caught up in the resistance to the Stuart Pretender.

1746 December, established a dispensary for the poor.

1747 August, made the first of twenty-one preaching tours in Ireland.

1749 Entered a form of engagement with Grace Murray. (For the course of this relationship and her subsequent marriage to John Bennet on 3 October, see Appendix B.)

1751 February, Wesley married a well-to-do widow, Mrs Molly Vazeille, mother of four children, without thoroughly consulting the Society or his brother, whose interference had cost him his intended marriage to Grace Murray.

   April, first visited Scotland, where, against his original intention, he was prevailed upon to preach.

1758 January, Wesley's wife left him, unable to cope with the competition for his time and devotion presented by his work and followers. She was to return and leave him again on several occasions before their final separation (see, for instance, *Journal* entry for 23 January 1771).

1768 First Methodist chapel built in New York.

1775 Wesley published *A Calm Address to our American Colonies*. His initial sympathy with American grievances did not survive the armed opposition to the English Crown.

1781 8 October, John Wesley's wife died. He did not learn of this till several days later.

1783 June, Wesley took the first of two 'little excursions' to Holland.

1784 Whilst continuing to proclaim his allegiance to the Anglican Church, Wesley ordained men for the American ministry (and subsequently for other areas where a strong need was expressed), in effect establishing an alternative ecclesiastical hierarchy to that provided by the Church of England.

1787 August, first tour of the Channel Islands.

1788 29 March, Charles Wesley died.

1790 24 October, *Journal* entries abruptly terminated.

1791 23 February, Wesley preached his last sermon.
   2 March, John Wesley died.

INTRODUCTION

In my way to Perth, I read over the first volume of Dr. Robertson's 'History of Charles the Fifth'. I know not when I have been so disappointed. It might as well be called the History of Alexander the Great. Here is a quarto volume of eight or ten shillings' price, containing dry, verbose dissertations on feudal government, the substance of all which might be comprised in half a sheet of paper! But 'Charles the Fifth'! Where is Charles the Fifth?

8 April 1772

The newcomer to Wesley's *Journal* could well be forgiven for experiencing the same kind of disappointment. A million or more words fail to yield an intimate glimpse of Wesley's private emotional life. The reader who relishes diaries for the delightful indiscretions, contemporary gossip, private malice, or personal soul-searching they can provide will find few such pleasures here. The reasons for this have to do with Wesley's temperament, the kind of life he led, and the type of document he was engaged in writing. It is perhaps easiest to explore these factors in reverse order.

The *Journal* was conceived as a public document which drew upon, but did not exactly replicate, the material in Wesley's personal diaries. The function of the diary which Wesley had begun to keep in 1725 was to provide a systematized method for spiritual self-examination and a record of the progress made in attempting to live the Christian life. The diary took the form of coded entries which preserved secrecy and made easier the regular charting of his moral and spiritual progress. Wesley imparted his diary-keeping method to at least fifteen other Methodists in Oxford and these records were sometimes produced and compared at meetings where discussion of individual spiritual progress took place. Even the diary, then, despite the secrecy lent by the code, was not an unambiguously private document.

In his Preface to the first number of the *Journal* Wesley explained how he had taken extracts from his diary, 'adding here and there such little reflections as occurred to my mind. It not being my design to relate all those particularities, which I wrote for my own use only; and which would answer no valuable end to others, however important they were to me.' Just as Wesley valued Methodism for being compatible with a variety of religious positions and personal opinions because it supplied a practical guide to faith rather than the only route to holiness, so he judged it unfitting to parade his personal prejudices in a work of encouragement for the faithful. Yet every page of the *Journal*, like first-generation Methodism itself, is shaped and coloured by Wesley's authoritarian personality and his absolute conviction of his duty to pronounce God's Word to whomever he encountered, be they rich or poor, willing or unwilling hearers, and to oversee the lives of all those whom he and his followers converted.

The *Journal* began as a public vindication of his doings, both at Oxford, where the Holy Club, of which he became the leading member, had been charged with self-destructive asceticism, and in America, which he had been forced to leave as a virtual outlaw. Wesley uses the *Journal* to record the part played by the example of Moravian teaching and practice upon his own daily endeavours to preach the religion of the heart. It remained a means of public communication, so that those who want to come closer to the Wesley whose confidences to and concern for his most devoted followers so disturbed his wife, may find richer quarry in his letters. Since the *Journal* was an extension to his mission Wesley did not hestitate to include edited accounts of riots or conversions of which he had not himself been a witness, yet he described the *Journal* as an attempt 'to relate simple truth in as inoffensive a manner as I can'. The doggedly tenacious attention to reporting the truth as he saw it, which cannot fail to impress readers, derives, in part, from Wesley's allowing the *Journal* to stand as independent testimony, unaffected by the light of subsequent events. His friend and sometime collaborator, George Whitefield, withdrew some of the material in his seven journals, published between 1738 and 1741, before issuing a revised version in 1756. Wesley's *Journal* is, in effect, a textbook of the experiential religion he proclaimed, not a theological treatise. It contains the raw evidence of God's interceding on man's behalf, in sudden conversions, instant answer to prayer, and through the inexplicable, mysterious leadings of dreams, which remained close to the heart of Wesley's faith, along with the means of grace the Church provided. The passion for rational analysis which led him to tabulate possible explanations for these seemingly miraculous events should not blind us to the fact that this process ultimately took him back to admitting the limitations of the human intellect and the realization that behind all 'natural causes' stood the First Cause Himself. Designed, then, as an instrument of conversion the *Journal* also provided a handle for those who wished to resist what they saw as a dangerous new form of fanaticism.

Over the years the *Journal* also became an instrument for strengthening the cohesive force of Methodism, keeping an isolated community in touch with the progress other remote outposts were making in 'the way of salvation'. It must also have become a means of exercising discipline and awarding praise or rebuke, since Wesley never minced his words when he encountered backsliding or laxity of conduct in the various societies whose spiritual health he so carefully monitored.

Wesley may not have relaxed his pastoral vigilance over the years from the first Methodist Conference in 1744 to his death in 1791, and he remained suspiciously alert for any signs that Methodism had become complacent with its undoubted growth in numbers and social acceptability, nevertheless the *Journal* does reveal a change of tone. Initially the reaction of relations and his former Oxford colleagues to his itinerant preaching encouraged Wesley to use the *Journal* as a forum in which to conduct a spirited defence. Gradually the element of personal apologia recedes and the *Journal* reads less like the communiqué from the leader of a persecuted society as Wesley finds time to record attendance at an oratorio by Handel or conversations with famous contemporaries like the Corsican patriot, General Paoli, or sight-seeing visits to country houses and gardens. Whilst he never lost his sense of the distance Methodism had travelled in his own lifetime, remarking on 27 December 1789:

I preached in St. Luke's, our parish church, in the afternoon, to a very numerous congregation, on 'The Spirit and the Bride say, Come'. So are the tables turned, that I have now more invitations to preach in churches than I can accept of.

even he regarded it as worthy remark when on 19 February 1786 he 'preached in Horsleydown church, where (to my no small surprise) no man, woman or child seemed to know me either by face or by name!'

These two entries were chosen to illustrate Wesley's consciousness of Methodism's changed fortunes, but coincidentally they also serve to suggest the way in which the manner of Wesley's life contributed to the curious impersonality of the *Journal*. Hundreds of entries began like these two by noting the date and place and text of a sermon, followed often by some brief note in which Wesley assesses the numbers attending, or attempts to gauge how effective his preaching has been. Few individuals emerge from the mass of his congregation and if they do, often appear as 'a soldier', 'a butcher', 'the town crier', 'the Mayor', 'one who . . .', not as individualized characters. Augustan literary convention, of course, plays a part here. Particularity and idiosyncrasy of appearance or manner were normally considered the prerogative of the satirist, and the descriptive writer was entitled to rely more heavily than our pluralist society permits upon the appeals to normative judgement contained in adjectives such as 'pleasant', 'elegant', 'exceeding grand', 'very agreeable', 'foolish'. Yet at the end of the century Jane Austen, relying upon similar generic terms of praise or blame, managed to create distinctive characters, and so some other explanation needs to be sought. In the course of his travels Wesley must have met more men and women than almost any other man of his day, and, whilst he cared deeply for their souls, he rarely had the time to form intimate relationships. Indeed, on the few occasions that he records staying with particular friends he almost always reminds himself that he must be off and about God's business rather than luxuriating in private enjoyment. Dr Johnson testified both to Wesley's capacity to charm cultivated acquaintances and to the fact that Wesley never allowed himself to put pleasure before business, remarking, 'John Wesley's conversation is good, but he is never at leisure. He is always obliged to go at a certain hour. This is very disagreeable to a man who loves to fold his legs and have out his talk, as I do.' The life of an itinerant preacher, constantly needing to adjust to fresh faces and circumstances may well have reinforced a natural tendency to reticence in expressing private emotion. Though prompt to deliver judgments in his capacity as a spiritual leader, Wesley seldom allows us to witness inner reactions. The phrase 'to my no small surprise' in his account of his visit to Horsleydown is in fact a very terse expression which covers a range of possible emotions from an initial blow to his self-esteem to his consequent self-reproach for regarding himself as any more than a vehicle for God's message— an emotion perhaps hinted at in the final sentence of this entry: 'But before I had done, many of the numerous congregation knew that God was there of a truth.'

Literary convention and necessary tact combined to restrain Wesley from exercising descriptive talents upon the people he met, but what of the places he visited? Travel writing was, after all, one of the most popular literary forms of the day. In the *Journal* Wesley mentions reading Johnson's *Tour to the Western Isles of Scotland* and Boswell's *Tour to the Hebrides* and *Journal of a Tour to Corsica*. In the course of his evangelizing work he travelled some quarter of a million miles, bringing the Gospel to new areas and then tirelessly revisiting to ensure that converts grew in the faith. Arminianism, which admitted the possibility of backsliding into perdition, placed a greater strain in this respect upon preacher and flock alike than did Calvinism. The *Journal* does contain some descriptive set-pieces such as Wesley's account of Georgia (December 1737, not reprinted here) or his comparison of the three great landscaped gardens at Stourhead, Cobham, and Stow (8–13 October 1779). These passages, however, are almost entirely devoid of the individual response to environment which lend the best travellers' tales their charm. Wesley's account of Georgia forms a practical guide to prevailing conditions for the aspiring emigrant, covering seasons, soils, crops, variety of terrain, chief settlements, and indigenous population. One looks in vain for aesthetic impressions. The second passage on gardens is a curious exercise. Wesley's appraisal is conducted in the manner of a balance sheet, assessing the natural advantages of the various sites, the landscape features of human contrivance and the choice of decorative building. The would-be visitor learns little from an account drawn up in a form which bears the hallmarks of Wesley's obsessional organizational talents. He allows that the overall prospect offered is of primary importance, but his judgment in favour of Stourhead is made according to idiosyncratic criteria: cleanliness and moral taste. There is perhaps an analogy to be drawn between Wesley's desire to see what had been so carefully nurtured preserved in pristine purity, and his perpetual supervision of the souls he had harvested. His objections to classically inspired statuary and temples which recalled less desirable aspects of pagan morality stems from his theocentric vision of life. Travelling the length and breadth of the kingdom Wesley kept constantly in mind the test, 'For where your treasure is, there will your heart be also', and invariably offered a comment upon the folly of human vanity when contemplating the money and effort expended by noblemen in building up estates frequently neglected or reworked by their heirs. To the modern reader these repeated epitaphs upon human endeavour are inclined to strike a sour note, but they are best seen, not as the product of cynicism, but as reflecting Wesley's desire to use every experience as part of his work for God. Contemporary projects served as well as graveyards and cathedral monuments as a *memento mori*. 'Having a little leisure, I thought I could not employ it better than in taking a walk through the gardens.' The deliberative phrase with which this passage opens demonstrates Wesley's habitual sense of accountability. He could endorse unreflective sight-seeing neither for himself nor his readers.

This heavy sense of responsibility often results in accounts of sight-seeing excursions purposely undertaken being the most disappointing. Consider for instance Wesley's remarks upon first seeing Land's End:

We went afterwards down, as far as we could go safely, toward the point of the rocks at the Land's-End. It was an awful sight! But how will these melt away, when God ariseth to judgment! The sea between does indeed 'boil like a pot'. 'One would think the deep to be hoary.' But 'though they swell, yet can they not prevail. He hath set their bounds, which they cannot pass.'

10 September 1743

Such a passage helps us to understand what Wesley meant when he wrote, 'The Bible is my standard of *language* as well as sentiment' (Letters, 1 April 1766), but would convey little in the way of the visual experience to a land-locked reader, though Wesley himself retained a clear enough memory to be able to comment on his second visit, 'I cannot think but the sea has gained some hundred yards since I was here forty years ago' (22 August 1785). Just occasionally Wesley happened upon a prospect so delightful or dramatic that he was driven to record it (e.g. 5 August 1747; 29 August 1765; 12 June 1778) but it is often possible for the reader to follow Wesley from Bath to Newcastle-upon-Tyne without any great awareness of the changing terrain. So accustomed was he to ceaseless travel that only the extraordinary merited mention: Cornish caves (15 September 1755), turfs cut from beneath the sand on the beach at Newport (14 July 1777) the largest elm-tree he has ever seen (11 October 1773) the observation that no singing birds were to be found in the vicinity of Dublin (3 July 1787). His taste was, in fact, that of an eighteenth-century gentleman and he would have found little to quarrel with in Alexander Pope's opinion:

> In prospects thus, some objects please our eyes,
> Which out of Nature's common order rise,
> The shapeless rock, or hanging precipice.

Like Pope too, he approved of 'Nature methodized', whether in the form of agricultural advances or in elegantly landscaped gardens. His appreciation of the latter made the two trips to Holland undertaken towards the end of his life particularly pleasant, and after all the years of laborious travel he still hankered after the formal beauty of college gardens: '*Thursday, 13* [October], *1785.* Returning to Oxford, I once more surveyed many of the gardens and delightful walks. What is wanting but the love of God, to make this place an earthly paradise?'

The Hall at Christ Church, where he had spent his undergraduate days, continued to supply him with a standard of measurement when surveying country houses for the rest of his life. Indeed the comparisons that haunt the pages of the *Journal* seem to confirm the need Wesley's orderly mind felt to give some framework to the apparently random experiences of his disjointed life.

The endeavour to keep up with the punishing schedule of visits to scattered societies made the practical circumstances of the two or three sermons he preached each day seem more important than leisurely contemplation of the scenery. Wesley developed a good eye for sites which offered good natural acoustics, shade from the sun, or shelter from the rain, but would preach above a hog-sty if it proved the only available venue. The *Journal* comes into its own as an account of climatic conditions in England between 1738 and 1790. Wesley was undeterred by snow that made Gateshead Fell appear 'a great pathless waste' (23 February 1745) or rain that fell so heavily on his way to Wapping that it 'put out the candle in our lantern' and shattered the tiles of the chapel so 'that the vestry was all in a float' (17 November 1755). Two summers spent in Georgia remained his standard for judging extreme heat in England or Ireland.

For someone who had experienced the rigours of the eighteenth-century transatlantic crossing (January 1736), the Irish Sea could hold no worse threat. This was especially so because the absolute reliance upon Christ and contempt for mortal concerns that Wesley found after his conversion enabled him to emulate the serenity of the German voyagers he had so admired on the ship bound for America. (cf. January 1736 and 23 July 1750.)

If Wesley's spare, emphatic style did not lend itself to descriptive lyricism it served as the perfect tool for dramatic narrative. Amongst the many accounts of anti-Methodist riots and accidents sustained while travelling it is worth singling out two episodes which Wesley reported in detail: the Staffordshire riots of October 1743, and a potentially fatal coaching accident of 20 June 1774. In both Wesley conveys the rapid flow of events by means of a series of short sentences and clauses in which the verbs carry the weight of the action. The metaphors he employs gain cogency from their freshness and their comparative infrequency. Two angry Staffordshire rioters are 'ready to swallow the ground with rage'. Stampeding horses career through a farmyard gate 'as if it had been a cobweb'. Wesley's habit of giving a verbatim account of any dialogue, occasionally essaying dialect, lends immediacy and further verisimilitude to his accounts.

The dramatic tension of these and other similar episodes, however, derives not just from the danger in which Wesley found himself, but from the counterpointing of the impassive central figure with the raging forces without. Even when he is being dragged along by a mob or in imminent danger of being dashed over a precipice he emerges as the dominant figure, his calm assurance providing a tower of strength to frightened supporters or relatives. Time and again his thought processes and considered action are pitted in the narrative against the unreasoning, instinctive behaviour of the mob or nature itself.

The direct narration of these two particular events is followed by an analysis of 'the remarkable circumstances' which ensured his deliverance and produced 'convincing proofs, that the hand of God is on every person and thing, over-ruling all as it seemeth him good'. Wesley has become an actor in God's divine drama. It is this consciousness of himself as playing a role in a drama written and stage-managed by God Himself that divests Wesley of self-consciousness. Reports of his own coolness in danger 'finding the same presence of mind, as if I had been sitting in my own study', that can seem boastful to the secular observer, are, for Wesley, merely an objective record of God's interposition on His servant's behalf. The almost inevitable alternation of these perspectives as one reads the *Journal* can make Wesley seem maddeningly self-obsessed at the very moment when his intention is to be self-effacing.

The *Journal*, like Wordsworth's *Prelude*, easily invites the charge of an 'egotistical sublime' in their authors. Wordsworth, setting out to describe the 'Growth of a Poet's Mind', inevitably found his own his most illuminating source and proceeded to make it the all-consuming object of his study. Wesley, intent on expounding 'practical religion' by demonstrating the ways of God to man, by a similar process emerged as the hero of his own epic. This decision to use his own life as an example of God's means of working out His purpose on earth sometimes makes Wesley's self-assessments read like a Headmaster's report, which for all its examination of character traits and actual progress made somehow fails to identify the features that make that child unique to friends and relations.

We are sometimes left with the feeling that for all his rigorous self-examination and self-discipline, either Wesley did not know himself very well, or chose to ignore certain aspects of his personality as running counter to the mould he believed God required.

The sins of 'idleness', of 'intemperate sleep', or 'loving women or company more than God', which his early Oxford Diaries record, scarcely distinguish Wesley from his contemporary, Dr Johnson. Moreover these are all faults of behaviour, capable of being easily identified and remedied by reorganizing the daily timetable. What is missing is the emotional life, the uncertainties and confusion of the uniquely personal reaction to the suspicion that one 'loves women or company more than God'. Another early Diary entry sheds more light: 'sins of thought: hence useless or sinful anger'. In religious parlance 'useless' can be interpreted as 'not spiritually profitable' rather than 'pointless'. By implication time spent exploring these feelings would be further time wasted. The *Journal*, as first published, gives no hint of the vacillation that marked Wesley's successive emotional entanglements. Wesley did, in fact, write accounts of two very intense relationships with women, one with Sophia Hopkey which expedited his departure from Georgia, and the second in 1749 with Grace Murray. Since they reveal something of the inner turmoil taking place behind the relentless regime of daily travel, pastoral admonishment, and preaching I have included extracts in the form of appendices.

Although Sophia and Grace were from very different social backgrounds, the first being a niece to Savannah's chief magistrate, the second the widow of a master mariner, there was one remarkable similarity in their positions. Both were already involved with another suitor and in both cases the intimate, yet indecisive relationship with Wesley was only terminated by the woman marrying another man with dramatic speed. Wesley had reason to feel that the contract *de praesenti* that he twice made with Grace Murray was legally binding and a sufficient guarantee of his affections, nevertheless, in the face of Charles Wesley's importunate interference, she remained uncertain enough to be persuaded that John had in fact renounced her. Wesley's intimacy with both women developed out of his initial role as their spiritual guide and mentor and in what followed he seems never to have been able to distinguish between pastoral responsibility and human affection.

From Wesley's own vantage point this is wholly intelligible since any marriage could only be between two individuals who saw themselves primarily as God's servants. Whilst 'Miss Sophy' seemed to provide suitable material to work on—she is praised for her teachability, humility, and uncomplaining efforts to combat physical weakness—an eighteen-year old from one of the most prominent families in the area could scarcely be considered the ideal choice as wife for a man who thought himself committed to the rigours of missionary life. In Grace Murray Wesley had proof of a capable nurse, an indefatigable travelling companion and an efficient organizer of female Methodist bands. He failed to see that if he found her educational and social inferiority of no conse-quence, others would not. It was one thing for his converts and associates to accept the authority of an Oxford don who had chosen to make his chief work among the poor, but a very different matter to accept the authority and respect that Grace Murray would have to command as Wesley's wife rather than as a particularly favoured helper.

At one level, then, his records of these relationships read as extraordinary self-centred agonizings about the potential suit-ability of these women as wives, and yet they do also convey genuine human misery. In Miss Sophy's case the wounded lover emerges in the persistence with which he charges her with insincer-ity when he attempted to resume his role as pastor after her marriage. In Grace Murray's case perhaps more telling than the literary flourish with which he records his refusal to give his brother the emotional scene Charles so clearly desired ('I felt little Emotion. It was only adding a drop of water to a drowning man.') is the absence of explanation, excuse, or comment, with which he records what, in retrospect turned out to be the catastrophic moment of decision ('I need add no more, then that if I had had more Regard for her I loved, than for ye Work of God, I sh^d now have gone on strait to Newcastle, & not back to Whitehaven. I knew this was giving up all: But I knew GOD call'd'.). Instead the ensuing account of his journey to Whitehaven, which he published as part of his public narrative, acquires a quasi-symbolic status,

telling us of the turmoil and pain which lay behind the oblique
reticence of the terse record of his decision.

The storm was exceeding high, and drove full in my face, so that it was
not without difficulty I could sit my horse; particularly as I rode over the
broad, bare backs of those enormous mountains which lay in my way.
However, I kept on as I could, till I came to the brow of Hatside. So thick
a fog then fell, that I was quickly out of all road, and knew not which way
to turn. But I knew where help was to be found, in either great difficulties
or small.

It is scarcely surprising that neither Sophia nor Grace's husband
found himself able to tolerate Wesley's continued pastoral supervision of his wife since Wesley never seems to have recognized the
distinction between spiritual and emotional reproof.

   One cannot doubt Wesley's desire to be honest in his records of
these incidents, yet it is difficult not to convict him of culpable
naïveté and, what is perhaps the same thing, a lack of imaginative
sympathy. Sophy's uncle was clearly anxious to marry her off and
if Wesley could not be got up to scratch then both the girl and her
relations must have seen that her eligibility would not be enhanced
by a continuation of this dangerous intimacy. A member of the
Newcastle Methodist society was exceptionally forthright in
expressing the disrepute into which Wesley's conduct with Grace
was in danger of bringing the movement. 'Good God! What will
the world say: He is tired of her, and so thrusts his whore into a
corner! Sister Murray, will you consent to this?' True unworldli-
ness might blind Wesley to social pressures such as these, but far
more disturbing is the almost total absence of comment on the
difficulties and emotional confusion his prospective brides must
have been experiencing. He seems constantly surprised that Sophy
might be depressed by her position between an engagement to a
ne'er-do-well, devotion to a man whose expressions of love were
always ambiguous, and the solid offer from Mr Williamson, 'a
person' according to Wesley's biased eye, 'not remarkable for
handsomeness, neither for greatness, or knowledge, or sense, and
least of all for religion'. It is easy to feel sympathy for the injured
pride behind Mrs Williamson's response to a third party's advice

to her to go and clear herself of the offences Wesley had charged her with in openly refusing to admit her to Holy Communion earlier that day: 'No, I will not show such meanness of spirit as to speak to him about it myself, but somebody else shall.'

The way in which Wesley managed to continue with the strenuous demands of his daily life during and after these episodes have led most commentators to detect an essential coldness about the man: 'granite in aspic' as V. H. H. Green so strikingly phrased it. This variety of personal criticism bears an interesting relationship to a strand of socially concerned commentary which sees in Methodism a force delaying urgently needed humanitarian reforms. In both cases it appears that concentrating upon a dimension beyond time, God's eternal plans, can encourage a myopia akin to indifference about present tribulation. In later years Wesley was to claim that his resignation stemmed from a God-given evenness of temper. 'I *feel* and I grieve; but, by the grace of God I *fret* at nothing' (28 June 1776). His puritanical upbringing in the Rectory at Epworth (*Journal*, 1 August 1742), where children of a year and under 'were taught to fear the rod, and to cry softly', probably had much to do with this emotional self-control, and in any case the vagaries of weather, accommodation, and transport which Wesley constantly encountered would have made such stoicism a necessary survival mechanism. Furthermore, the absolute conviction of God's special providence watching over him enabled Wesley to accept obstacles, upsets, and enforced changes of plan as evidence that all things work together for good to them that love Him.

Nevertheless, when we hear Wesley repeatedly attributing his longevity to a firm routine, undisturbed patterns of sleep, and unfailing equanimity, we cannot but be aware that the *Journal* sometimes tells another tale. Sleepless nights are rare enough to deserve recording, but occur they do, and the equable temperament reigned just as long as Wesley's will or perception of God's will went unchallenged. Spending his life almost exclusively amongst the less well-educated and socially inferior accustomed Wesley to unquestioning acceptance of his decisions and in turn he developed the omnicompetence of a paternalistic dictator, entirely sure of his own judgement in matters spiritual, medical, or architectural. The following account of a visit to the society at Deptford seems to convey Wesley's manner particularly succinctly.

Tuesday, January 2, 1787. I went over to Deptford; but it seemed, I was got into a den of lions. Most of the leading men of the society were mad for separating from the Church. I endeavoured to reason with them, but in vain; they had neither sense nor even good manners left. At length, after meeting the whole society, I told them, 'If you are resolved, you may have your services in church-hours; but remember, from that time you will see my face no more.' This struck deep; and from that hour I have heard no more of separating from the Church.

The image of Daniel cast into the lions' den and the language in which the ultimatum is couched suggest that not only did the Bible supply Wesley with a working vocabulary but that, by this stage in his life, his self-assimilation into the world of the prophets had become almost complete. Any fleeting picture of a leonine prophet distinguished by straggling white locks and contempt for conventional clothing should, however, be instantly dismissed. Despite, or perhaps because of, his itinerant life Wesley remained fastidious about his appearance. This excerpt proves the prophetic role to have been entirely compatible, in Wesley's case, with the mental set of an eighteenth-century gentleman. Suspicious of 'enthusiasm' (an eighteenth-century synonym for 'fanaticism') Wesley resorts first to the powers of reason and, when those fail, takes his stand upon courtesy and civilized behaviour. When it becomes apparent that he cannot rely upon the assumptions underlying reasonable discussion or polite social intercourse, then he feels justified in treating the leaders of the Deptford society as children, and there is a grim satisfaction in the way he records his complete quelling of the dispute.

If the world was Wesley's parish, his flock was his family. Those who carped when the childless Wesley presumed to preach upon the upbringing of children swiftly had their argument dismissed as a feeble quibble, but perhaps their complaint had some force to it. Despite his marriage to a widow with children Wesley retained in many ways the cast of mind of a bachelor don, devoted to his pupils, endlessly prepared to draw up reading lists and give the necessary instruction to his largely uneducated preaching assistants and stewards, yet never entirely prepared to recognize that they had metaphorically speaking 'come of age' and might be entitled to make decisions that differed from his. In the early years Wesley's acknowledgments of the success others achieved in their preaching was often accompanied by an expression of surprise at the use God can make of those with little education and small natural talents. With those he had trained himself the teacher-pupil relationship was rarely outgrown. The constant awareness of playing for eternal stakes made it well-nigh impossible to allow others to make their own mistakes.

The delegation of responsibility could only be limited when Wesley remained supremely conscious that at the end he would be accountable for the souls he saved. Just occasionally towards the end of his life the sheer immensity of the task of personal supervision required over an ever-growing flock seems to have struck Wesley, as in this entry about one of his pet projects, the school at Kingswood.

Friday, September 7, 1781. I went over to Kingswood, and made a particular inquiry into the management of the school, I found some of the Rules had not been observed at all; particularly that of rising in the morning. Surely Satan has a peculiar spite at this school! What trouble has it cost me for above these thirty years! I can *plan*; but who will *execute*? I know not; God help me!

Kingswood seems to have given joy and pain about equally over the years, but in other cases it is difficult to assess whether a local society had a self-perpetuating character or whether Wesley quickly developed self-confirming expectations which marked certain societies out as either promising or recalcitrant disciples. A visit to Witney, for instance, never failed to raise his spirits, whilst the society at Norwich became a byword for fickleness and backsliding.

Perhaps finally Wesley was isolated from others by his passion for committing his thoughts to paper. Letters and diaries became perforce his chief means of communication both with those to whom he was bound by the closest ties and with mere acquaintances. The ease with which modern devices like the telephone can restore a form of direct contact makes us less aware of the temptations of solipsism ever open to those who make the written word their chief medium. Wesley's humour, as sparsely conveyed by the *Journal* entries, seems to have been intrinsically self-communing. His shafts of irony or perceptions of the pathos of human eccentricities seem to be the product of a mind that knows that his immediate companions will probably not share his taste for understatement and veiled wit. Against this, however, must be set the memorial tribute of Samuel Bradburn, a constant travelling companion of Wesley's for some seventeen years, who claimed that, 'Few men had a greater share of vivacity, when in company with those he loved, especially on his journies.' Recalling Wesley's efforts to cheer fellow travellers in moments of hardship, Bradburn also spoke of his 'almost inexhaustible fund of stories and anecdotes, adapted to all kinds of people, and to every occurrence in life'.

Wesley's passion for observation, his educated yet eclectic interest in everything he saw, mean that the social history embedded in the *Journal* almost compensates for its obdurate silence on more personal matters. In the course of his itinerant ministry, undertaken at first by foot or on horseback and later by the post-chaise purchased for him by his friends, he visited Ireland on twenty-one occasions, and regularly penetrated England's other Celtic fringes. Perhaps even more significant was the triangle he habitually described between the three main centres of Methodism: Bristol, Newcastle, and London. This journey between great trading ports encompassed also the areas of swiftest change, industrially speaking. Although characteristically the *Journal* speaks more of orphanages, workhouses, and jails than of visits to factories, Wesley found himself in a peculiarly favourable position for collecting data and refuting current demographical mythology. In 1776 he tried two methods of assessing the population (1 May and 9 September) and came to the triumphant conclusion that England's population was increasing rather than decreasing and that talk of a decline in rural areas ran against the evidence as he saw it. Unemployment in particular areas and trades also concerned Wesley in as much as it affected the welfare of his flock. Although he welcomed upper and middle class converts, the lower classes remained his chief concern. For all his reputation as a Tory paternalist, he expended much effort on enabling the lower classes to be self-sufficient in relieving the needs of their own class. The publication of his *Primitive Physick; or an Easy and Natural Method of Curing Most Diseases (1747)*, which ran to twenty-three editions in his lifetime, must have gone some way to freeing poor Methodists either from dependence for treatment of their ailments, (upon the squire or parson's family) or from fees payable to the physicians and apothecaries whom Wesley by and large distrusted. Wesley seems to have placed enormous faith in the beneficial effects of being 'electrified daily' and between 1756 and 1758 set up four machines in London alone for this purpose.

The *Journal* does record Wesley's reaction to such major political events as the Jacobite rising of 1745 and the American War of Independence, but it remains more interesting for the impression it offers of the way in which such events affected people's daily domestic lives. During the '45, rumour and fear were rife, and Wesley found himself in beleaguered Newcastle. Despite his own frequently proclaimed loyalty to the reigning monarch, Wesley and his itinerant preachers formed easy targets for the press-gang, and everywhere the *Journal* gives testimony to the influential presence of the militia in many a major port and town.

The incidental vignettes of the rougher side of eighteenth-century life: bull-baiting, Cornish smuggling, highway robberies, or the record of a journey to London on 22 July 1779 where, 'I was nobly attended; behind the coach were ten convicted felons, loudly blaspheming and rattling their chains; by my side sat a man with a loaded blunderbuss, and another upon the coach'—all help to explain why Evelyn Waugh alighted on Wesley's life as a suitable vehicle for his account of the making of the sensationally awful religious film, 'A Brand from the Burning' in *Vile Bodies* (1930). On its first showing a peculiar feature of early cinematographic technique results in the film getting faster and faster whenever dramatic action like riots or elopements takes place, whereas any scene of repose or inaction seems unendurably prolonged. Finally even the film's most enthusiastic shareholder feels compelled to cut a bit 'after Wesley had sat uninterrupted composing a pamphlet for four and a half minutes'.

In making a selection which roughly decimates Wesley's own

composition, I have tried for a mean between these two extremes of the frenetic and wholly fragmentary and the longeurs of mere place names, sermon titles, and polemical pamphlet material. By scything ruthlessly through doctrinal controversy I have inevitably underplayed one element of Wesley's life, and some will undoubtedly feel that in attempting to tailor the work for that Protean figure 'the general reader' I have come dangerously near catering for the tastes of George Eliot's character, Mrs Linnet, who,

On taking up the biography of a celebrated preacher ... immediately turned to the end to see what disease he died of; and if his legs swelled, as her own occasionally did, she felt a stronger interest in ascertaining any earlier facts in the history of the dropsical divine—whether he had ever fallen off a stage-coach, whether he had married more than one wife ... She then glanced over the letters and diary, and wherever there was a predominance of Zion, the River of Life, and notes of exclamation, she turned over to the next page; but any passages in which she saw such promising nouns as 'small-pox', 'pony', or 'boots and shoes', at once arrested her.

Nor can this selection do complete justice to Wesley's voracious reading habits. In choosing which of his comments on the books he read to reprint I settled on the policy of confining attention, in the main, to those books which became classics and where we therefore have both the means and the interest to assess Wesley's judgment for ourselves. Whenever I have felt unduly awed by the temerity of this enterprise I have comforted myself by recollecting Wesley's own habit of abridging and editing any books which he felt should enjoy a wider readership and by turning to an entry for 17 February 1769 which reads 'I abridged Dr. Watts's pretty "Treatise on the Passions". His hundred and seventy-seven pages will make a useful tract of four-and-twenty. Why do persons who treat the same subjects with me, write so much larger books?'

A NOTE ON THE TEXT

Wesley's *Journal* was originally published in a series of twenty-one extracts, starting in or about 1739 and ending some months after his death in 1791.

This selection is largely based upon the text prepared by Thomas Jackson in the first four volumes of *The Works of the Rev. John Wesley*, 5th edn. (14 vols, 1829–31).* It was this corrected edition which formed the basis for *The Standard Edition of the Journal of the Rev. John Wesley*, ed. N. Curnock (8 vols, 1909–16). Curnock's edition, although valuable to the Wesleyan scholar, is inordinately complicated to follow, often employing as many as four different typefaces on one page as he weaves back and forth between the extracts as initially published, interpolations from contemporary manuscript documents, and his own explanatory notes. As a source for biographical material and the history of early Methodism his notes offer fascinating, though at times laborious reading. Curnock's edition has been used to supply the extracts from the Frederica and Savannah Journals reproduced in Appendix B, which cover the Sophia Hopkey episode, and to supply names which Wesley deleted in the extracts he published. The latter insertions are always indicated within square brackets. The extracts in Appendix C, covering John Wesley's relationship with Grace Murray, are taken from J. A. Leger, *John Wesley's Last Love* (1910).

For an authoritative, scholarly edition we must await the publication of the *Journal* as edited by Professor W. R. Ward.

* Some aspects of the original punctuation have been modernized for this edition.

THE JOURNAL

Preface

1. IT was in pursuance of an advice given by Bishop Taylor, in his 'Rules for Holy Living and Dying', that, about fifteen years ago, I began to take a more exact account than I had done before, of the manner wherein I spent my time, writing down how I had employed every hour. This I continued to do wherever I was, till the time of my leaving England. The variety of scenes which I then passed through, induced me to transcribe, from time to time, the more material parts of my diary, adding here and there such little reflections as occurred to my mind. Of this journal thus occasionally compiled, the following is a short extract: It not being my design to relate all those particulars, which I wrote for my own use only; and which would answer no valuable end to others, however important they were to me.

2. Indeed I had no design or desire to trouble the world with any of my little affairs: As cannot but appear to every impartial mind, from my having been so long 'as one that heareth not'; notwithstanding the loud and frequent calls I have had to answer for myself. Neither should I have done it now, had not Captain Williams's[1] affidavit, published *as soon as he had left England*, laid an obligation upon me, to do what in me lies, in obedience to that command of God, 'Let not the good which is in you be evil spoken of.' With this view I do at length 'give an answer to every man that asketh me a reason of the hope which is in me', that in all these things 'I have a conscience void of offence toward God and toward men.'

3. I have prefixed hereto a letter, wrote several years since, containing a plain account of the rise of that little society in Oxford, which has been so variously represented. Part of this was published in 1733; but without my consent or knowledge. It now stands as it was wrote; without any addition, diminution, or amendment; it being my only concern herein nakedly to 'declare the thing as it is'.

4. Perhaps my employments of another kind may not allow me to give any farther answer to them who 'say all manner of evil of me falsely', and seem to 'think that they do God service'. Suffice it, that both they and I shall shortly 'give an account to Him that is ready to judge the quick and the dead'

Introductory Letter [2]

SIR,   OXON, *October 18th*, 1732

THE occasion of my giving you this trouble is of a very extraordinary nature. On Sunday last I was informed (as no doubt you will be ere long) that my brother and I had killed your son: That the rigorous fasting which he had imposed upon himself, by our advice, had increased his illness and hastened his death. Now though, considering it in itself, 'it is a very small thing with me to be judged by man's judgment'; yet as the being thought guilty of so mischievous an imprudence might make me the less able to do the work I came into the world for, I am obliged to clear myself of it, by observing to you, as I have done to others, that your son left off fasting about a year and a half since; and that it is not yet half a year since I began to practise it.

I must not let this opportunity slip of doing my part towards giving you a juster notion of some other particulars, relating both to him and myself, which have been industriously misrepresented to you.

In March last he received a letter from you, which, not being able to read, he desired me to read to him; several of the expressions whereof I perfectly remember, and shall do, till I too am called hence. I then determined, that if God was pleased to take away your son before me, I would justify him and myself, which I now do with all plainness and simplicity, as both my character and cause required.

In one practice for which you blamed your son, I am only concerned as a friend, not as a partner. That, therefore, I shall consider first. Your own account of it was in effect this: 'He frequently went into poor people's houses, in the villages about Holt, called their children together, and instructed them in their duty to God, their neighbour, and themselves. He likewise explained to them the necessity of private as well as public prayer, and provided them with such forms as were best suited to their several capacities: And being well apprized how much the success of his endeavours depended on their good-will towards him, to win upon their affections, he sometimes distributed among them a little of that money which he had saved from gaming, and the other fashionable expenses of the place.' This is the first charge against him; upon which all that I shall observe is, that I will refer it to your own judgment, whether it be fitter to have a place in the catalogue of his faults, or of those virtues for which he is now 'numbered among the sons of God'.

If all the persons concerned in 'that ridiculous society, whose follies you have so often heard repeated', could but give such a proof of their deserving the glorious title [the Holy Club] which was once bestowed upon them, they would be contented that their 'lives' too should be 'counted madness, and their end' thought to be 'without honour'. But the truth is, their title to holiness stands upon much less stable foundations; as you will easily perceive when you know the ground of this wonderful outcry, which it seems England is not wide enough to contain

In November, 1729, at which time I came to reside at Oxford, your son, my brother, myself, and one more, agreed to spend three or four evenings in a week together. Our design was to read over the classics, which we had before read in private, on common nights, and on Sunday some book in divinity. In the summer following, Mr. M. told me he had called at the gaol, to see a man who was condemned for killing his wife; and that, from the talk he had with one of the debtors, he verily believed it would do much good, if any one would be at the pains of now and then speaking with them. This he so frequently repeated, that on the 24th of August, 1730, my brother and I walked with him to the castle. We were so well satisfied with our conversation there, that we agreed to go thither once or twice a week; which we had not done long, before he desired me to go with him to see a poor woman in the town, who was sick. In this employment too, when we came to reflect upon it, we believed it would be worth while to spend an hour or two in a week; provided the Minister of the parish, in which any such person was, were not against it. But that we might not depend wholly on our own judgments, I wrote an account to my father of our whole design; withal begging that he, who had lived seventy years in the world, and seen as much of it as most private men have ever done, would advise us whether we had yet gone too far, and whether we should now stand still, or go forward.

Part of his answer, dated September 21st, 1730, was this:

'And now, as to your own designs and employments, what can I say less of them than, *Valde probo* [I greatly approve]. And that I have the highest reason to bless God, that he has given me two sons together at Oxford, to whom he has given grace and courage to turn the war against the world and the devil, which is the best way to conquer them. They have but one more enemy to combat with, the flesh; which if they take care to subdue by fasting and prayer, there will be no more for them to do, but to proceed steadily in the same course, and expect 'the crown which fadeth not away'. You have reason to bless God, as I do, that you have so fast a friend as Mr. M., who, I see, in the most difficult service, is ready to break the ice for you. You do not know of how much good that poor wretch who killed his wife has been the providential occasion. I think I must adopt Mr. M., to be my son, together with you and your brother Charles; and when I have such a ternion[3] to prosecute that war, wherein I am now *miles emeritus* [a retired soldier], I shall not be ashamed when they speak with their enemies in the gate.

'I am afraid lest the main objection you make against your going on in the business with the prisoners may secretly proceed from flesh and blood. For "who can harm you if you are followers of that which is so good"; and which will be one of the marks by which the Shepherd of Israel will know his sheep at the last day?— though if it were possible for you to suffer a little in the cause, you would have a confessor's reward. You own, none but such as are out of their senses would be prejudiced against your acting in this manner; but say, "These are they that need a physician." But what if they will not accept of one, who will be welcome to the poor prisoners? Go on then, in God's name, in the path to which your Saviour has directed you, and that track wherein your father has gone before you! For when I was an undergraduate at Oxford, I visited those in the castle there, and reflect on it with great satisfaction to this day. Walk as prudently as you can, though not fearfully, and my heart and prayers are with you.

'Your first regular step is, to consult with him (if any such there be) who has a jurisdiction over the prisoners; and the next is, to obtain the direction and approbation of your Bishop. This is Monday morning, at which time I shall never forget you. If it be possible, I should be glad to see you all three here in the fine end of the summer. But if I cannot have that satisfaction, I am sure I can reach you every day, though you were beyond the Indies. Accordingly, to Him who is every where I now heartily commit you as being

'Your most affectionate and joyful father.' ...

Soon after, a gentleman of Merton College, who was one of our little company, which now consisted of five persons, acquainted us that he had been much rallied the day before for being a member of *The Holy Club*; and that it was become a common topic of mirth at his college, where they had found out several of our customs, to which we were ourselves utter strangers ... But the outcry daily increasing, that we might show what ground there was for it, we proposed to our friends, or opponents, as we had opportunity, these or the like questions:

I. Whether it does not concern all men of all conditions to imitate Him, as much as they can, 'who went about doing good'?

Whether all Christians are not concerned in that command, 'While we have time, let us do good to all men'?

Whether we shall not be more happy hereafter, the more good we do now?

Whether we can be happy at all hereafter, unless we have, according to our power, 'fed the hungry, clothed the naked, visited those that are sick, and in prison'; and made all these actions subservient to a higher purpose, even the saving of souls from death?

Whether it be not our bounden duty always to remember, that He did more for us than we can do for him, who assures us, 'Inasmuch as ye have done it unto one of the least of these my brethren, ye have done it unto me'?

II. Whether, upon these considerations, we may not try to do good to our acquaintance? Particularly, whether we may not try to convince them of the necessity of being Christians?

Whether of the consequent necessity of being scholars?

Whether of the necessity of method and industry, in order to either learning or virtue?

Whether we may not try to persuade them to confirm and increase their industry, by communicating as often as they can?

Whether we may not mention to them the authors whom we conceive to have wrote the best on those subjects?

Whether we may not assist them, as we are able, from time to time, to form resolutions upon what they read in those authors, and to execute them with steadiness and perseverance?

III. Whether, upon the considerations above-mentioned, we may not try to do good to those that are hungry, naked, or sick? In particular, whether, if we know any necessitous family, we may not give them a little food, clothes, or physic, as they want?

Whether we may not give them, if they can read, a Bible, Common-Prayer Book, or Whole Duty of Man?

Whether we may not, now and then, inquire how they have used them; explain what they do not understand, and enforce what they do?

Whether we may not enforce upon them, more especially, the necessity of private prayer, and of frequenting the church and sacrament?

Whether we may not contribute, what little we are able, toward having their children clothed and taught to read?

Whether we may not take care that they be taught their catechism, and short prayers for morning and evening?

IV. Lastly: Whether, upon the considerations above-mentioned, we may not try to do good to those that are in prison? In particular, Whether we may not release such well-disposed persons as remain in prison for small sums?

Whether we may not lend smaller sums to those that are of any trade, that they may procure themselves tools and materials to work with?

Whether we may not give to them who appear to want it most, a little money, or clothes, or physic?

Whether we may not supply as many as are serious enough to read, with a Bible, and Whole Duty of Man?

Whether we may not, as we have opportunity, explain and enforce these upon them, especially with respect to public and private prayer, and the blessed sacrament?

I do not remember that we met with any person who answered any of these questions in the negative; or who even doubted, whether it were not lawful to apply to this use that time and money which we should else have spent in other diversions. But several we met with who increased our little stock of money for the prisoners and the poor, by subscribing something quarterly to it; so that the more persons we proposed our designs to, the more we were confirmed in the belief of their innocency, and the more determined to pursue them, in spite of the ridicule, which increased fast upon us during the winter. However, in spring I thought it could not be improper to desire farther instructions from those who were wiser and better than ourselves; and accordingly (on May 18th, 1731), I wrote a particular account of all our proceedings to a Clergyman of known wisdom and integrity.[4] After having informed him of all the branches of our design, as clearly and simply as I could, I next acquainted him with the success it had met with, in the following words: 'Almost as soon as we had made our first attempts this way, some of the men of wit in Christ Church entered the lists against us; and, between mirth and anger, made a pretty many reflections upon the Sacramentarians, as they were pleased to call us. Soon after, their allies at Merton changed our title, and did us the honour of styling us, The Holy Club. But most of them being persons of well-known characters, they had not the good fortune to gain any proselytes from the sacrament, till a gentleman, eminent for learning, and well esteemed for piety, joining them, told his nephew, that if he dared to go to the weekly communion any longer, he would immediately turn him out of doors. That argument, indeed, had no success: The young gentleman communicated next week; upon which his uncle, having again tried to convince him that he was in the wrong way, by shaking him by the throat to no purpose, changed his method, and by mildness prevailed upon him to absent from it the Sunday following; as he has done five Sundays in six ever since. This much delighted our gay opponents, who increased their number apace; especially when, shortly after, one of the seniors of the college having been with the Doctor, upon his return from him sent for two young gentlemen severally, who had communicated weekly for some time, and was so successful in his exhortations, that for the future they promised to do it only three times a year . . .

Your son was now at Holt: However, we continued to meet at our usual times, though our little affairs went on but heavily without him. But at our return from Lincolnshire, in September last, we had the pleasure of seeing him again; when, though he could not be so active with us as formerly, yet we were exceeding glad to spend what time we could in talking and reading with him . . .

The two points whereunto, by the blessing of God and your son's help, we had before attained, we endeavoured to hold fast: I mean, the doing what good we can; and, in order thereto, communicating as often as we have opportunity. To these, by the advice of Mr. Clayton,[5] we have added a third—the observing the fasts of the Church; the general neglect of which we can by no means apprehend to be a lawful excuse for neglecting them. And in the resolution to adhere to these and all things else which we are convinced God requires at our hands, we trust we shall persevere till he calls us to give an account of our stewardship. As for the names of Methodists, Supererogation-men,[6] and so on, with which some of our neighbours are pleased to compliment us, we do not conceive ourselves to be under any obligation to regard them, much less to take them for arguments. 'To the law and to the testimony' we appeal, whereby we ought to be judged. If by these it can be proved we are in an error, we will immediately and gladly retract it: If not, we 'have not so learned Christ', as to renounce any part of his service, though men should 'say all manner of evil against us', with more judgment and as little truth as hitherto. We do, indeed, use all the lawful means we know, to prevent 'the good which is in us from being evil spoken of': But if the neglect of known duties be the one condition of securing our reputation, why, fare it well; we know whom we have believed, and what we thus lay out He will pay us again. Your son already stands before

the judgment-seat of Him who judges righteous judgment; at the
brightness of whose presence the clouds remove: His eyes are open,
and he sees clearly whether it was 'blind zeal, and a thorough
mistake of true religion, that hurried him on in the error of his
way'; or whether he acted like a faithful and wise servant, who,
from a just sense that his time was short, made haste to finish his
work before his Lord's coming, that 'when laid in the balance' he
might not 'be found wanting'.

I have now largely and plainly laid before you the real ground
of all the strange outcry you have heard; and am not without hope
that by this fairer representation of it than you probably ever
received before, both you and the Clergyman you formerly
mentioned may have a more favourable opinion of a good cause,
though under an ill name. Whether you have or no, I shall ever
acknowledge my best services to be due to yourself and your
family, both for the generous assistance you have given my father,
and for the invaluable advantages your son has (under God)
bestowed on,

Sir,

Your ever obliged

and most obedient servant.

JOURNAL

Tuesday, October 14, 1735. Mr. Benjamin Ingham,[7] of Queen's College, Oxford, Mr. Charles Delamotte, son of a merchant, in London, who had offered himself some days before, my brother Charles Wesley, and myself took boat for Gravesend, in order to embark for Georgia. Our end in leaving our native country was not to avoid want (God having given us plenty of temporal blessings), nor to gain the dung or dross of riches or honour; but singly this—to save our souls; to live wholly to the glory of God. In the afternoon we found the Simmonds off Gravesend, and immediately went on board.

Wednesday and *Thursday* we spent with one or two of our friends, partly on board and partly on shore, in exhorting one another 'to shake off every weight, and to run with patience the race set before us'.

Fri. 17. I began to learn German, in order to converse with the Germans, six-and-twenty of whom we had on board. On Sunday, the weather being fair and calm we had the Morning Service on quarter-deck. I now first preached *extempore*, and then administered the Lord's supper to six or seven communicants. A little flock. May God increase it!

Mon. 20. Believing the denying ourselves, even in the smallest instances, might, by the blessing of God, be helpful to us, we wholly left off the use of flesh and wine, and confined ourselves to vegetable food—chiefly rice and biscuit. In the afternoon, David Nitschman, Bishop of the Germans, and two others, began to learn English. O may we be, not only of one tongue, but of one mind and of one heart!

Tues. 21. We sailed from Gravesend. When we were past about half the Goodwin Sands, the wind suddenly failed. Had the calm continued till ebb, the ship had probably been lost. But the gale sprung up again in an hour, and carried us into the Downs.

We now began to be a little regular. Our common way of living was this: From four in the morning till five, each of us used private prayer. From five to seven we read the Bible together, carefully comparing it (that we might not lean to our own understandings) with the writings of the earliest ages. At seven we breakfasted. At eight were the public prayers. From nine to twelve, I usually learned German, and Mr. Delamotte, Greek. My brother writ sermons, and Mr. Ingham instructed the children. At twelve we met to give an account to one another what we had done since our last meeting, and what we designed to do before our next. About one we dined. The time from dinner to four, we spent in reading to those whom each of us had taken in charge, or in speaking to them severally, as need required. At four were the evening prayers; when either the second lesson was explained (as it always was in the morning), or the children were catechised and instructed before the congregation. From five to six we again used private prayer. From six to seven I read in our cabin to two or three of the passengers (of whom there were about eighty English on board); and each of my brethren to a few more in theirs. At seven I joined with the Germans in their public service; while Mr. Ingham was reading between the decks, to as many as desired to hear. At eight we met again, to exhort and instruct one another. Between nine and ten we went to bed, where neither the roaring of the sea, nor the motion of the ship, could take away the refreshing sleep which God gave us.

Fri. 24. Having a rolling sea, most of the passengers found the effects of it. Mr. Delamotte was exceeding sick for several days; Mr. Ingham, for about half an hour. My brother's head ached much. Hitherto it hath pleased God, the sea has not disordered me at all; nor have I been hindered one quarter of an hour from reading, writing, composing, or doing any business I could have done on shore.

During our stay in the Downs, some or other of us went, as often as we had opportunity, on board the ship that sailed in company with us, where also many were glad to join in prayer and hearing the word.

Fri. 31. We sailed out of the Downs. At eleven at night I was waked by a great noise. I soon found there was no danger. But the bare apprehension of it gave me a lively conviction what manner of men those ought to be who are every moment on the brink of eternity.

Saturday, November 1. We came to St Helen's harbour, and the next day into Cowes road. The wind was fair, but we waited for the man-of-war which was to sail with us. This was a happy opportunity of instructing our fellow-travellers. May He whose seed we sow, give it the increase! . . .

Saturday, January 17, 1736. Many people were very impatient at the contrary wind. At seven in the evening they were quieted by a storm. It rose higher and higher till nine. About nine the sea broke over us from stem to stern; burst through the windows of the state cabin, where three or four of us were, and covered us all over, though a bureau sheltered me from the main shock. About eleven I lay down in the great cabin, and in a short time fell asleep, though very uncertain whether I should wake alive, and much ashamed of my unwillingness to die. O how pure in heart must he be, who would rejoice to appear before God at a moment's warning! Toward morning, 'He rebuked the winds and the sea, and there was a great calm.'

Sun. 18. We returned God thanks for our deliverance, of which a few appeared duly sensible. But the rest (among whom were most of the sailors) denied we had been in any danger. I could not have believed that so little good would have been done by the terror they were in before. But it cannot be that they should long obey God from fear, who are deaf to the motives of love.

Fri. 23. In the evening another storm began. In the morning it increased, so that they were forced to let the ship drive. I could not but say to myself, 'How is it that thou hast no faith?' being still unwilling to die. About one in the afternoon, almost as soon as I had stepped out of the great cabin-door, the sea did not break as usual, but came with a full, smooth tide over the side of the ship. I was vaulted over with water in a moment, and so stunned that I scarce expected to lift up my head again, till the sea should give up her dead. But thanks be to God, I received no hurt at all. About midnight the storm ceased.

Sun. 25. At noon our third storm began. At four it was more violent than before. Now, indeed, we could say, 'The waves of the sea were mighty, and raged horribly. They rose up to the heavens above, and' clave 'down to hell beneath.' The winds roared round about us, and (what I never heard before) whistled as distinctly as if it had been a human voice. The ship not only rocked to and fro with the utmost violence, but shook and jarred with so unequal, grating a motion, that one could not but with great difficulty keep one's hold of any thing, nor stand a moment without it. Every ten minutes came a shock against the stern or side of the ship, which one would think should dash the planks in pieces. At this time a child, privately baptized before, was brought to be received into the church. It put me in mind of Jeremiah's buying the field, when the Chaldeans were on the point of destroying Jerusalem, and seemed a pledge of the mercy God designed to show us, even in the land of the living.

We spent two or three hours after prayers, in conversing suitably to the occasion, confirming one another in a calm submission to the wise, holy, gracious will of God. And now a storm did not appear so terrible as before. Blessed be the God of all consolation!

At seven I went to the Germans. I had long before observed the great seriousness of their behaviour. Of their humility they had given a continual proof, by performing those servile offices for the other passengers, which none of the English would undertake; for which they desired, and would receive no pay, saying, 'it was good for their proud hearts', and 'their loving Saviour had done more for them'. And every day had given them occasion of showing a meekness which no injury could move. If they were pushed, struck, or thrown down, they rose again and went away; but no complaint was found in their mouth. There was now an opportunity of trying whether they were delivered from the spirit of fear, as well as from that of pride, anger, and revenge. In the midst of the psalm wherewith their service began, the sea broke over, split the main-sail in pieces, covered the ship, and poured in between the decks, as if the great deep had already swallowed us up. A terrible scream-ing began among the English. The Germans calmly sung on. I asked one of them afterwards, 'Was you not afraid?' He answered, 'I thank God, no.' I asked, 'But were not your women and children afraid?' He replied mildly, 'No; our women and children are not afraid to die.'

From them I went to their crying, trembling neighbours, and pointed out to them the difference in the hour of trial, between him that feareth God, and him that feareth him not. At twelve the wind fell. This was the most glorious day which I have hitherto seen.

Mon. 26. We enjoyed the calm. I can conceive no difference comparable to that between a smooth and a rough sea, except that which is between a mind calmed by the love of God, and one torn up by the storms of earthly passions.

Thur. 29. About seven in the evening, we fell in with the skirts of a hurricane. The rain as well as the wind was extremely violent. The sky was so dark in a moment, that the sailors could not so much as see the ropes, or set about furling the sails. The ship must, in all probability, have overset, had not the wind fell as suddenly as it rose. Toward the end of it, we had that appearance on each of the masts, which (it is thought) the ancients called Castor and Pollux. It was a small ball of white fire, like a star. The mariners say, it appears either in a storm (and then commonly upon the deck), or just at the end of it; and then it is usually on the masts or sails ...

Friday, February 6. About eight in the morning, we first set foot on American ground. It was a small uninhabited island, over against Tybee. Mr. Oglethorpe led us to a rising ground, where we all kneeled down to give thanks. He then took boat for Savannah. When the rest of the people were come on shore, we called our little flock together to prayers. Several parts of the Second Lesson (Mark vi.) were wonderfully suited to the occasion; in particular, the account of the courage and sufferings of John the Baptist; our Lord's directions to the first Preachers of his Gospel, and their toiling at sea, and deliverance; with these comfortable words: 'It is I, be not afraid.' ...

Tuesday, March 30. Mr. Ingham, coming from Frederica, brought me letters, pressing me to go thither. The next day Mr. Delamotte and I began to try, whether life might not as well be sustained by one sort as by a variety of food. We chose to make the experiment with bread; and were never more vigorous and healthy than while we tasted nothing else. 'Blessed are the pure in heart'; who, whether they eat or drink, or whatever they do, have no end therein but to please God! To them all things are pure. Every creature is good to them, and nothing to be rejected. But let them who know and feel that they are not thus pure, use every help, and remove every hinderance; always remembering, 'He that despiseth little things shall fall by little and little.'

Sunday, April 4. About four in the afternoon I set out for Frederica, in a pettiawga—a sort of flat-bottomed barge. The next evening we anchored near Skidoway Island, where the water, at flood, was twelve or fourteen foot deep. I wrapped myself up from head to foot, in a large cloak, to keep off the sand-flies, and lay down on the quarter-deck. Between one and two I waked under water, being so fast asleep that I did not find where I was till my mouth was full of it. Having left my cloak, I know not how, upon deck, I swam round to the other side of the pettiawga, where a boat was tied, and climbed up by the rope without any hurt, more than wetting my clothes. Thou art the God of whom cometh salvation: Thou art the Lord by whom we escape death . . .

Thursday, June 10. We began to execute at Frederica what we had before agreed to do at Savannah. Our design was, on Sundays, in the afternoon, and every evening, after public service, to spend some time with the most serious of the communicants, in singing, reading, and conversation. This evening we had only Mark Hird. But on Sunday Mr. Hird and two more desired to be admitted. After a psalm and a little conversation, I read Mr. Law's 'Christian Perfection', and concluded with another psalm.

Sat. 12. Being with one who was very desirous to converse with me, but not upon religion, I spoke to this effect: 'Suppose you was going to a country where every one spoke Latin, and understood no other language, neither would converse with any that did not understand it: Suppose one was sent to stay here a short time, on purpose to teach it you; suppose that person, pleased with your company, should spend his time in trifling with you, and teach you nothing of what he came for: Would that be well done? Yet this is our case. You are going to a country where every one speaks the love of God. The citizens of heaven understand no other language. They converse with none who do not understand it. Indeed none such are admitted there. I am sent from God to teach you this. A few days are allotted us for that purpose. Would it then be well done in me, because I was pleased with your company, to spend this short time in trifling, and teach you nothing of what I came for? God forbid! I will rather not converse with you at all. Of the two extremes, this is the best.' ...

Tuesday, July 20. Five of the Chicasaw Indians (twenty of whom had been in Savannah several days) came to see us, with Mr. Andrews, their interpreter. They were all warriors, four of them head men. The two chief were Paustoobee and Mingo Mattaw. Our conference was as follows:

Q. Do you believe there is One above who is over all things?
Paustoobe answered. We believe there are four beloved things above;—the clouds, the sun, the clear sky, and He that lives in the clear sky.
Q. Do you believe there is but One that lives in the clear sky?
A. We believe there are two with him, three in all.
Q. Do you think he made the sun, and the other beloved things?
A. We cannot tell. Who hath seen?
Q. Do you think he made you?
A. We think he made all men at first.
Q. How did he make them at first?
A. Out of the ground.
Q. Do you believe he loves you?
A. I do not know. I cannot see him.
Q. But has he not often saved your life?
A. He has. many bullets have gone on this side, and many on that side; but he would never let them hurt me. And many bullets have gone into these young men; and yet they are alive.
Q. Then, cannot he save you from your enemies now?
A. Yes, but we know not if he will. We have now so many enemies round about us, that I think of nothing but death. And if I am to die, I shall die, and I will die like a man. But if he will have me to live, I shall live. Though I had ever so many enemies, he can destroy them all.
Q. How do you know that?
A. From what I have seen. When our enemies came against us before, then the beloved clouds came for us. And often much rain, and sometimes hail, has come upon them; and that in a very hot day. And I saw, when many French, and Choctaws, and other

nations came against one of our towns; and the ground made a noise under them, and the beloved ones in the air behind them; and they were afraid, and went away, and left their meat and drink, and their guns. I tell no lie. All these saw it too.

Q. Have you heard such noises at other times?

A. Yes, often; before and after almost every battle.

Q. What sort of noises were they?

A. Like the noise of drums, and guns, and shouting.

Q. Have you heard any such lately?

A. Yes; four days after our last battle with the French.

Q. Then you heard nothing before it?

A. The night before. I dreamed I heard many drums up there; and many trumpets there, and much stamping of feet and shouting. Till then I thought we should all die. But then I thought the beloved ones were come to help us. And the next day I heard above a hundred guns go off before the fight began; and I said, 'When the sun is there, the beloved ones will help us; and we shall conquer our enemies.' And we did so.

Q. Do you often think and talk of the beloved ones?

A. We think of them always, wherever we are. We talk of them and to them, at home and abroad; in peace, in war, before and after we fight; and, indeed, whenever and wherever we meet together.

Q. Where do you think your souls go after death?

A. We believe the souls of red men walk up and down, near the place where they died, or where their bodies lie; for we have often heard cries and noises near the place where any prisoners had been burned.

Q. Where do the souls of white men go after death?

A. We cannot tell. We have not seen.

Q. Our belief is, that the souls of bad men only walk up and down; but the souls of good men go up.

A. I believe so too. But I told you the talk of the nation.

(Mr. Andrews.—They said at the burying, they knew what you was doing. You was speaking to the beloved ones above, to take up the soul of the young woman.)

Q. We have a book that tells us many things of the beloved ones above; would you be glad to know them?

A. We have no time now but to fight. If we should ever be at peace, we should be glad to know.

Q. Do you expect ever to know what the white men know?

(Mr. Andrews.—They told Mr. O., they believed the time will come when the red and white men will be one.)

Q. What do the French teach you?

A. The French black kings[8] never go out. We see you go about;—we like that;—that is good.

Q. How came your nation by the knowledge they have?

A. As soon as ever the ground was sound and fit to stand upon, it came to us, and has been with us ever since. But we are young men; our old men know more: But all of them do not know. There are but a few who the beloved one chooses from a child, and is in them, and takes care of them, and teaches them: They know these things; and our old men practise; therefore they know. But I do not practise; therefore I know little . . .

After having beaten the air in this unhappy place for twenty days, on *January 26th* [1737] I took my final leave of Frederica. It was not any apprehension of my own danger, though my life had been threatened many times, but an utter despair of doing good there, which made me content with the thought of seeing it no more.

In my passage home, having procured a celebrated book (The Works of Nicholas Machiavel), I set myself carefully to read and consider it. I began with a prejudice in his favour; having been informed, he had often been misunderstood, and greatly misrepresented. I weighed the sentiments that were less common; transcribed the passages wherein they were contained; compared one passage with another, and endeavoured to form a cool, impartial judgment. And my cool judgment is, that if all the other doctrines of devils which have been committed to writing since letters were in the world were collected together in one volume, it would fall short of this; and, that should a Prince form himself by this book, so calmly recommending hypocrisy, treachery, lying, robbery, oppression, adultery, whoredom, and murder of all kinds, Domitian or Nero would be an angel of light, compared to that man . . .

Wednesday, August 3. We returned to Savannah. *Sunday, 7,* I repelled Mrs. Williamson from the holy communion.[9] And *Mon-*

day, 8, Mr. Recorder, of Savannah, issued out the warrant following:

Georgia. Savannah ss.

'*To all Constables, Tithingmen, and others, whom these may concern*:

'You, and each of you, are hereby required to take the body of John Wesley, Clerk:

'And bring him before one of the bailiffs of the said town, to answer the complaint of William Williamson and Sophia his wife, for defaming the said Sophia, and refusing to administer to her the Sacrament of the Lord's Supper, in a public congregation, without cause; by which the said William Williamson is damaged one thousand pounds sterling: And for so doing, this is your warrant, certifying what you are to do in the premises. Given under my hand and seal the 8th day of August, *Anno Dom.* 1737.

THO. CHRISTIE.'

Tues. 9. Mr. Jones, the Constable, served the warrant, and carried me before Mr. Bailiff Parker and Mr. Recorder. My answer to them was, that the giving or refusing the Lord's Supper being a matter purely ecclesiastical, I could not acknowledge their power to interrogate me upon it. Mr. Parker told me, 'However, you must appear at the next Court, holden for Savannah.' Mr. Williamson, who stood by, said, 'Gentlemen, I desire Mr. Wesley may give bail for his appearance.' But Mr. Parker immediately replied, 'Sir, Mr. Wesley's word is sufficient.'

Wed. 10. Mr. Causton (from a just regard, as his letter expressed it, to the friendship which had subsisted between us till this affair) required me to give the reasons in the Courthouse, why I repelled Mrs. Williamson from the holy communion. I answered, 'I apprehend many ill consequences may arise from so doing: Let the cause be laid before the Trustees.'

Thur. 11. Mr. Causton came to my house, and among many other sharp words, said, 'Make an end of this matter: Thou hadst best. My niece to be used thus! I have drawn the sword, and I will never sheath it till I have satisfaction.'

Soon after, he added, 'Give the reasons of your repelling her before the whole congregation.' I answered, 'Sir, if you insist upon it, I will; and so you may be pleased to tell her.' He said, 'Write to her, and tell her so yourself.' I said, 'I will'; and after he went, I wrote as follows:

'*To Mrs. Sophia Williamson.*

'AT Mr. Causton's request, I write once more. The rules whereby I proceed are these:

' "So many as intend to be partakers of the holy communion, shall signify their names to the Curate, at least some time the day before." This you did not do.

' "And if any of these—have done any wrong to his neighbours, by word or deed, so that the congregation be thereby offended, the Curate——shall advertise him, that in any wise he presume not to come to the Lord's table, until he hath openly declared himself to have truly repented."

'If you offer yourself at the Lord's table on Sunday, I will advertise you (as I have done more than once), wherein you have done wrong. And when you have openly declared yourself to have truly repented, I will administer to you the mysteries of God.

JOHN WESLEY.

'August 11, 1737'

Mr. Delamotte carrying this, Mr. Causton said, among many other warm sayings, 'I am the person that am injured. The affront is offered to me; and I will espouse the cause of my niece. I am ill-used; and I will have satisfaction, if it be to be had in the world.'

Which way this satisfaction was to be had, I did not yet conceive. But on Friday and Saturday it began to appear: Mr. Causton declared to many persons, that 'Mr. Wesley had repelled Sophy from the holy communion, purely out of revenge; because he had made proposals of marriage to her, which she rejected, and married Mr. Williamson.' . . .

October 7. I consulted my friends, whether God did not call me to return to England? The reason for which I left it had now no force; there being no possibility, as yet, of instructing the Indians; neither had I, as yet, found or heard of any Indians on the continent of America who had the least desire of being instructed. And as to Savannah, having never engaged myself, either by word or letter, to stay there a day longer than I should judge convenient, nor ever taken charge of the people any otherwise than as in my passage to the Heathens, I looked upon myself to be fully discharged therefrom, by the vacating of that design. Besides, there was a probability of doing more service to that unhappy people, in England, than I could do in Georgia, by representing, without fear or favour to the Trustees, the real state the colony was in. After deeply considering these things, they were unanimous, 'That I ought to go; but not yet.' So I laid the thoughts of it aside for the present: Being persuaded, that when the time was come, God would 'make the way plain before my face'. . . .

Friday, December 2. I proposed to set out for Carolina about noon, the tide then serving. But about ten, the Magistrates sent for me, and told me, I must not go out of the province; for I had not answered the allegations laid against me. I replied, 'I have appeared at six or seven Courts successively, in order to answer them. But I was not suffered so to do, when I desired it time after time.' Then they said, however, I must not go, unless I would give security to answer those allegations at their Court. I asked, 'What security?' After consulting together about two hours, the Recorder showed me a kind of bond, engaging me, under a penalty of fifty pounds, to appear at their Court when I should be required. He added, 'But Mr. Williamson too has desired of us, that you should give bail to answer his action.' I then told him plainly, 'Sir, you use me very ill, and so you do the Trustees. I will give neither any bond, nor any bail at all. You know your business, and I know mine.'

In the afternoon, the Magistrates published an order, requiring all the officers and centinels to prevent my going out of the province; and forbidding any person to assist me so to do. Being now only a prisoner at large, in a place where I knew by experience, every day would give fresh opportunity to procure evidence of words I never said, and actions I never did; I saw clearly the hour was come for leaving this place: And as soon as Evening Prayers were over, about eight o'clock, the tide then serving, I shook off the dust of my feet, and left Georgia, after having preached the Gospel there (not as I ought, but as I was able) one year, and nearly nine months . . .

Sat. 3. We came to Purrysburg early in the morning, and endeavoured to procure a guide to Port-Royal. But none being to be had, we set out without one, an hour before sunrise. After walking two or three hours, we met with an old man, who led us into a small path, near which was a line of *blazed* trees (that is, marked by cutting off part of the bark), by following which, he said, we might easily come to Port-Royal in five or six hours.

We were four in all; one of whom intended to go to England with me; the other two to settle in Carolina. About eleven we came into a large swamp, where we wandered about till near two. We then found another *blaze*, and pursued it, till it divided into two: One of these we followed through an almost impassable thicket, a mile beyond which it ended. We made through the thicket again, and traced the other *blaze* till that ended too. It now grew toward sunset; so we sat down, faint and weary, having had no food all day, except a gingerbread cake, which I had taken in my pocket. A third of this we had divided among us at noon; another third we took now; the rest we reserved for the morning; but we had met with no water all the day. Thrusting a stick into the ground, and finding the end of it moist, two of our company fell a digging with their hands, and, at about three feet depth, found water. We thanked God, drank, and were refreshed. The night was sharp; however, there was no complaining among us; but after having commended ourselves to God, we lay down close together, and (I at least) slept till near six in the morning.

Sun. 4. God renewing our strength, we arose neither faint nor weary, and resolved to make one trial more to find out a path to Port-Royal. We steered due east; but finding neither path nor blaze, and the woods growing thicker and thicker, we judged it would be our best course to return, if we could, by the way we came. The day before, in the thickest part of the woods, I had broke many young trees, I knew not why, as we walked along: These we found a great help in several places, where no path was to be seen; and between one and two God brought us safe to Benjamin Arieu's house, the old man we left the day before.

In the evening I read French prayers to a numerous family, a mile from Arieu's; one of whom undertook to guide us to Port-Royal. In the morning we set out. About sunset, we asked our guide if he knew where he was; who frankly answered, No. However, we pushed on till, about seven, we came to a plantation, and the next evening (after many difficulties and delays) we landed on Port-Royal Island . . .

February 1738. It is now two years and almost four months since I left my native country, in order to teach the Georgian Indians the nature of Christianity: But what have I learned myself in the mean time? Why (what I the least of all suspected), that I who went to America to convert others, was never myself converted to God.[10] 'I am not mad,' though I thus speak; but 'I speak the words of truth and soberness,' if haply some of those who still dream may awake, and see, that as I am, so are they.

Are they read in philosophy? So was I. In ancient or modern tongues? So was I also. Are they versed in the science of divinity? I too have studied it many years. Can they talk fluently upon spiritual things? The very same could I do. Are they plenteous in alms? Behold, I gave all my goods to feed the poor. Do they give of their labour as well as of their substance? I have laboured more abundantly than they all. Are they willing to suffer for their brethren? I have thrown up my friends, reputation, ease, country; I have put my life in my hand, wandering into strange lands; I have given my body to be devoured by the deep, parched up with heat, consumed by toil and weariness, or whatsoever God should please to bring upon me. But does all this (be it more or less, it matters not) make me acceptable to God? Does all I ever did or can know, say, give, do, or suffer, justify me in his sight? Yea, or the constant use of all the means of grace? (Which, nevertheless, is meet, right, and our bounden duty.) Or that I know nothing of myself; that I am, as touching outward, moral righteousness blameless? Or (to come closer yet) the having a rational conviction of all the truths of Christianity? Does all this give me a claim to the holy, heavenly, divine character of a Christian? By no means. If the Oracles of God are true, if we are still to abide by 'the law and the testimony'; all these things, though, when ennobled by faith in Christ, they are holy and just and good, yet without it are 'dung and dross', meet only to be purged away by 'the fire that never shall be quenched'.

This, then, have I learned in the ends of the earth—That I 'am fallen short of the glory of God'; That my whole heart is 'altogether corrupt and abominable'; and, consequently, my whole life (seeing it cannot be, that an 'evil tree' should 'bring forth good fruit'): That 'alienated' as I am from the life of God', I am 'a child of wrath', an heir of hell: That my own works, my own sufferings, my own righteousness, are so far from reconciling me to an offended God, so far from making any atonement for the least of those sins, which 'are more in number than the hairs of my head', that the most specious of them need an atonement themselves, or they cannot abide his righteous judgment; that 'having the sentence of death' in my heart, and having nothing in or of myself to plead, I have no hope, but that of being justified freely, 'through the redemption that is in Jesus'; I have no hope, but that if I seek I shall find Christ, and 'be found in him not having my own righteousness, but that which is through the faith of Christ, the righteousness which is of God by faith'. (Phil. iii. 9.)

If it be said, that I have faith (for many such things have I heard, from many miserable comforters), I answer, So have the devils—a sort of faith; but still they are strangers to the covenant of promise. So the apostles had even at Cana in Galilee, when Jesus first 'manifested forth his glory', even then they, in a sort, 'believed on him'; but they had not then 'the faith that over-cometh the world'. The faith I want is 'a sure trust and confidence in God, that, through the merits of Christ, my sins are forgiven, and I reconciled to the favour of God'. I want that faith which St. Paul recommends to all the world, especially in his Epistle to the Romans: That faith which enables every one that hath it to cry out, 'I live not; but Christ liveth in me; and the life which I now live, I live by faith in the Son of God, who loved me, and gave himself for me.' I want that faith which none can have without knowing that he hath it (though many imagine they have it, who have it not); for whosoever hath it, is 'freed from sin, the' whole 'body of sin is destroyed' in him; He is freed from fear, 'having peace with God through Christ, and rejoicing in hope of the glory of God'. And he is freed from doubt, 'having the love of God shed abroad in his heart, through the Holy Ghost which is given unto him', which 'Spirit itself beareth witness with his spirit, that he is a child of God' . . . .

Tuesday, February 7. (A day much to be remembered.) At the house of Mr. Weinantz, a Dutch merchant, I met Peter Böhler, Schulius Richter, and Wensel Neiser, just then landed from Germany. Finding they had no acquaintance in England, I offered to procure them a lodging, and did so near Mr. Hutton's, where I then was. And from this time I did not willingly lose any opportunity of conversing with them, while I stayed in London . . .

Tues. 28. I saw my mother once more. The next day I prepared for my journey to my brother at Tiverton. But on *Thursday* morning, *March 2d*, a message that my brother Charles was dying at Oxford, obliged me to set out for that place immediately. Calling at an odd house[11] in the afternoon, I found several persons there who seemed well-wishers to religion to whom I spake plainly; as I did in the evening, both to the servants and strangers at my inn.

With regard to my own behaviour, I now renewed and wrote down my former resolutions.

1. To use absolute openness and unreserve, with all I should converse with.

2. To labour after continual seriousness, not willingly indulging myself in any the least levity of behaviour, or in laughter—no, not for a moment.

3. To speak no word which does not tend to the glory of God; in particular, not to talk of worldly things. Others may, nay, must. But what is that to thee? And,

4. To take no pleasure which does not tend to the glory of God; thanking God every moment for all I do take, and therefore rejecting every sort and degree of it, which I feel I cannot so thank him *in* and *for*.

Sat. 4. I found my brother at Oxford, recovering from his pleurisy; and with him Peter Böhler; by whom (in the hand of the great God) I was, on *Sunday, the 5th*, clearly convinced of unbelief, of the want of that faith whereby alone we are saved.

Immediately it struck into my mind, 'Leave off preaching. How can you preach to others, who have not faith yourself?' I asked Böhler, whether he thought I should leave it off or not. He answered, 'By no means.' I asked, 'But what can I preach?' He said, 'Preach faith *till* you have it; and then, *because* you have it, you *will* preach faith.'

Accordingly, *Monday, 6*, I began preaching this new doctrine, though my soul started back from the work. The first person to whom I offered salvation by faith alone, was a prisoner under sentence of death. His name was Clifford. Peter Böhler had many times desired me to speak to him before. But I could not prevail on myself so to do; being still (as I had been many years) a zealous assertor of the impossibility of a death-bed repentance . . .

Monday, May 1. The return of my brother's illness obliged me again to hasten to London. In the evening I found him at James Hutton's, better as to his health than I expected; but strongly averse from what he called 'the new faith'.

This evening our little society began, which afterwards met in Fetter-Lane. Our fundamental rules were as follows:

IN obedience to the command of God by St. James, and by the advice of Peter Böhler, it is agreed by us,

1. That we will meet together once a week to 'confess our faults one to another, and pray one for another, that we may be healed'.

2. That the persons so meeting be divided into several *bands*, or little companies, none of them consisting of fewer than five, or more than ten persons.

3. That every one in order speak as freely, plainly, and concisely as he can, the real state of his heart, with his several temptations and deliverances, since the last time of meeting.

4. That all the bands have a conference at eight every Wednesday evening, begun and ended with singing and prayer.

5. That any who desire to be admitted into this society be asked, 'What are your reasons for desiring this? Will you be entirely open; using no kind of reserve? Have you any objection to any of our orders?' (which may then be read).

6. That when any new member is proposed, every one present speak clearly and freely whatever objection he has to him.

7. That those against whom no reasonable objection appears, be, in order for their trial, formed into one or more distinct bands, and some person agreed on to assist them.

8. That after two months' trial, if no objection then appear, they may be admitted into the society.

9. That every fourth Saturday be observed as a day of general intercession.

10. That on the Sunday seven-night following be a general love-feast, from seven till ten in the evening.

11. That no particular member be allowed to act in any thing contrary to any order of the society: And that if any persons, after being thrice admonished, do not conform thereto, they be not any longer esteemed as members.

Wed. 3. My brother had a long and particular conversation with Peter Böhler. And it now pleased God to open his eyes; so that he also saw clearly what was the nature of that one true living faith, whereby alone, 'through grace, we are saved' ...

What occurred on *Wednesday, 24,* I think best to relate at large, after premising what may make it the better understood. Let him that cannot receive it ask of the Father of lights, that He would give more light to him and me.

1. I believe, till I was about ten years old I had not sinned away that 'washing of the Holy Ghost' which was given me in baptism; having been strictly educated and carefully taught, that I could only be saved 'by universal obedience, by keeping all the commandments of God'; in the meaning of which I was diligently instructed. And those instructions, so far as they respected outward duties and sins, I gladly received, and often thought of. But all that was said to me of inward obedience, or holiness, I neither understood nor remembered. So that I was indeed as ignorant of the true meaning of the Law, as I was of the Gospel of Christ.

2. The next six or seven years were spent at school; where, outward restraints being removed, I was much more negligent than before, even of outward duties, and almost continually guilty of outward sins, which I knew to be such, though they were not scandalous in the eye of the world. However, I still read the Scriptures, and said my prayers, morning and evening. And what I now hoped to be saved by, was, 1. Not being so bad as other

people. 2. Having still a kindness for religion. And, 3. Reading the Bible, going to church, and saying my prayers.

3. Being removed to the University for five years, I still said my prayers both in public and in private, and read, with the Scriptures, several other books of religion, especially comments on the New Testament. Yet I had not all this while so much as a notion of inward holiness; nay, went on habitually, and, for the most part, very contentedly, in some or other known sin: Indeed, with some intermission and short struggles, especially before and after the holy communion, which I was obliged to receive thrice a year. I cannot well tell what I hoped to be saved by now, when I was continually sinning against that little light I had; unless by those transient fits of what many Divines taught me to call repentance.

4. When I was about twenty-two, my father pressed me to enter into holy orders. At the same time, the providence of God directed me to Kempis's 'Christian Pattern', I began to see, that true religion was seated in the heart, and that God's law extended to all our thoughts as well as words and actions. I was, however, very angry at Kempis, for being too strict; though I read him only in Dean Stanhope's translation. Yet I had frequently much sensible comfort in reading him, such as I was an utter stranger to before: And meeting likewise with a religious friend, which I never had till now, I began to alter the whole form of my conversation, and to set in earnest upon a new life. I set apart an hour or two a day for religious retirement. I communicated every week. I watched against all sin, whether in word or deed. I began to aim at, and pray for, inward holiness. So that now, 'doing so much, and living so good a life', I doubted not but I was a good Christian.

5. Removing soon after to another College, I executed a resolution which I was before convinced was of the utmost importance—shaking off at once all my trifling acquaintance. I began to see more and more the value of time. I applied myself closer to study. I watched more carefully against actual sins; I advised others to be religious, according to that scheme of religion by which I modelled my own life. But meeting now with Mr. Law's 'Christian Perfection' and 'Serious Call', although I was much offended at many parts of both, yet they convinced me more than ever of the exceeding height and breadth and depth of the

law of God. The light flowed in so mightily upon my soul, that every thing appeared in a new view. I cried to God for help, and resolved not to prolong the time of obeying Him as I had never done before. And by my continued endeavour to keep His whole law, inward and outward, to the utmost of my power, I was persuaded that I should be accepted of Him, and that I was even then in a state of salvation.

6. In 1730 I began visiting the prisons; assisting the poor and sick in town; and doing what other good I could, by my presence, or my little fortune, to the bodies and souls of all men. To this end I abridged myself of all superfluities, and many that are called necessaries of life. I soon became a by-word for so doing, and I rejoiced that my name was cast out as evil. The next spring I began observing the Wednesday and Friday Fasts, commonly observed in the ancient Church; tasting no food till three in the afternoon. And now I knew not how to go any farther. I diligently strove against all sin. I omitted no sort of self-denial which I thought lawful: I carefully used, both in public and in private, all the means of grace at all opportunities. I omitted no occasion of doing good: I for that reason suffered evil. And all this I knew to be nothing, unless as it was directed toward inward holiness. Accordingly this, the image of God, was what I aimed at in all, by doing his will, not my own. Yet when, after continuing some years in this course, I apprehended myself to be near death, I could not find that all this gave me any comfort, or any assurance of acceptance with God. At this I was then not a little surprised; not imagining I had been all this time building on the sand, nor considering that 'other foundation can no man lay, than that which is laid' by God, 'even Christ Jesus'.

7. Soon after, a contemplative man convinced me still more than I was convinced before, that outward works are nothing, being alone; and in several conversations instructed me, how to pursue inward holiness, or a union of the soul with God. But even of his instructions (though I then received them as the words of God) I cannot but now observe, 1. That he spoke so incautiously against trusting in outward works, that he discouraged me from doing them at all. 2. That he recommended (as it were, to supply what was wanting in them) *mental prayer*, and the like exercises, as

the most effectual means of purifying the soul, and uniting it with God. Now these were, in truth, as much my own works as visiting the sick or clothing the naked; and the union with God thus pursued, was as really my own righteousness, as any I had before pursued under another name.

8. In this refined way of trusting to my own works and my own righteousness (so zealously inculcated by the mystic writers), I dragged on heavily, finding no comfort or help therein, till the time of my leaving England. On shipboard, however, I was again active in outward works; where it pleased God of his free mercy to give me twenty-six of the Moravian brethren for companions, who endeavoured to show me 'a more excellent way'. But I understood it not at first. I was too learned and too wise. So that it seemed foolishness unto me. And I continued preaching, and following after, and trusting in, that righteousness whereby no flesh can be justified.

9. All the time I was at Savannah I was thus beating the air. Being ignorant of the righteousness of Christ, which, by a living faith in Him, bringeth salvation 'to every one that believeth', I sought to establish my own righteousness; and so laboured in the fire all my days. I was now properly 'under the law'; I knew that 'the law' of God was 'spiritual; I consented to it that it was good'. Yea, 'I delighted in it, after the inner man.' Yet was I 'carnal, sold under sin'. Every day was I constrained to cry out, 'What I do, I allow not: For what I would, I do not; but what I hate, that I do. To will is' indeed 'present with me: But how to perform that which is good, I find not. For the good which I would, I do not; but the evil which I would not, that I do. I find a law, that when I would do good, evil is present with me': Even 'the law in my members, warring against the law of my mind', and still 'bringing me into captivity to the law of sin'.

10. In this vile, abject state of bondage to sin, I was indeed fighting continually, but not conquering. Before, I had willingly served sin; now it was unwillingly; but still I served it. I fell, and rose, and fell again. Sometimes I was overcome, and in heaviness: Sometimes I overcame, and was in joy. For as in the former state I had some foretastes of the terrors of the law, so had I in this, of the comforts of the Gospel. During this whole struggle between nature

and grace, which had now continued above ten years, I had many remarkable returns to prayer; especially when I was in trouble: I had many sensible comforts; which are indeed no other than short anticipations of the life of faith. But I was still 'under the law', not 'under grace' (the state most who are called Christians are content to live and die in): For I was only striving with, not freed from, sin: Neither had I the witness of the Spirit with my spirit, and indeed could not; for I 'sought it not by faith, but as it were by the works of the law'.

11. In my return to England, January, 1738, being in imminent danger of death, and very uneasy on that account, I was strongly convinced that the cause of that uneasiness was unbelief; and that the gaining a true, living faith was the 'one thing needful' for me. But still I fixed not this faith on its right object: I meant only faith in God, not faith in or through Christ. Again, I knew not that I was wholly void of this faith; but only thought, I had not enough of it. So that when Peter Böhler, whom God prepared for me as soon as I came to London, affirmed of true faith in Christ (which is but one), that it had those two fruits inseparably attending it, 'Dominion over sin, and constant Peace from a sense of forgiveness', I was quite amazed, and looked upon it as a new Gospel. If this was so, it was clear I had not faith. But I was not willing to be convinced of this. Therefore, I disputed with all my might, and laboured to prove that faith might be where these were not; especially where the sense of forgiveness was not: For all the Scriptures relating to this I had been long since taught to construe away; and to call all Presbyterians who spoke otherwise. Besides, I well saw, no one could, in the nature of things, have such a sense of forgiveness, and not *feel* it. But I felt it not. If then there was no faith without this, all my pretensions to faith dropped at once.

12. When I met Peter Böhler again, he consented to put the dispute upon the issue which I desired, namely, Scripture and experience. I first consulted the Scripture. But when I set aside the glosses of men, and simply considered the words of God, comparing them together, endeavouring to illustrate the obscure by the plainer passages; I found they all made against me, and was forced to retreat to my last hold, 'that experience would never agree with the *literal interpretation* of those scriptures. Nor could I therefore

allow it to be true, till I found some living witnesses of it.' He replied, he could show me such at any time; if I desired it, the next day. And accordingly, the next day he came again with three others, all of whom testified, of their own personal experience, that a true living faith in Christ is inseparable from a sense of pardon for all past, and freedom from all present, sins. They added with one mouth, that this faith was the gift, the free gift of God; and that he would surely bestow it upon every soul who earnestly and perseveringly sought it. I was now throughly convinced; and, by the grace of God, I resolved to seek it unto the end, 1. By absolutely renouncing all dependence, in whole or in part, upon *my own* works or righteousness; on which I had really grounded my hope of salvation, though I knew it not, from my youth up. 2. By adding to the constant use of all the other means of grace, continual prayer for this very thing, justifying, saving faith, a full reliance on the blood of Christ shed for *me*; a trust in Him, as *my* Christ, as *my* sole justification, sanctification, and redemption.

13. I continued thus to seek it (though with strange indifferecne, dulness, and coldness, and unusually frequent relapses into sin), till Wednesday, May 24. I think it was about five this morning, that I opened my Testament on those words, *Τα μεγιστα ημιν και τιμια επαγγελματα δεδωρηται, ινα γενησθε θειας κοινωνοι φυσεως.* 'There are given unto us exceeding great and precious promises, even that ye should be partakers of the divine nature.' (2 Pet. i. 4.) Just as I went out, I opened it again on those words, 'Thou art not far from the kingdom of God.' In the afternoon I was asked to go to St. Paul's. The anthem was, 'Out of the deep have I called unto thee, O Lord: Lord, hear my voice. O let thine ears consider well the voice of my complaint. If thou, Lord, wilt be extreme to mark what is done amiss, O Lord, who may abide it? For there is mercy with thee; therefore shalt thou be feared. O Israel, trust in the Lord: For with the Lord there is mercy, and with him is plenteous redemption. And He shall redeem Israel from all his sins.'

14. In the evening I went very unwillingly to a society in Aldersgate-Street, where one was reading Luther's preface to the Epistle to the Romans. About a quarter before nine, while he was describing the change which God works in the heart through faith

in Christ, I felt my heart strangely warmed. I felt I did trust in Christ, Christ alone for salvation: And an assurance was given me, that he had taken away *my* sins, even *mine*, and saved *me* from the law of sin and death ...

Wednesday, June 7. I determined, if God should permit, to retire for a short time into Germany. I had fully proposed, before I left Georgia, so to do, if it should please God to bring me back to Europe. And I now clearly saw the time was come. My weak mind could not bear to be thus sawn asunder. And I hoped the conversing with those holy men who were themselves living witnesses of the full power of faith, and yet able to bear with those that are weak, would be a means, under God, of so establishing my soul, that I might go on from faith to faith, and 'from strength to strength' ...

We reached the Mease at eight on *Thursday morning* [15 June], and in an hour and a half landed at Rotterdam.

We were eight in all; five English, and three Germans. Dr. Koker, a Physician of Rotterdam, was so kind, when we set forward in the afternoon, as to walk an hour with us on our way. I never before saw any such road as this. For many miles together, it is raised for some yards above the level, and paved with a small sort of brick, as smooth and clean as the Mall in St. James's. The walnut-trees stand in even rows on either side, so that no walk in a gentleman's garden is pleasanter. About seven we came to Goudart, where we were a little surprised at meeting with a treatment which is not heard of in England. Several inns utterly refused to entertain us; so that it was with difficulty we at last found one, where they did us the favour to take our money for some meat and drink, and the use of two or three bad beds. They pressed us much in the morning to see their church, but were displeased at our pulling off our hats when we went in; telling us, we must not do so; it was not the custom there. It is a large old building, of the Gothic kind, resembling some of our English cathedrals. There is much history-painting in the windows, which, they told us, is greatly admired. About eight we left Goudart, and in a little more than six hours reached Ysselstein.

Here we were at Baron Wattevil's, as at home. We found with him a few German brethren and sisters, and seven or eight of our

English acquaintance, who had settled here some time before. They lodged just without the town, in three or four little houses, till one should be built that would contain them all. *Saturday, 17*, was their Intercession-day. In the morning, some of our English brethren desired me to administer the Lord's Supper: The rest of the day we spent with all the brethren and sisters, in hearing the wonderful work which God is beginning to work over all the earth; and in making our requests known unto Him, and giving Him thanks for the mightiness of his kingdom.

At six in the morning we took boat. The beautiful gardens lie on both sides the river, for great part of the way to Amsterdam, whither we came about five in the evening. The exact neatness of all the buildings here, the nice cleanness of the streets (which, we were informed, were all washed twice a week), and the canals which run through all the main streets, with rows of trees on either side, make this the pleasantest city which I have ever seen . . .

Mon. 26. We breakfasted at Reinberg; left it at half an hour past ten, and at four came to Urding. Being much tired, we rested here, so that it was near ten at night before we came to Neus. Having but a few hours' walk from hence to Cölen, we went thither easily, and came at five the next evening into the ugliest, dirtiest city I ever yet saw with my eyes.

Wed. 28. We went to the cathedral, which is mere heaps upon heaps: a huge, mis-shapen thing, which has no more of symmetry than of neatness belonging to it. I was a little surprised to observe, that neither in this, nor in any other of the Romish churches where I have been, is there, properly speaking, any such thing as joint worship; but one prays at one shrine or altar, and another at another, without any regard to, or communication with, one another. As we came out of the church, a procession began on the other side of the church-yard. One of our company scrupling to pull off his hat, a zealous Catholic presently cried out, 'Knock down the Lutheran dog.' But we prevented any contest, by retiring into the church . . .

At four we took boat, when I could not but observe the decency of the Papists above us who are called Reformed. As soon as ever we were seated (and so every morning after), they all pulled off their hats, and each used by himself a short prayer for our prosperous journey. And this justice I must do to the very boatmen (Who upon the Rhine are generally wicked even to a proverb): I never heard one of them take the name of God in vain, or saw any one laugh when anything of religion was mentioned. So that I believe the glory of sporting with sacred things is peculiar to the English nation! . . . We set out early in the morning on *Tuesday, the 4th* [July], and about one came to Marienborn. But I was so ill, that, after talking a little with Count Zinzendorf,[12] I was forced to lie down the rest of the day.

The family at Marienborn consists of about ninety persons, gathered out of many nations. They live for the present in a large house hired by the Count, which is capable of receiving a far greater number; but are building one about three English miles off, on the top of a fruitful hill. 'O how pleasant a thing it is for brethren to dwell together in unity!'

Thur. 6. The Count carried me with him to the Count of Solmes, where I observed with pleasure the German frugality. Three of the young Countesses (though grown up) were dressed in linen; the Count and his son in plain cloth. At dinner, the next day, a glass of wine and a glass of water were set by every one, and if either were emptied, a second. They all conversed freely and unaffectedly. At ten at night we took coach again, and in the morning reached Marienborn.

I lodged with one of the brethren at Eckershausen, an English mile from Marienborn, where I usually spent the day, chiefly in conversing with those who could speak either Latin or English; not being able, for want of more practice, to speak German readily. And here I continually met with what I sought for, viz., living proofs of the power of faith: Persons saved from inward as well as outward sin, by 'the love of God shed abroad in their hearts'; and from all doubt and fear, by the abiding witness of 'the Holy Ghost given unto them' . . .

Sunday, August 6 . . . After the Evening Service at Hernhuth was ended, all the unmarried men (as is their custom) walked quite round the town, singing praise with instruments of music; and then on a small hill, at a little distance from it, casting themselves into a ring, joined in prayer. Thence they returned into the great Square, and, a little after eleven, commended each other to God.

Tues. 8. A child was buried. The burying-ground (called by them Gottes Acker, that is, God's ground) lies a few hundred yards out of the town, under the side of a little wood. There are distinct Squares in it for married men and unmarried; for married and unmarried women; for male and female children, and for widows. The corpse was carried from the chapel, the children walking first; next the orphan-father (so they call him who has the chief care of the Orphan-house), with the Minister of Bertholsdorf; then four children bearing the corpse; and after them, Martin Döber and the father of the child. Then followed the men; and last of all the women and girls. They all sung as they went. Being come into the Square where the male children are buried, the men stood on two sides of it, the boys on the third, and the women and girls on the fourth. There they sung again: After which the Minister used (I think read) a short prayer and concluded with that blessing, 'Unto God's gracious mercy and protection I commit you.'

Seeing the father (a plain man, a tailor by trade) looking at the grave, I asked, 'How do you find yourself?' He said, 'Praised be the Lord, never better. He has taken the soul of my child to himself. I have seen, according to my desire, his body committed to holy ground. And I know that when it is raised again, both he and I shall be ever with the Lord.' ...

[Wesley returned to England on *Saturday 16 September* and immediately resumed his preaching and private exhortation.]

Friday, November 10. I set out, and *Saturday, 11,* spent the evening with a little company at Oxford. I was grieved to find prudence had made them leave off singing psalms. I fear it will not stop here. God deliver me, and all that seek Him in sincerity, from what the world calls Christian prudence!

Sun. 12. I preached twice at the Castle. In the following week, I began more narrowly to inquire what the doctrine of the Church of England is, concerning the much controverted point of justification by faith; and the sum of what I found in the Homilies, I extracted and printed for the use of others.

Sun. 19. I only preached in the afternoon, at the Castle. On *Monday night* I was greatly troubled in dreams; and about eleven o'clock, waked in an unaccountable consternation, without being able to sleep again. About that time (as I found in the morning), one who had been designed to be my pupil, but was not, came into the Porter's lodge (where several persons were sitting), with a pistol in his hand. He presented this, as in sport, first at one, and then at another. He then attempted twice or thrice to shoot himself; but it would not go off. Upon his laying it down, one took it up, and blew out the priming. He was very angry, went and got fresh prime, came in again, sat down, beat the flint with his key, and about twelve, pulling off his hat and wig, said he would die like a gentleman, and shot himself through the head . . .

Wednesday, March 28, 1739. Perhaps it may be a satisfaction to some, if before I enter upon this new period of my life, I give the reasons why I preferred for so many years an University life before any other. Then especially, when I was earnestly pressed by my father to accept of a cure of souls. I have here, therefore, subjoined the letter I wrote several years ago on that occasion:

'DEAR SIR,   OXON, *December 10, 1734*

'THE authority of a parent and the call of Providence are things of so sacred a nature, that a question in which these are any way concerned deserves the most serious consideration . . .

'However, when two ways of life are proposed, I would choose to consider first, Which have I reason to believe will be best for *my own soul?* will most forward me in holiness? By holiness meaning, not fasting (as you seem to suppose), or bodily austerities; but the mind that was in Christ: A renewal of soul in the image of God. And I believe the state wherein I am will most forward me in this, because of the peculiar advantages I now enjoy.

'The first of these is, daily converse with my friends. I know no other place under heaven, where I can have some always at hand, of the same judgment, and engaged in the same studies; persons who are awakened into a full conviction, that they have but one work to do upon earth; who see at a distance what that one work is, even the recovery of a single eye and a clean heart; who, in order to this, have, according to their power, absolutely devoted themselves to God, and follow after their Lord, denying themselves, and taking up their cross daily. To have even a small number of such friends constantly watching over my soul, and administering, as need is, reproof or advice with all plainness and gentleness, is a blessing I know not where to find in any other part of the kingdom.

'Another blessing which I enjoy here in a greater degree than I could expect elsewhere, is retirement. I have not only as much, but as little, company as I please. Trifling visitants I have none. No one takes it into his head to come within my doors unless I desire him, or he has business with me. And even then, as soon as his business is done, he immediately goes away . . .

'Freedom from care is yet another invaluable blessing. And where could I enjoy this as I do now? I *hear* of such a thing as the cares of the world; but I *feel* them not. My income is ready for me on so many stated days: All I have to do is to carry it home. The grand article of my expense is food. And this too is provided without any care of mine. The servants I employ are always ready at quarter-day; so I have no trouble on their account. And what I occasionally need to buy, I can immediately have, without any expense of thought. Here, therefore, I can be 'without careful-ness'. I can 'attend upon the Lord without distraction'. And I know what a help this is to the being holy both in body and spirit.

'To quicken me in making a diligent and thankful use of these peculiar advantages, I have the opportunity of communicating weekly, and of public prayer twice a day. It would be easy to mention many more; as well as to show many disadvantages, which one of greater courage and skill than me, could scarce separate from the way of life you speak of. But whatever others could do, I could not. I could not stand my ground one month against intemperance in sleep, self-indulgence in food, irregularity in study; against a general lukewarmness in my affections, and remissness in my actions; against a softness directly opposite to the character of a good soldier of Jesus Christ . . .

Here is indeed a large scene of various action: Here is room for charity in all its forms: There is scarce any possible way of doing good, for which here is not daily occasion. I can now only touch on the several heads. Here are poor families to be relieved: Here are children to be educated: Here are workhouses, wherein both young and old gladly receive the word of exhortation: Here are prisons, and therein a complication of all human wants: And, lastly, here are the Schools of the Prophets. Of these, in particular, we must observe, that he who gains one, does thereby do as much service to the world, as he could do in a parish in his whole life; for his name is Legion: In him are contained all those who shall be converted to God by him: He is not a single drop of the dew of heaven, but a river to make glad the city of God.

'But "Epworth", you say, "is a larger sphere of action than this: There I should have the care of two thousand souls." Two thousand souls! I see not how it is possible for such a one as me, to take care of one hundred. Because the weight that is now upon me is almost more than I can bear, shall I increase it ten-fold? . . .'

Thur. 29. I left London, and in the evening expounded to a small company at Basingstoke. *Saturday, 31.* In the evening I reached Bristol, and met Mr. Whitefield there. I could scarce reconcile myself at first to this strange way of preaching in the fields, of which he set me an example on Sunday; having been all my life (till very lately) so tenacious of every point relating to decency and order, that I should have thought the saving of souls almost a sin, if it had not been done in a church.

April 1. In the evening (Mr. Whitefield being gone) I begun expounding our Lord's Sermon on the Mount (one pretty remarkable precedent of field-preaching, though I suppose there were churches at that time also), to a little society which was accustomed to meet once or twice a week in Nicholas-Street.

Mon. 2. At four in the afternoon, I submitted to be more vile, and proclaimed in the highways the glad tidings of salvation, speaking from a little eminence in a ground adjoining to the city, to about three thousand people . . .

Wednesday, May 9 [Bristol]. We took possession of a piece of ground, near St. James's church-yard, in the Horse Fair, where it was designed to build a room, large enough to contain both the societies of Nicholas and Baldwin-Street, and such of their acquaintance as might desire to be present with them, at such times as the Scripture was expounded. And on *Saturday, 12*, the first stone was laid, with the voice of praise and thanksgiving.

I had not at first the least apprehension or design of being personally engaged, either in the expense of this work, or in the direction of it: Having appointed eleven feoffees, on whom I supposed these burdens would fall of course. But I quickly found my mistake; first with regard to the expense: For the whole undertaking must have stood still, had not I immediately taken upon myself the payment of all the workmen; so that before I knew where I was, I had contracted a debt of more than a hundred and fifty pounds. And this I was to discharge how I could; the subscriptions of both societies not amounting to one quarter of the sum. And as to the direction of the work, I presently received letters from my friends in London, Mr. Whitefield in particular, backed with a message by one just come from thence, that neither he nor they would have any thing to do with the building, neither contribute any thing towards it, unless I would instantly discharge all feoffees, and do every thing in my own name. Many reasons they gave for this; but one was enough, viz., 'that such feoffees always would have it in their power to control me; and if I preached not as they liked, to turn me out of the room I had built'. I accordingly yielded to their advice, and calling all the feoffees together, cancelled (no man opposing) the instrument made before, and took the whole management into my own hands. Money, it is true, I had not, nor any human prospect or probability of procuring it: But I knew 'the earth is the Lord's and the fulness thereof'; and in his name set out, nothing doubting . . .

Sun. 13 . . . My ordinary employment, in public, was now as follows: Every morning I read prayers and preached at Newgate. Every evening I expounded a portion of Scripture at one or more of the societies. On Monday, in the afternoon, I preached abroad, near Bristol; on Tuesday, at Bath and Two-Mile-Hill alternately; on Wednesday, at Baptist-Mills; every other Thursday, near Pensford; every other Friday, in another part of Kingswood; on Saturday, in the afternoon, and Sunday morning, in the Bowling-Green (which lies near the middle of the city); on Sunday, at eleven, near Hannam-Mount; at two, at Clifton; and at five on Rose-Green: And hitherto, as my days, so my strength hath been . . .

Tuesday, June 5. There was great expectation at Bath of what a noted man was to do to me there,[13] and I was much entreated not to preach; because no one knew what might happen. By this report

I also gained a much larger audience, among whom were many of the rich and great. I told them plainly, the Scripture had concluded them all under sin—high and low, rich and poor, one with another. Many of them seemed to be a little surprised, and were sinking apace into seriousness, when their champion appeared, and coming close to me, asked by what authority I did these things. I replied, 'By the authority of Jesus Christ, conveyed to me by the (now) Archbishop of Canterbury, when he laid hands upon me, and said, "Take thou authority to preach the Gospel." ' He said, 'This is contrary to Act of Parliament: This is a conventicle.' I answered, 'Sir, the conventicles mentioned in that Act (as the preamble shows) are seditious meetings: But this is not such; here is no shadow of sedition; therefore it is not contrary to that Act.' He replied, 'I say it is: And, beside, your preaching frightens people out of their wits.' 'Sir, did you ever hear me preach?' 'No.' 'How then can you judge of what you never heard?' 'Sir, by common report.' 'Common report is not enough. Give me leave, Sir, to ask, Is not your name Nash?' 'My name is Nash.' 'Sir, I dare not judge of you by common report: I think it not enough to judge by.' Here he paused awhile, and, having recovered himself, said, 'I desire to know what this people comes here for'; On which one replied, 'Sir, leave him to me: Let an old woman answer him. You, Mr. Nash, take care of your body; we take care of our souls; and for the food of our souls we come here.' He replied not a word, but walked away.

As I returned, the street was full of people, hurrying to and fro, and speaking great words. But when any of them asked, 'Which is he?' and I replied, 'I am he,' they were immediately silent. Several ladies following me into Mr. Merchant's house, the servant told me there were some wanted to speak to me. I went to them, and said, 'I believe, ladies, the maid mistook; you only wanted to look at me.' I added, 'I do not expect that the rich and great should want either to speak with me, or to hear me; for I speak the plain truth;—a thing you hear little of, and do not desire to hear.' A few more words passed between us, and I retired . . .

Mon. 11 . . . Yet during this whole time, I had many thoughts concerning the unusual manner of my ministering among them. But after frequently laying it before the Lord, and calmly weighing whatever objections I heard against it, I could not but adhere to what I had some time since wrote to a friend, who had freely spoken his sentiments concerning it. An extract of that letter I here subjoin; that the matter may be placed in a clear light.

'DEAR SIR,

'THE best return I can make for the kind freedom you use, is to use the sâme to you. O may the God whom we serve sanctify it to us both, and teach us the whole truth as it is in Jesus! . . . You ask, 'How is it that I assemble Christians who are none of my charge, to sing psalms, and pray, and hear the Scriptures expounded?' and think it hard to justify doing this in other men's parishes, upon Catholic principles . . .

'Suffer me now to tell you my principles in this matter. I look upon all the world as my parish; thus far I mean, that, in whatever part of it I am, I judge it meet, right, and my bounden duty, to declare unto all that are willing to hear, the glad tidings of salvation. This is the work which I know God has called me to; and sure I am, that his blessing attends it. Great encouragement have I, therefore, to be faithful in fulfilling the work He hath given me to do. His servant I am, and, as such, am employed according to the plain direction of his word, "As I have opportunity, doing good unto all men": And his providence clearly concurs with his word; which has disengaged me from all things else, that I might singly attend on this very thing, "and go about doing good" ' . . .

Tuesday, July 17. I rode to Bradford, five miles from Bath, whither I had been long invited to come. I waited on the Minister, and desired leave to preach in his church. He said, it was not usual to preach on the week-days; but if I could come thither on a Sunday, he should be glad of my assistance. Thence I went to a gentleman in the town, who had been present when I preached at Bath, and, with the strongest marks of sincerity and affection, wished me good luck in the name of the Lord. But it was past. I found him now quite cold. He began disputing on several heads; and at last told me plainly, one of our own College had informed him they always took me to be a little crack-brained at Oxford . . .

Sat. 21. I began expounding, a second time, our Lord's Sermon on the Mount. In the morning, *Sunday, 22,* as I was explaining, 'Blessed are the poor in spirit', to about three thousand people, we had a fair opportunity of showing all men, what manner of spirit we were of: For in the middle of the sermon, the press-gang came, and seized on one of the hearers (ye learned in the law, what becomes of Magna Charta, and of English liberty and property? Are not these mere sounds, while, on any pretence, there is such a thing as a press-gang suffered in the land?); all the rest standing still, and none opening his mouth or lifting up his hand to resist them ...

Thursday, September 13. A serious Clergyman desired to know, in what points we differed from the Church of England. I answered, 'To the best of my knowledge, in none. The doctrines we preach are the doctrines of the Church of England; indeed, the fundamental doctrines of the Church, clearly laid down, both in her Prayers, Articles, and Homilies.'

He asked, 'In what points, then, do you differ from the other Clergy of the Church of England?' I answered, 'In none from that part of the Clergy who adhere to the doctrines of the Church; but from that part of the Clergy who dissent from the Church (though they own it not), I differ in the points following:

'First, They speak of justification, either as the same thing with sanctification, or as something consequent upon it. I believe justification to be wholly distinct from sanctification, and necessarily antecedent to it.

'Secondly, They speak of our own holiness, or good works, as the cause of our justification; or, that for the sake of which, on account of which, we are justified before God. I believe, neither our own holiness, nor good works, are any part of the cause of our justification; but that the death and righteousness of Christ are the whole and sole cause of it; or, that for the sake of which, on account of which, we are justified before God.

'Thirdly, They speak of good works as a condition of justification, necessarily previous to it. I believe no good work can be previous to justification, nor, consequently, a condition of it; but that we are justified (being till that hour ungodly, and, therefore, incapable of doing any good work) by faith alone, faith without works, faith (though producing all, yet) including no good work.

'Fourthly, They speak of sanctification (or holiness) as if it were an outward thing; as if it consisted chiefly, if not wholly, in those two points, 1. The doing no harm; 2. The doing good (as it is called), that is, the using the means of grace, and helping our neighbour.

'I believe it to be an inward thing, namely, the life of God in the soul of man; a participation of the divine nature; the mind that was in Christ; or, the renewal of our heart, after the image of Him that created us.

'Lastly, They speak of the new birth as an outward thing; as if it were no more than baptism; or, at most, a change from outward wickedness to outward goodness; from a vicious to (what is called) a virtuous life. I believe it to be an inward thing; a change from inward wickedness to inward goodness; an entire change of our inmost nature from the image of the devil (wherein we are born) to the image of God; a change from the love of the creature to the love of the Creator; from earthly and sensual, to heavenly and holy affections;—in a word, a change from the tempers of the spirits of darkness, to those of the angels of God in heaven.

There is, therefore, a wide, essential, fundamental, irreconcilable difference between us; so that if they speak the truth as it is in Jesus, I am found a false witness before God. But if I teach the way of God in truth, they are blind leaders of the blind.' . . .

Tuesday, November 27. I writ a short account of what had been done in Kingswood, and of our present undertaking there. The account was as follows:

'Few persons have lived long in the West of England, who have not heard of the colliers of Kingswood; a people famous, from the beginning hitherto, for neither fearing God nor regarding man: So ignorant of the things of God, that they seemed but one remove from the beasts that perish; and therefore utterly without desire of instruction, as well as without the means of it.

'Many last winter used tauntingly to say of Mr. Whitefield, "If he will convert Heathens, why does not he go to the colliers of Kingswood?" In spring he did so. And as there were thousands who resorted to no place of public worship, he went after them into their own wilderness, 'to seek and save that which was lost'. When he was called away, others went into 'the highways and hedges, to compel them to come in'. And, by the grace of God, their labour was not in vain. The scene is already changed. Kingswood does not now, as a year ago, resound with cursing and blasphemy. It is no more filled with drunkenness and uncleanness, and the idle diversions that naturally lead thereto. It is no longer full of wars and fightings, of clamour and bitterness, of wrath and envyings. Peace and love are there. Great numbers of the people are mild, gentle, and easy to be intreated. They 'do not cry, neither strive', and hardly is their 'voice heard in the streets', or indeed in their own wood; unless when they are at their usual evening diversion, singing praise unto God their Saviour.

'That their children too might know the things which make for their peace, it was some time since proposed to build a house in Kingswood; and after many foreseen and unforeseen difficulties, in June last the foundation was laid. The ground made choice of was in the middle of the wood, between the London and Bath roads, not far from that called Two-mile-Hill, about three measured miles from Bristol.

'Here a large room was begun for the school, having four small rooms at either end for the Schoolmasters (and, perhaps, if it should please God, some poor children) to lodge in. Two persons are ready to teach, so soon as the house is fit to receive them, the shell of which is nearly finished; so that it is hoped the whole will be completed in spring, or early in the summer.

'It is true, although the masters require no pay, yet this undertaking is attended with great expense. But let Him that "feedeth the young ravens" see to that. He hath the hearts of all men in his hand. If He put it into your heart, or into that of any of your friends, to assist in bringing this his work to perfection, in this world look for no recompence; but it shall be remembered in that day, when our Lord shall say, 'Inasmuch as ye did it unto the least of these my brethren, ye did it unto me.'' . . .

Monday, December 31. I had a long and particular conversation with Mr. Molther himself.[14] I weighed all his words with the utmost care; desired him to explain what I did not understand; asked him again and again, 'Do I not mistake what you say? Is this your meaning, or is it not?' So that I think, if God has given me any measure of understanding, I could not mistake him much.

As soon as I came home, I besought God to assist me, and not suffer 'the blind to go out of the way'. I then wrote down what I conceived to be the difference between us, in the following words:

'As to faith, you believe,

'1. There are no degrees of faith, and that no man has any degree of it, before all things in him are become new, before he has the full assurance of faith, the abiding witness of the Spirit, or the clear perception that Christ dwelleth in him.

'2. Accordingly you believe, there is no justifying faith,[15] or state of justification, short of this.

'3. Therefore you believe, our brother Hutton, Edmonds, and others, had no justifying faith before they saw you.

'4. And, in general, that that gift of God, which many received since Peter Böhler came into England, viz., "a sure confidence of the love of God" to them, was not justifying faith.

'5. And that the joy and love attending it were from animal spirits, from nature or imagination; not "joy in the Holy Ghost", and the real "love of God shed abroad in their hearts".

"Whereas I believe,

'1. There are degrees in faith; and that a man may have some degree of it, before all things in him are become new; before he has the full assurance of faith, the abiding witness of the Spirit, or the clear perception that Christ dwelleth in him.

'2. Accordingly, I believe there is a degree of justifying faith (and consequently, a state of justification) short of, and commonly antecedent to, this.

'3. And I believe our brother Hutton, with many others, had justifying faith long before they saw you.

'4. And, in general, that the gift of God, which many received since Peter Böhler came into England, viz., 'a sure confidence of the love of God to them', was justifying faith.

'5. And that the joy and love attending it, were not from animal spirits, from nature or imagination; but a measure of "joy in the Holy Ghost", and of "the love of God shed abroad in their hearts".

'As to the way to faith, you believe,

'That the way to attain it is, to wait for Christ, and be still; that is,

'Not to use (what we term) the means of grace;

'Not to go to church;

'Not to communicate;

'Not to fast;

'Not to use so much private prayer;

'Not to read the Scripture;

'(Because you believe, these are not means of grace; that is, do not ordinarily convey God's grace to unbelievers; and,

'That it is impossible for a man to use them without trusting in them);

'Not to do temporal good;

'Nor to attempt doing spiritual good.

'(Because you believe, no fruit of the Spirit is given by those who have it not themselves;

'And, that those who have not faith are utterly blind, and therefore unable to guide other souls.)

'Whereas I believe,

'The way to attain it is, to wait for Christ and be still;

'In using all the means of grace.

'Therefore I believe it right, for him who knows he has not faith (that is, that conquering faith),

'To go to church;

'To communicate;

'To fast;

'To use as much private prayer as he can, and

'To read the Scripture;

'(Because I believe, these are "means of grace"; that is, do ordinarily convey God's grace to unbelievers; and

'That it is possible for a man to use them, without trusting in them);

'To do all the temporal good he can;

'And to endeavour after doing spiritual good.

'(Because I know, many fruits of the Spirit are given by those who have them not themselves;

'And that those who have not faith, or but in the lowest degree may have more light from God, more wisdom for the guiding of other souls, than many that are strong in faith.)

'As to the manner of propagating the faith, you believe (as I have also heard others affirm)

'That we may, on some accounts, use guile:

'By saying what we know will deceive the hearers, or lead them to think the thing which is not.

'By describing things a little beyond the truth, in order to their coming up to it.

'By speaking as if we meant what we do not.

'But I believe,

'That we may not "use guile" on any account whatsoever;

'That we may not, on any account, say what we know will, and design should, deceive the hearers;

'That we may not describe things one jot beyond the truth, whether they come up to it, or no; and,

'That we may not speak, on any pretence, as if we meant what indeed we do not.

'Lastly, as to the fruits of your thus propagating the faith in England, you believe,

'Much good has been done by it;

'Many unsettled from a false foundation;

'Many brought into true stillness, in order to their coming to the true foundation;

'Some grounded thereon who were wrong before, but are right now.

'On the contrary, I believe that very little good, but much hurt, has been done by it.

'Many who were beginning to build holiness and good works, on the true foundation of faith in Jesus, being now wholly unsettled and lost in vain reasonings and doubtful disputations;

'Many others being brought into a false unscriptural stillness; so that they are not likely to come to any true foundation;

'And many being grounded on a faith which is without works; so that they who were right before, are wrong now.'

Tuesday, January 1, 1740. I endeavoured to explain to our brethren the true, Christian, scriptural stillness, by largely unfold-

ing those solemn words, 'Be still, and know that I am God.'
Wednesday, 2, I earnestly besought them all to 'stand in the old
paths', and no longer to subvert one another's souls by idle
controversies, and strife of words. They all seemed convinced. We
then cried to God to heal all our backslidings: And sent forth such
a spirit of peace and love, as we had not known for many months
before.

Thur. 3. I left London, and the next evening came to Oxford:
Where I spent the two following days, in looking over the letters
which I had received for the sixteen or eighteen years last past.
How few traces of inward religion are here! I found but one
among all my correspondents who declared, (what I well remember, at that time I knew not how to understand), that God had
'shed abroad his love in his heart', and given him the 'peace that
passeth all understanding'. But, who believed his report? Should I
conceal a sad truth, or declare it for the profit of others? He was
expelled out of his society, as a madman; and, being disowned by
his friends, and despised and forsaken of all men, lived obscure
and unknown for a few months, and then went to Him whom his
soul loved.

Tuesday, April 1 [Bristol]. While I was expounding the former
part of the twenty-third chapter of the Acts (how wonderfully
suited to the occasion! though not by my choice), the floods
began to lift up their voice. Some or other of the children of Belial
had laboured to disturb us several nights before: But now it seemed
as if all the host of the aliens were come together with one consent.
Not only the court and the alleys, but all the street, upwards and
downwards, was filled with people, shouting, cursing and swearing, and ready to swallow the ground with fierceness and rage. The
Mayor sent order, that they should disperse. But they set him at
nought. The chief Constable came next in person, who was, till
then, sufficiently prejudiced against us. But they insulted him also
in so gross a manner, as, I believe, fully opened his eyes. At length
the Mayor sent several of his officers, who took the ringleaders
into custody, and did not go till all the rest were dispersed. Surely
he hath been to us 'the Minister of God for good'.

Wed. 2. The rioters were brought up to the Court, the Quarter
Sessions being held that day. They began to excuse themselves by

saying many things of me. But the Mayor cut them all short, saying, 'What Mr. Wesley is, is nothing to you. I will keep the peace: I will have no rioting in this city.'

Calling at Newgate in the afternoon, I was informed that the poor wretches under sentence of death were earnestly desirous to speak with me; but that it could not be; Alderman Beecher having just then sent an express order that they should not. I cite Alderman Beecher to answer for these souls at the judgment-seat of Christ ...

Sat. 12. After preaching at Lanvachas in the way, in the afternoon I came to Bristol, and heard the melancholy news, that ——, one of the chief of those who came to make the disturbance on the 1st instant, had hanged himself. He was cut down, it seems, alive; but died in less than an hour. A second of them had been for some days in strong pain; and had many times sent to desire our prayers. A third came to me himself and confessed, he was hired that night, and made drunk on purpose; but when he came to the door, he knew not what was the matter, he could not stir, nor open his mouth ...

Saturday, August 23. A gentlewoman (one Mrs. C——) desired to speak with me, and related a strange story: On Saturday, the 16th instant (as she informed me), one Mrs. G., of Northampton, deeply convinced of sin, and therefore an abomination to her husband, was by him put into Bedlam. On Tuesday she slipped out of the gate with some other company; and after awhile, not knowing whither to go, sat down at Mrs. C.'s door. Mrs. C., knowing nothing of her, advised her the next day to go to Bedlam again; and went with her, where she was then chained down, and treated in the usual manner.—This is the justice of men! A poor highwayman is hanged; and Mr. G. esteemed a very honest man!

Thur. 28. I desired one who had seen affliction herself to go and visit Mrs. G in Bedlam; where it pleased God greatly to knit their hearts together, and with his comforts to refresh their souls ...

Tuesday, November 25 [London]. After several methods proposed for employing those who were out of business, we determined to make a trial of one which several of our brethren recommended to us. Our aim was, with as little expense as possible, to keep them at once from want and from idleness; in order to which, we took twelve of the poorest, and a teacher, into the society-room, where they were employed for four months, till spring came on, in carding and spinning of cotton: And the design answered: They were employed and maintained with very little more than the produce of their own labour . . .

Saturday, March 28, 1741. Having heard much of Mr. White-field's unkind behaviour, since his return from Georgia, I went to him to hear him speak for himself, that I might know how to judge. I much approved of his plainness of speech. He told me, he and I preached two different gospels, and therefore he not only would not join with, or give me the right hand of fellowship, but was resolved publicly to preach against me and my brother, wheresoever he preached at all. Mr. Hall (who went with me) put him in mind of the promise he had made but a few days before, that, whatever his private opinion was, he would never publicly preach against us. He said, that promise was only an effect of human weakness, and he was now of another mind.

Mon. 30. I fixed an hour every day for speaking with each of the Bands, that no disorderly walker might remain among them, nor any of a careless or contentious spirit. And the hours from ten to two, on every day but Saturday, I set apart for speaking with any who should desire it . . .

Tuesday, August 25. I explained, at Chelsea, the nature and necessity of the new birth. One (who, I afterwards heard was a Dissenting Teacher) asked me when I had done, '*Quid est tibi nomen?*' And on my not answering, turned in triumph to his companions, and said, 'Ay, I told you he did not understand Latin!' . . .

Sunday, February 21, 1742 [Bath]. In the evening I explained the 'exceeding great and precious promises' which are given us: A strong confirmation whereof I read, in a plain artless account of a child, whose body then lay before us. The substance of this was as follows:

'JOHN WOOLLEY was for some time in your school; but was turned out for his ill behaviour: Soon after he ran away from his parents, lurking about for several days and nights together, and hiding himself in holes and corners, that his mother might not find him. During this time he suffered both hunger and cold. Once he was three whole days without sustenance, sometimes weeping and praying by himself, and sometimes playing with other loose boys.

'One night he came to the new-room. Mr. Wesley was then speaking of disobedience to parents. He was quite confounded, and thought there never was in the world so wicked a child as himself. He went home, and never ran away any more. His mother saw the change in his whole behaviour, but knew not the cause. He would often get up stairs by himself to prayer, and often go alone into the fields, having done with all his idle companions.

'And now the devil began to set upon him with all his might, continually tempting him to self-murder: Sometimes he was vehemently pressed to hang himself; sometimes to leap into the river: But this only made him the more earnest in prayer; in which, after he had been one day wrestling with God, he saw himself, he said, surrounded on a sudden with an inexpressible light, and was so filled with joy and the love of God, that he scarce knew where he was; and with such love to all mankind, that he could have laid himself on the ground, for his worst enemies to trample upon.

'From this time his father and mother were surprised at him, he was so diligent to help them in all things. When they went to the preaching, he was careful to give their supper to the other children; and when he had put them to bed, hurried away to the room, to light his father or mother home. Meantime he lost no opportunity of hearing the preaching himself, or of doing any good he could, either at home or in any place where he was.

'One day, walking in the fields, he fell into talk with a farmer, who spoke very slightly of religion. John told him, he ought not to talk so; and enlarged upon that word of the Apostle (which he begged him to consider deeply), 'Without holiness no man shall see the Lord.' The man was amazed, caught the child in his arms, and knew not how to part with him.

'His father and mother once hearing him speak pretty loud in the next room, listened to hear what he said. He was praying thus: 'Lord, I do not expect to be heard for my much speaking. Thou knowest my heart; thou knowest my wants.' He then descended to particulars. Afterward he prayed very earnestly for his parents, and for his brothers and sisters by name; then for Mr. John and Charles Wesley, that God would set their faces as a flint, and give them to go on conquering and to conquer; then for all the other Ministers he could remember by name, and for all that were, or desired to be, true Ministers of Christ.

'In the beginning of his illness his mother asked him if he wanted any thing. He answered, 'Nothing but Christ; and I am as sure of him as if I had him already.' He often said, 'O mother, if all the world believed in Christ, what a happy world would it be!—And they may; for Christ died for every soul of man: I was the worst of sinners, and he died for *me*. O thou that callest the worst sinners, call *me*! O, it is a free gift! I am sure I have done nothing to deserve it.'

'On Wednesday he said to his mother, 'I am in very great trouble for my father; he has always taken an honest care of his family, but he does not know God; if he dies in the state he is in now, he cannot be saved. I have prayed for him, and will pray for him. If God should give him the true faith, and then take him to himself, do not you fear—do not you be troubled: God has promised to be *a father to the fatherless, and a husband to the widow.* I will pray for him and you in heaven; and I hope we shall sing Hallelujah in heaven together.'

'To his eldest sister he said, 'Do not puff yourself up with pride. When you receive your wages, which is not much, lay it out in plain necessaries. And if you are inclined to be merry, do not sing songs; that is the devil's diversion; there are many lies and ill things in those idle songs: Do you sing psalms and hymns. Remember your Creator in the days of your youth. When you are at work, you may lift up your heart to God; and be sure never to rise or go to bed without asking his blessing.'

'He added, "I shall die; but do not cry for me. Why should you cry for me? Consider what a joyful thing it is, to have a brother go to heaven. I am not a man; I am but a boy. But is it not in the Bible, *Out of the mouths of babes and sucklings thou hast ordained strength*? I know where I am going: I would not be without this knowledge for a thousand worlds; for though I am not in heaven yet, I am as sure of it as if I was."

'On Wednesday night he wrestled much with God in prayer. At last, throwing his arms open, he cried, "Come, come, Lord Jesus! I am thine. Amen and Amen!" He said, "God answers me in my heart, *Be of good cheer, thou hast overcome the world*"; and immediately after, he was filled with love and joy unspeakable.

'He said to his mother, "That school was the saving of my soul; for there I began to seek the Lord. But how is it, that a person no sooner begins to seek the Lord, but Satan straight stirs up all his instruments against him?"

'When he was in agony of pain, he cried out, "O Saviour, give me patience! Thou hast given me patience, but give me more. Give me thy love, and pain is nothing: I have deserved all this, and a thousand times more; for there is no sin but I have been guilty of."

'A while after he said, "O mother, how is this? If a man does not do his work, the masters in the world will not pay him his wages. But it is not so with God; he gives me good wages, and yet I am sure I have done nothing to gain them. O it is a free gift; it is free for every soul, for Christ has died for all."

'On Thursday morning his mother asked him how he did: He said, "I have had much struggling to-night, but my Saviour is so loving to me, I do not mind it; it is no more than nothing to me."

'Then he said, "I desire to be buried from the Room; and I desire Mr. Wesley would preach a sermon over me, on those words of David (unless he thinks any other to be more fit), *Before I was afflicted I went astray; but now I have kept thy word.*"

'I asked him, "How do you find yourself now?" He said, "In great pain, but full of love." I asked him, "But does not the love of God overcome pain?" He answered, "Yes! pain is nothing to me: I did sing praises to the Lord in the midst of my greatest pain; and I could not help it." I asked him, if he was willing to die: He replied, "O yes, with all my heart." I said, "But if life and death were set before you, what would you choose then?" He answered, "To die, and to be with Christ: I long to be out of this wicked world."

'On Thursday night he slept much sweeter than he had done for some time before. In the morning he begged to see Mr. John

Wesley. When Mr. Wesley came, and, after some other questions, asked him what he should pray for; he said, that God would give him a clean heart, and renew a right spirit within him. When prayer was ended, he seemed much enlivened, and said, "I thought I should have died to-day: But I must not be in haste; I am content to stay. I will tarry the Lord's leisure."

'On Saturday, one asked, if he still chose to die: He said, "I have no will; my will is resigned to the will of God. But I shall die: Mother, be not troubled; I shall go away like a lamb."

'On Sunday he spoke exceeding little. On Monday his speech began to falter: On Tuesday it was gone; but he was fully in his senses, almost continually lifting up his eyes to heaven. On Wednesday, his speech being restored, his mother said, "Jacky, you have not been with your Saviour to-night": He replied, "Yes, I have." She asked, "What did he say?" He answered, "He bid me not be afraid of the devil; for he had no power to hurt me at all, but I should tread him under my feet." He lay very quiet on Wednesday night. The next morning he spent in continual prayer; often repeating the Lord's Prayer, and earnestly commending his soul into the hands of God.

'He then called for his little brother and sister, to kiss them; and for his mother, whom he desired to kiss him: Then (between nine and ten) he said, "Now let me kiss you", which he did, and immediately fell asleep.

'He lived some months above thirteen years.' . . .

Friday, March 19. I rode once more to Pensford, at the earnest request of several serious people. The place where they desired me to preach, was a little green spot, near the town. But I had no sooner begun, than a great company of rabble, hired (as we afterwards found) for that purpose, came furiously upon us, bringing a bull, which they had been baiting, and now strove to drive in among the people. But the beast was wiser than his drivers; and continually ran either on one side of us, or the other, while we quietly sang praise to God, and prayed for about an hour. The poor wretches, finding themselves disappointed, at length seized upon the bull, now weak and tired, after having been so long torn and beaten, both by dogs and men; and, by main strength, partly dragged and partly thrust him in among the people. When they had forced their way to the little table on which I stood, they strove several times to throw it down, by thrusting the helpless beast against it; who, of himself, stirred no more than a log of wood. I once or twice put aside his head with my hand, that the blood might not drop upon my clothes; intending to go on, as soon as the hurry should be a little over. But the table falling down, some of our friends caught me in their arms, and carried me right away on their shoulders; while the rabble wreaked their vengeance on the table, which they tore bit from bit. We went a little way off, where I finished my discourse, without any noise or interruption . . .

Friday, June 4. At noon I preached at Birstal once more. All the hearers were deeply attentive; whom I now confidently and cheerfully committed to 'the great Shepherd and Bishop of souls'.

Hence I rode to Beeston. Here I met once more with the works of a celebrated author, of whom many great men cannot speak without rapture, and the strongest expressions of admiration—I mean Jacob Behmen. The book I now opened was his 'Mysterium Magnum', or Exposition of Genesis. Being conscious of my ignorance, I earnestly besought God to enlighten my understanding. I seriously considered what I read, and endeavoured to weigh it in the balance of the sanctuary. And what can I say concerning the part I read? I can and must say thus much (and that with as full evidence as I can say, that two and two make four), it is most sublime nonsense; inimitable bombast; fustian not to be paralleled![16] All of a piece with his inspired interpretation of the word *Tetragrammaton*; on which (mistaking it for the unutterable name itself, whereas it means only a word consisting of four letters) he comments with such exquisite gravity and solemnity, telling you the meaning of every *syllable* of it.

Sat. 5. I rode for Epworth. Before we came thither, I made an end of Madam Guyon's, 'Short Method of Prayer', and 'Les Torrents Spirituelles'.[17] Ah, my brethren! I can answer your riddle, now I have ploughed with your heifer. The very words I have so often heard some of you use, are not your own, no more than they are God's. They are only retailed from this poor Quietist; and that with the utmost faithfulness. O that ye knew how much God is wiser than man! Then would you drop Quietists and Mystics together, and at all hazards keep to the plain, practical, written word of God.

It being many years since I had been in Epworth before, I went to an inn, in the middle of the town, not knowing whether there were any left in it now who would not be ashamed of my acquaintance. But an old servant of my father's, with two or three poor women, presently found me out. I asked her, 'Do you know any in Epworth who are in earnest to be saved?' She answered, 'I am, by the grace of God; and I know I am saved through faith.' I asked, 'Have you then the peace of God? Do you know that He has forgiven your sins?' She replied, 'I thank God, I know it well. And many here can say the same thing.'

Sun. 6. A little before the Service began, I went to Mr. Romley, the Curate, and offered to assist him either by preaching or reading Prayers. But he did not care to accept of my assistance. The church was exceeding full in the afternoon, a rumour being spread, that I was to preach. But the sermon on, 'Quench not the Spirit', was not suitable to the expectation of many of the hearers. Mr. Romley told them, one of the most dangerous ways of quenching the Spirit was by enthusiasm; and enlarged on the character of an enthusiast, in a very florid and oratorical manner. After sermon John Taylor stood in the church-yard, and gave notice, as the people were coming out, 'Mr. Wesley, not being permitted to preach in the church, designs to preach here at six o'clock.'

Accordingly at six I came, and found such a congregation as I believe Epworth never saw before. I stood near the east end of the church, upon my father's tomb-stone, and cried, 'The kingdom of heaven is not meat and drink; but righteousness, and peace, and joy in the Holy Ghost' ...

Sat. 12. I preached on the righteousness of the Law and the righteousness of faith. While I was speaking, several dropped down as dead; and among the rest, such a cry was heard, of sinners groaning for the righteousness of faith, as almost drowned my voice. But many of these soon lifted up their heads with joy, and broke out into thanksgiving; being assured they now had the desire of their soul—the forgiveness of their sins.

I observed a gentleman there, who was remarkable for not

pretending to be of any religion at all. I was informed he had not been at public worship of any kind for upwards of thirty years. Seeing him stand as motionless as a statue, I asked him abruptly, 'Sir, are you a sinner?' He replied, with a deep and broken voice, 'Sinner enough', and continued staring upwards till his wife and a servant or two, who were all in tears, put him into his chaise and carried him home.

Sun. 13. At seven I preached at Haxey, on, 'What must I do to be saved?' Thence I went to Wroote, of which (as well as Epworth) my father was Rector for several years. Mr. Whitelamb offering me the church, I preached in the morning, on, 'Ask, and it shall be given you'. In the afternoon, on the difference between the righteousness of the Law and the righteousness of faith. But the church could not contain the people, many of whom came from far; and, I trust, not in vain.

At six I preached for the last time in Epworth church-yard (being to leave the town the next morning), to a vast multitude gathered together from all parts, on the beginning of our Lord's Sermon on the Mount. I continued among them for near three hours; and yet we scarce knew how to part. O let none think his labour of love is lost because the fruit does not immediately appear! Near forty years did my father labour here; but he saw little fruit of all his labour. I took some pains among this people too; and my strength also seemed spent in vain: But now the fruit appeared. There were scarce any in the town on whom either my father or I had taken any pains formerly, but the seed, sown so long since, now sprung up, bringing forth repentance and remission of sins ... I left Bristol in the evening of *Sunday, July 18*, and on *Tuesday* came to London. I found my mother on the borders of eternity. But she had no doubt or fear; nor any desire but (as soon as God should call) 'to depart, and to be with Christ'.

Fri. 23. About three in the afternoon I went to my mother, and found her change was near. I sat down on the bed-side. She was in her last conflict; unable to speak, but I believe quite sensible. Her look was calm and serene, and her eyes fixed upward, while we commended her soul to God. From three to four, the silver cord was loosing, and the wheel breaking at the cistern; and then, without any struggle, or sigh, or groan, the soul was set at liberty. We stood round the bed, and fulfilled her last request, uttered a little before she lost her speech: 'Children, as soon as I am released, sing a psalm of praise to God.'

Sunday, August 1. Almost an innumerable company of people being gathered together, about five in the afternoon, I committed to the earth the body of my mother, to sleep with her fathers. The portion of Scripture from which I afterwards spoke was, 'I saw a great white throne, and him that sat on it, from whose face the earth and the heaven fled away; and there was found no place for them. And I saw the dead, small and great, stand before God; and the books were opened: And the dead were judged out of those things which were written in the books, according to their works.' It was one of the most solemn assemblies I ever saw, or expect to see on this side eternity.

We set up a plain stone at the head of her grave, inscribed with the following words:

𝕳𝖊𝖗𝖊 𝖑𝖎𝖊𝖘 𝖙𝖍𝖊 𝕭𝖔𝖉𝖞
OF
MRS. SUSANNAH WESLEY,

THE YOUNGEST AND LAST SURVIVING DAUGHTER OF
DR. SAMUEL ANNESLEY.

IN sure and steadfast hope to rise,
And claim her mansion in the skies,
A Christian here her flesh laid down,
The cross exchanging for a crown.

True daughter of affliction, she,
Inured to pain and misery,
Mourn'd a long night of griefs and fears,
A legal night of seventy years.

The Father then reveal'd his Son,
Him in the broken bread made known;
She knew and felt her sins forgiven,
And found the earnest of her heaven.

Meet for the fellowship above,
She heard the call, 'Arise, my love!'
'I come,' her dying looks replied,
And lamb-like, as her Lord, she died.

I cannot but further observe, that even she (as well as her father, and grandfather, her husband, and her three sons) had been, in her measure and degree, a preacher of righteousness. This I learned from a letter, wrote long since to my father; part of which I have here subjoined:

'February 6, 1711–12

'——As I am a woman, so I am also mistress of a large family. And though the superior charge of the souls contained in it, lies upon you; yet, in your absence, I cannot but look upon every soul you leave under my care, as a talent committed to me under a trust, by the great Lord of all the families, both of heaven and earth. And if I am unfaithful to him or you, in neglecting to improve these talents, how shall I answer unto him, when he shall command me to render an account of my stewardship?

'As these, and other such like thoughts, made me at first take a more than ordinary care of the souls of my children and servants, so—knowing our religion requires a strict observation of the Lord's day, and not thinking that we fully answered the end of the institution by going to church, unless we filled up the intermediate spaces of time by other acts of piety and devotion—I thought it my duty to spend some part of the day, in reading to and instructing my family: And such time I esteemed spent in a way more acceptable to God, than if I had retired to my own private devotions.

'This was the beginning of my present practice. Other people's coming and joining with us was merely accidental. Our lad told his parents: They first desired to be admitted; then others that heard of it, begged leave also: So our company increased to about thirty; and it seldom exceeded forty last winter.

'But soon after you went to London last, I light on the account of the Danish Missionaries. I was, I think, never more affected with any thing; I could not forbear spending good part of that evening in praising and adoring the divine goodness, for inspiring them with such ardent zeal for his glory. For several days I could think or speak of little else. At last it came into my mind, Though I am not a man, nor a Minister, yet if my heart were sincerely devoted to God, and I was inspired with a true zeal for his glory, I

might do somewhat more than I do. I thought I might pray more
for them, and might speak to those with whom I converse with
more warmth of affection. I resolved to begin with my own
children; in which I observe the following method: I take such a
proportion of time as I can spare every night, to discourse with
each child apart. On Monday, I talk with Molly; on Tuesday, with
Hetty; Wednesday, with Nancy; Thursday, with Jacky; Friday,
with Patty; Saturday, with Charles; and with Emily and Suky
together on Sunday.

'With those few neighbours that then came to me, I discoursed
more freely and affectionately. I chose the best and most awaken-
ing sermons we have. And I spent somewhat more time with them
in such exercises, without being careful about the success of my
undertaking. Since this, our company increased every night; for I
dare deny none that ask admittance.

'Last Sunday I believe we had above two hundred. And yet
many went away, for want of room to stand.

'We banish all temporal concerns from our society. None is
suffered to mingle any discourse about them with our reading or
singing. We keep close to the business of the day; and when it is
over, all go home.

'I cannot conceive, why any should reflect upon you, because
your wife endeavours to draw people to church, and to restrain
them from profaning the Lord's day, by reading to them, and
other persuasions. For my part, I value no censure upon this
account. I have long since shook hands with the world. And I
heartily wish, I had never given them more reason to speak against
me.

'As to its looking particular, I grant it does. And so does almost
any thing that is serious, or that may any way advance the glory of
God, or the salvation of souls.

'As for your proposal, of letting some other person read: Alas!
you do not consider what a people these are. I do not think one
man among them could read a sermon, without spelling a good
part of it. Nor has any of our family a voice strong enough to be
heard by such a number of people.

'But there is one thing about which I am much dissatisfied; that
is, their being present at family prayers. I do not speak of any

concern I am under, barely because so many are present; for those who have the honour of speaking to the Great and Holy God, need not be ashamed to speak before the whole world: But because of my sex. I doubt if it is proper for me to present the prayers of the people to God. Last Sunday I would fain have dismissed them before prayers; but they begged so earnestly to stay, I durst not deny them.

'To the Rev. Mr. Wesley.
  '*In St. Margaret's Church-Yard, Westminster.*'

For the benefit of those who are entrusted, as she was, with the care of a numerous family, I cannot but add one letter more, which I received from her many years ago:

'Dear Son,   *July 24, 1732*

'According to your desire, I have collected the principal rules I observed in educating my family; which I now send you as they occurred to my mind, and you may (if you think they can be of use to any) dispose of them in what order you please.

'The children were always put into a regular method of living, in such things as they were capable of, from their birth; as in dressing, undressing, changing their linen, &c. The first quarter commonly passes in sleep. After that, they were, if possible, laid into their cradles awake, and rocked to sleep; and so they were kept rocking, till it was time for them to awake. This was done to bring them to a regular course of sleeping; which at first was three hours in the morning, and three in the afternoon: Afterward two hours, till they needed none at all.

'When turned a year old (and some before), they were taught to fear the rod, and to cry softly; by which means they escaped abundance of correction they might otherwise have had; and that most odious noise of the crying of children was rarely heard in the house; but the family usually lived in as much quietness, as if there had not been a child among them.

'As soon as they were grown pretty strong, they were confined to three meals a day. At dinner their little table and chairs were set by ours, where they could be overlooked; and they were suffered to eat and drink (small beer) as much as they would; but not to call for any thing. If they wanted aught, they used to whisper to the maid which attended them, who came and spake to me; and as soon as they could handle a knife and fork, they were set to our table. They were never suffered to choose their meat, but always made to eat such things as were provided for the family.

'Mornings they had always spoon-meat; sometimes at nights. But whatever they had, they were never permitted to eat, at those meals, of more than one thing; and of that sparingly enough. Drinking or eating between meals was never allowed, unless in case of sickness; which seldom happened. Nor were they suffered to go into the kitchen to ask any thing of the servants, when they were at meat; if it was known they did, they were certainly beat, and the servants severely reprimanded.

'At six, as soon as family prayers were over, they had their supper; at seven, the maid washed them; and, beginning at the youngest, she undressed and got them all to bed by eight; at which time she left them in their several rooms awake; for there was no such thing allowed of in our house, as sitting by a child till it fell asleep.

'They were so constantly used to eat and drink what was given them, that when any of them was ill, there was no difficulty in making them take the most unpleasant medicine: For they durst not refuse it, though some of them would presently throw it up. This I mention, to show that a person may be taught to take any thing, though it be never so much against his stomach.

'In order to form the minds of children, the first thing to be done is to conquer their will, and bring them to an obedient temper. To inform the understanding is a work of time, and must with children proceed by slow degrees as they are able to bear it; but the subjecting the will, is a thing which must be done at once; and the sooner the better. For by neglecting timely correction, they will contract a stubbornness and obstinacy, which is hardly ever after conquered; and never, without using such severity as would be as painful to me as to the child. In the esteem of the world they pass for kind and indulgent, whom I call cruel, parents, who permit their children to get habits, which they know must be afterwards broken. Nay, some are so stupidly fond, as in sport to teach their children to do things which in a while after, they have severely beaten them for doing. Whenever a child is corrected, it must be conquered; and this will be no hard matter to do, if it be not grown headstrong by too much indulgence. And when the will of a child is totally subdued, and it is brought to revere and stand in awe of the parents, then a great many childish follies and inadvertences may be passed by. Some should be overlooked and taken no notice of, and others mildly reproved; but no wilful transgression ought ever to be forgiven children, without chastisement, less or more, as the nature and circumstances of the offence require.

'I insist upon conquering the will of children betimes, because this is the only strong and rational foundation of a religious education; without which both precept and example will be ineffectual. But when this is thoroughly done, then a child is capable of being governed by the reason and piety of its parents, till its own understanding comes to maturity, and the principles of religion have taken root in the mind.

'I cannot yet dismiss this subject. As self-will is the root of all sin and misery, so whatever cherishes this in children, insures their after-wretchedness and irreligion: Whatever checks and mortifies it, promotes their future happiness and piety. This is still more evident, if we farther consider, that religion is nothing else than the doing the will of God, and not our own: That the one grand impediment to our temporal and eternal happiness being this self-will, no indulgences of it can be trivial, no denial unprofitable. Heaven or hell depends on this alone. So that the parent who studies to subdue it in his child, works together with God in the renewing and saving a soul. The parent who indulges it does the devil's work, makes religion impracticable, salvation unattainable; and does all that in him lies to damn his child, soul and body for ever.

'The children of this family were taught, as soon as they could speak, the Lord's Prayer, which they were made to say at rising and bed-time constantly; to which, as they grew bigger, were added a short prayer for their parents, and some Collects; a short Catechism, and some portion of Scripture, as their memories could bear.

'They were very early made to distinguish the Sabbath from

other days; before they could well speak or go. They were as soon taught to be still at family prayers, and to ask a blessing immediately after, which they used to do by signs, before they could kneel or speak.

'They are quickly made to understand, they might have nothing they cried for, and instructed to speak handsomely for what they wanted. They were not suffered to ask even the lowest servant for aught without saying, "Pray give me such a thing"; and the servant was chid, if she ever let them omit that word. Taking God's name in vain, cursing and swearing, profaneness, obscenity, rude, ill-bred names, were never heard among them. Nor were they ever permitted to call each other by their proper names, without the addition of brother or sister.

'None of them were taught to read till five years old, except Kezzy, in whose case I was overruled; and she was more years learning, than any of the rest had been months. The way of teaching was this: The day before a child began to learn, the house was set in order, every one's work appointed them, and a charge given, that none should come into the room from nine till twelve, or from two till five; which, you know, were our school-hours. One day was allowed the child wherein to learn its letters; and each of them did in that time know all its letters, great and small, except Molly and Nancy, who were a day and a half before they knew them perfectly; for which I then thought them very dull; but since I have observed how long many children are learning the hornbook, I have changed my opinion. But the reason why I thought them so then was, because the rest learned so readily; and your brother Samuel, who was the first child I ever taught, learned the alphabet in a few hours. He was five years old on the 10th of February; the next day he began to learn; and as soon as he knew the letters, began at the first chapter of Genesis. He was taught to spell the first verse, then to read it over and over, till he could read it off-hand without any hesitation; so on to the second, &c., till he took ten verses for a lesson, which he quickly did. Easter fell low that year; and by Whitsuntide he could read a chapter very well; for he read continually, and had such a prodigious memory, that I cannot remember ever to have told him the same word twice.

'What was yet stranger, any word he had learned in his lesson, he knew, wherever he saw it, either in his Bible, or any other book; by which means he learned very soon to read an English author well.

'The same method was observed with them all. As soon as they knew the letters, they were put first to spell, and read one line, then a verse; never leaving, till perfect in their lesson, were it shorter or longer. So one or other continued reading at school-time, without any intermission; and before we left school, each child read what he had learned that morning; and ere we parted in the afternoon, what they had learned that day.

'There was no such thing as loud talking or playing allowed of; but every one was kept close to their business, for the six hours of school: And it is almost incredible, what a child may be taught in a quarter of a year by a vigorous application, if it have but a tolerable capacity, and good health. Every one of these, Kezzy excepted, could read better in that time, than the most of women can do as long as they live.

'Rising out of their places, or going out of the room, was not permitted, unless for good cause; and running into the yard, garden, or street, without leave, was always esteemed a capital offence.

'For some years we went on very well. Never were children in better order. Never were children better disposed to piety, or in more subjection to their parents; till that fatal dispersion of them, after the fire, into several families. In those they were left at full liberty to converse with servants, which before they had always been restrained from; and to run abroad, and play with any children, good or bad. They soon learned to neglect a strict observation of the Sabbath, and got knowledge of several songs and bad things, which before they had no notion of. That civil behaviour which made them admired, when at home, by all which saw them, was, in great measure, lost; and a clownish accent, and many rude ways, were learned, which were not reformed without some difficulty.

'When the house was rebuilt, and the children all brought home, we entered upon a strict reform; and then was begun the custom of singing psalms at beginning and leaving school, morning and evening. Then also that of a general retirement at five o'clock was entered upon; when the oldest took the youngest that could speak, and the second the next, to whom they read the Psalms for the day, and a chapter in the New Testament; as, in the morning, they were directed to read the Psalms and a chapter in the Old: After which they went to their private prayers, before they got their breakfast, or came into the family. And, I thank God, the custom is still preserved among us.

'There were several by-laws observed among us, which slipped my memory, or else they had been inserted in their proper place; but I mention them here, because I think them useful.

'1. It had been observed, that cowardice and fear of punishment often lead children into lying, till they get a custom of it, which they cannot leave. To prevent this, a law was made, That whoever was charged with a fault, of which they were guilty, if they would ingenuously confess it, and promise to amend, should not be beaten. This rule prevented a great deal of lying, and would have done more, if one in the family would have observed it. But he could not be prevailed on, and therefore was often imposed on by false colours and equivocations; which none would have used (except one), had they been kindly dealt with. And some, in spite of all, would always speak truth plainly.

'2. That no sinful action, as lying, pilfering, playing at church, or on the Lord's day, disobedience; quarrelling, &c., should ever pass unpunished.

'3. That no child should ever be chid or beat twice for the same fault; and that if they amended, they should never be upbraided with it afterwards.

'4. That every signal act of obedience, especially when it crossed upon their own inclinations, should be always commended, and frequently rewarded, according to the merits of the cause.

'5. That if ever any child performed an act of obedience, or did any thing with an intention to please, though the performance was not well, yet the obedience and intention should be kindly accepted; and the child with sweetness directed how to do better for the future.

'6. That propriety be inviolably preserved, and none suffered to invade the property of another in the smallest matter, though it were but of the value of a farthing, or a pin; which they might not take from the owner, without, much less against, his consent. This rule can never be too much inculcated on the minds of children; and from the want of parents or governors doing it as they ought, proceeds that shameful neglect of justice which we may observe in the world.

'7. That promises be strictly observed; and a gift once bestowed, and so the right passed away from the donor, be not resumed, but left to the disposal of him to whom it was given; unless it were conditional, and the condition of the obligation not performed.

'8. That no girl be taught to work till she can read very well; and then that she be kept to her work with the same application, and for the same time, that she was held to in reading. This rule also is much to be observed; for the putting children to learn sewing before they can read perfectly, is the very reason, why so few women can read fit to be heard, and never to be well understood.'

Sun. 8. I cried aloud, in Ratcliffe-Square, 'Why will ye die, O house of Israel?' Only one poor man was exceeding noisy and turbulent; but in a moment God touched his heart: He hung down his head; tears covered his face, and his voice was heard no more.

I was constrained this evening to separate from the believers, some who did not show their faith by their works. One of these, Sam. Prig, was deeply displeased, spoke many very bitter words, and went abruptly away. The next morning he called; told me, neither my brother nor I preached the Gospel, or knew what it meant. I asked 'What do we preach then?' He said, 'Heathen morality: Tully's Offices,[18] and no more. So I wash my hands of you both. We shall see what you will come to in a little time.'

Wed. 11. He sent me a note, demanding the payment of one hundred pounds, which he had lent me about a year before, to pay the workmen at the Foundery. On Friday morning, at eight, he came and said, he wanted his money, and could stay no longer. I told him, I would endeavour to borrow it; and desired him to call in the evening. But he said, he could not stay so long, and must have it at twelve o'clock. Where to get it, I knew not. Between nine and ten one came and offered me the use of an hundred pounds for a year: But two others had been with me before, to make the same offer. I accepted the bank note which one of them brought; and saw that God is over all! . . .

Saturday, January 1, 1743. Between Doncaster and Epworth, I overtook one who immediately accosted me with so many and so impertinent questions, that I was quite amazed. In the midst of some of them, concerning my travels and my journey, I interrupted him, and asked, 'Are you aware that we are on a longer journey; that we are travelling toward eternity?' He replied instantly, 'O, I find you! I find you! I know where you are! Is not your name Wesley?—'Tis pity! 'Tis great pity. Why could not your father's religion serve *you*? Why must you have a *new* religion?' I was going to reply; but he cut me short by crying out in triumph, 'I am a Christian! I am a Christian! I am a Churchman! I am a Churchman! I am none of your Culamites';[19] as plain as he could speak; for he was so drunk, he could but just keep his seat. Having then clearly won the day, or, as his phrase was, 'put them all down', he began kicking his horse on both sides, and rode off as fast as he could.

In the evening I reached Epworth. *Sunday, 2.* At five, I preached on, 'So is every one that is born of the Spirit.' About eight I preached from my father's tomb, on Heb. viii. 11. Many from the neighbouring towns asked, if it would not be well, as it was sacrament Sunday, for them to receive it. I told them, 'By all means: But it would be more respectful first to ask Mr. Romley, the Curate's leave.' One did so, in the name of the rest; to whom he said, 'Pray tell Mr. Wesley, I shall not give *him* the sacrament; for he is not *fit*.'

How wise a God is our God! There could not have been so fit a place under heaven, where this should befal me first, as my father's house, the place of my nativity, and the very place where, 'according to the straitest sect of our religion', I had so long 'lived a Pharisee'! It was also fit, in the highest degree, that he who repelled me from that very table, where I had myself so often distributed the bread of life, should be one who owed his all in this world to the tender love which my father had shown to his, as well as personally to himself . . .

Tuesday, March 8. In the afternoon I preached on a smooth part of the Fell (or Common) near Chowden. I found we were got into the very Kingswood of the north. Twenty or thirty wild children ran round us, as soon as we came, staring as in amaze. They could not properly be said to be either clothed or naked. One of the largest (a girl, about fifteen) had a piece of a ragged, dirty blanket, some way hung about her, and a kind of cap on her head, of the same cloth and colour. My heart was exceedingly enlarged towards them; and they looked as if they would have swallowed me up; especially while I was applying these words, 'Be it known unto you, men and brethren, that through this man is preached unto you forgiveness of sins.'

Sat. 12. I concluded my second course of visiting, in which I inquired particularly into two things: 1. The case of those who had almost every night the last week cried out aloud, during the preaching. 2. The number of those who were separated from us, and the reason and occasion of it.

As to the former I found,

1. That all of them (I think, not one excepted) were persons in perfect health; and had not been subject to fits of any kind, till they were thus affected.

2. That this had come upon every one of them in a moment, without any previous notice, while they were either hearing the word of God, or thinking on what they had heard.

3. That in that moment they dropped down, lost all their strength, and were seized with violent pain.

This they expressed in different manners. Some said, they felt just as if a sword was running through them; others, that they thought a great weight lay upon them, as if it would squeeze them into the earth. Some said, they were quite choked, so that they could not breathe; that their hearts swelled ready to burst: Others, that it was as if their heart, as if their inside, as if their whole body, was tearing all to pieces.

These symptoms I can no more impute to any natural cause, than to the Spirit of God. I can make no doubt, but it was Satan tearing them, as they were coming to Christ. And hence proceeded those grievous cries, whereby he might design both to discredit the work of God, and to affright fearful people from hearing that word, whereby their souls might be saved.

I found, 4. That their minds had been as variously affected as their bodies. Of this some could give scarce any account at all; which also I impute to that wise spirit, purposely stunning and confounding as many as he could, that they might not be able to bewray his devices. Others gave a very clear and particular account, from the beginning to the end. The word of God pierced their souls, and convinced them of inward as well as outward sin. They saw and felt the wrath of God abiding on them, and were afraid of his judgments. And here the accuser came with great power, telling them, there was no hope, they were lost for ever. The pains of body then seized them in a moment, and extorted those loud and bitter cries.

As to the latter, I observed, the number of those who had left the society, since December 30, was seventy-six:

Fourteen of these (chiefly Dissenters) said they left it, because otherwise their Ministers would not give them the sacrament.

Nine more, because their husbands or wives were not willing they should stay in it.

Twelve, because their parents were not willing.

Five, because their master and mistress would not let them come.

Seven, because their acquaintance persuaded them to leave it.

Five, because people said such bad things of the society.

Nine, because they would not be laughed at.

Three, because they would not lose the poor's allowance.

Three more, because they could not spare time to come.

Two, because it was too far off.

One, because she was afraid of falling into fits.

One, because people were so rude in the street.

Two, because Thomas Naisbit was in the society.

One, because he would not turn his back on his baptism.

One, because we were mere Church of England men. And,

One, because it was time enough to serve God yet.

The number of those who were expelled the society was sixty-four:

Two for cursing and swearing.

Two for habitual Sabbath-breaking.

Seventeen for drunkenness.

Two for retailing spirituous liquors.

Three for quarrelling and brawling.

One for beating his wife.

Three for habitual, wilful lying.

Four for railing and evil-speaking.

One for idleness and laziness. And,

Nine-and-twenty for lightness and carelessness ...

Monday, August 22 [London]. After a few of us had joined in prayer, about four I set out, and rode softly to Snow-Hill; where, the saddle slipping quite upon my mare's neck, I fell over her head, and she ran back into Smithfield. Some boys caught her, and brought her to me again, cursing and swearing all the way. I spoke plainly to them, and they promised to amend. I was setting forward, when a man cried, 'Sir, you have lost your saddlecloth.' Two or three more would needs help me to put it on; but these too swore at almost every word. I turned to one and another, and spoke in love. They all took it well, and thanked me much. I gave them two or three little books, which they promised to read over carefully.

Before I reached Kensington, I found my mare had lost a shoe. This gave me an opportunity of talking closely, for near half an hour, both to the smith and his servant. I mention these little circumstances, to show how easy it is to redeem every fragment of time (if I may so speak), when we feel any love to those souls for which Christ died ...

Wed. 24 ... Having found, for some time, a strong desire to unite with Mr. Whitefield as far as possible, to cut off needless dispute, I wrote down my sentiments, as plain as I could, in the following terms:

There are three points in debate: 1. Unconditional Election. 2. Irresistible Grace. 3. Final Perseverance.

With regard to the First, Unconditional Election, I believe,

That God, before the foundation of the world, did unconditionally elect certain persons to do certain works, as Paul to preach the Gospel:

That He has unconditionally elected some nations to receive peculiar privileges, the Jewish nation in particular:

That He has unconditionally elected some nations to hear the Gospel, as England and Scotland now, and many others in past ages:

That He has unconditionally elected some persons to many peculiar advantages, both with regard to temporal and spiritual things:

And I do not deny (though I cannot prove it is so),

That He has unconditionally elected some persons to eternal glory.

But I cannot believe,

That all those who are not thus elected to glory, must perish everlastingly: Or,

That there is one soul on earth, who has not ever had a possibility of escaping eternal damnation.

With regard to the Second, Irresistible Grace, I believe,

That the grace which brings faith, and thereby salvation into the soul, is irresistible at that moment:

That most believers may remember some time when God did irresistibly convince them of sin:

That most believers do, at some other times, find God irresistibly acting upon their souls:

Yet I believe that the grace of God, both before and after those moments, may be, and hath been, resisted: And

That, in general, it does not act irresistibly; but we may comply therewith, or may not:

And I do not deny,

That, in some souls, the grace of God is so far irresistible, that they cannot but believe and be finally saved.

But I cannot believe.

That all those must be damned, in whom it does not thus irresistibly work: Or,

That there is one soul on earth, who has not, and never had, any other grace, than such as does, in fact, increase his damnation, and was designed of God so to do.

With regard to the Third, Final Perseverance, I incline to believe,

That there is a state attainable in this life, from which a man cannot finally fall: And

That he has attained this, who can say, 'Old things are passed away; all things' in me 'are become new'. ...

Monday, September 12. .... I had had for some time a great desire to go and publish the love of God our Saviour, if it were but for one day, in the Isles of Scilly: And I had occasionally mentioned it to several. This evening three of our brethren came and offered to carry me thither, if I could procure the Mayor's boat, which, they said, was the best sailer of any in the town. I sent, and he lent it me immediately. So the next morning, *Tuesday, 13* John Nelson, Mr. Shepherd, and I, with three men and a pilot, sailed from St. Ives. It seemed strange to me to attempt going in a fisher-boat, fifteen leagues upon the main ocean; especially when the waves began to swell, and hang over our heads. But I called to my companions, and we all joined together in singing lustily and with a good courage,

> When passing through the wat'ry deep,
>   I ask in faith his promis'd aid;
> The waves an awful distance keep,
>   And shrink from my devoted head;
> Fearless their violence I dare:
> They cannot harm,—for God is there.

About half an hour after one, we landed on St. Mary's, the chief of the inhabited islands.

We immediately waited upon the Governor, with the usual present, viz., a newspaper. I desired him, likewise, to accept of an 'Earnest Appeal'.[20] The Minister not being willing I should preach in the church, I preached, at six, in the street, to almost all the town, and many soldiers, sailors, and workmen, on, 'Why will ye die, O house of Israel?' It was a blessed time, so that I scarce knew how to conclude. After sermon I gave them some little books and hymns, which they were so eager to receive, that they were ready to tear both them and me to pieces.

For what *political reason* such a number of workmen were gathered together, and employed at so large an expense, to fortify a few barren rocks, which whosoever would take, deserves to have them for his pains, I could not possibly devise: But a *providential reason* was easy to be discovered. God might call them together to hear the Gospel, which perhaps otherwise they might never have thought of.

At five in the morning I preached again, on, 'I will heal their backsliding; I will love them freely.' And between nine and ten, having talked with many in private, and distributed both to them and others between two and three hundred hymns and little books, we left this barren, dreary place, and set sail for St. Ives, though the wind was strong, and blew directly in our teeth. Our pilot said we should have good luck, if we reached the land; but he knew not Him whom the winds and seas obey. Soon after three we were even with the Land's End, and about nine we reached St. Ives . . .

Thursday, October 20. After preaching to a small, attentive congregation, I rode to Wednesbury. At twelve I preached in a ground near the middle of the town, to a far larger congregation than was expected, on, 'Jesus Christ, the same yesterday, and today, and for ever.' I believe every one present felt the power of God; and no creature offered to molest us, either going or coming; but the Lord fought for us, and we held our peace.

I was writing at Francis Ward's, in the afternoon, when the cry arose, that the mob had beset the house. We prayed that God would disperse them; and it was so: One went this way, and another that; so that, in half an hour, not a man was left. I told our brethren, 'Now is the time for us to go'; but they pressed me exceedingly to stay. So, that I might not offend them, I sat down, though I foresaw what would follow. Before five the mob surrounded the house again, in greater numbers than ever. The cry of one and all was, 'Bring out the Minister; we will have the Minister.' I desired one to take their captain by the hand, and bring him into the house. After a few sentences interchanged between us, the lion was become a lamb. I desired him to go and bring one or two more of the most angry of his companions. He brought in two, who were ready to swallow the ground with rage; but in two minutes they were as calm as he. I then bade them make way, that I might go out among the people. As soon as I was in the midst of them, I called for a chair; and, standing up, asked, 'What do any of you want with me?' Some said, 'We want you to go with us to the Justice.' I replied, 'That I will, with all my heart.' I then spoke a few words, which God applied; so that they cried out, with might and main, 'The gentleman is an honest gentleman, and we will spill our blood in his defence.' I asked, 'Shall we go to the Justice to-night, or in the morning?' Most of them cried, 'To-night, to-night', on which I went before, and two or three hundred followed; the rest returning whence they came.

The night came on before we had walked a mile, together with heavy rain. However, on we went to Bentley-Hall, two miles from Wednesbury. One or two ran before, to tell Mr. Lane they had brought Mr. Wesley before his Worship. Mr. Lane replied, 'What have I to do with Mr. Wesley? Go and carry him back again.' By this time the main body came up, and began knocking at the door. A servant told them Mr. Lane was in bed. His son followed, and asked what was the matter. One replied, 'Why, an't please you, they sing psalms all day; nay, and make folks rise at five in the morning. And what would your Worship advise us to do?' 'To go home,' said Mr. Lane, 'and be quiet.'

Here they were at a full stop, till one advised, to go to Justice Persehouse, at Walsal. All agreed to this; so we hastened on, and about seven came to his house. But Mr. P—— likewise sent word, that he was in bed. Now they were at a stand again; but at last they all thought it the wisest course, to make the best of their way home. About fifty of them undertook to convoy me. But we had not gone a hundred yards, when the mob of Walsal came pouring in like a flood, and bore down all before them. The Darlaston mob made what defence they could; but they were weary, as well as out-numbered: So that in a short time, many being knocked down, the rest ran away, and left me in their hands.

To attempt speaking was vain, for the noise on every side was like the roaring of the sea. So they dragged me along till we came to the town; where seeing the door of a large house open, I attempted to go in; but a man, catching me by the hair, pulled me back into the middle of the mob. They made no more stop till they had carried me through the main street, from one end of the town to the other. I continued speaking all the time to those within hearing, feeling no pain or weariness. At the west end of the town, seeing a door half open, I made toward it, and would have gone in; but a gentleman in the shop would not suffer me, saying, they would pull the house down to the ground. However, I stood at the door, and asked, 'Are you willing to hear me speak?' Many cried out, 'No, no! knock his brains out; down with him; kill him at once.' Others said, 'Nay, but we will hear him first.' I began asking, 'What evil have I done? Which of you all have I wronged in word or deed?' And continued speaking for above a quarter of an hour, till my voice suddenly failed: Then the floods began to lift up their voice again; many crying out, 'Bring him away! Bring him away!'

In the mean time my strength and my voice returned, and I broke out aloud into prayer. And now the man who just before headed the mob, turned, and said, 'Sir, I will spend my life for you. Follow me, and not one soul here shall touch a hair of your head.' Two or three of his fellows confirmed his words, and got close to me immediately. At the same time, the gentleman in the shop cried out, 'For shame, for shame! Let him go.' An honest butcher, who was a little farther off, said, it was a shame they should do thus; and pulled back four or five, one after another, who were running on the most fiercely. The people then, as if it had been by common consent, fell back to the right and left; while those three or four men took me between them, and carried me through them all. But on the bridge the mob rallied again: We therefore went on one side, over the mill-dam, and thence through the meadows; till, a little before ten, God brought me safe to Wednesbury; having lost only one flap of my waistcoat, and a little skin from one of my hands.

I never saw such a chain of providences before; so many convincing proofs, that the hand of God is on every person and thing, over-ruling all as it seemeth him good.

The poor woman of Darlaston, who had headed that mob, and sworn, that none should touch me, when she saw her followers give way, ran into the thickest of the throng, and knocked down three or four men, one after another. But many assaulting her at once, she was soon overpowered, and had probably been killed in a few minutes (three men keeping her down and beating her with all their might), had not a man called to one of them, 'Hold, Tom, hold!' 'Who is there?' said Tom: 'What, honest Munchin? Nay, then, let her go.' So they held their hand, and let her get up and crawl home as well as she could.

From the beginning to the end I found the same presence of mind, as if I had been sitting in my own study. But I took no thought for one moment before another; only once it came into my mind, that if they should throw me into the river, it would spoil the papers that were in my pocket. For myself, I did not doubt but I should swim across, having but a thin coat, and a light pair of boots.

The circumstances that follow, I thought, were particularly remarkable: 1. That many endeavoured to throw me down while we were going down-hill on a slippery path to the town; as well judging, that if I was once on the ground, I should hardly rise any more. But I made no stumble at all, nor the least slip till I was entirely out of their hands. 2. That although many strove to lay hold on my collar or clothes, to pull me down, they could not fasten at all: Only one got fast hold of the flap of my waistcoat, which was soon left in his hand; the other flap, in the pocket of which was a bank note, was torn but half off. 3. That a lusty man just behind, struck at me several times, with a large oaken stick; with which if he had struck me once on the back part of my head, it would have saved him all farther trouble. But every time the blow was turned aside, I know not how; for I could not move to the right hand or left. 4. That another came rushing through the press, and raising his arm to strike, on a sudden let it drop, and only stroked my head, saying, 'What soft hair he has!' 5. That I stopped exactly at the Mayor's door, as if I had known it (which the mob doubtless thought I did), and found him standing in the shop, which gave the first check to the madness of the people. 6. That the very first men whose hearts were turned were the heroes of the town, the captains of the rabble on all occasions, one of them having been a prize-fighter at the bear-garden. 7. That, from first to last, I heard none give a reviling word, or call me by any opprobrious name whatever; but the cry of one and all was, 'The Preacher! The Preacher! The Parson! The Minister.' 8. That no creature, at least within my hearing, laid any thing to my charge, either true or false; having in the hurry quite forgot to provide themselves with an accusation of any kind. And, Lastly, That they were as utterly at a loss, what they should do with me; none proposing any determinate thing; only, 'Away with him! Kill him at once!'

By how gentle degrees does God prepare us for his will! Two years ago a piece of brick grazed my shoulders. It was a year after that the stone struck me between the eyes. Last month I received one blow, and this evening two; one before we came into the town, and one after we were gone out; but both were as nothing: For though one man struck me on the breast with all his might, and the other on the mouth with such a force that the blood gushed out immediately, I felt no more pain from either of the blows, than if they had touched me with a straw.

It ought not to be forgotten, that when the rest of the society made all haste to escape for their lives, four only would not stir, William Sitch, Edward Slater, John Griffiths, and Joan Parks; these kept with me, resolving to live or die together; and none of them received one blow, but William Sitch, who held me by the arm from one end of the town to the other. He was then dragged away, and knocked down; but he soon rose and got to me again. I afterwards asked him, what he expected when the mob came upon us. He said, 'To die for Him who had died for us': And he felt no hurry or fear: but calmly waited till God should require his soul of him.

I asked J. Parks, if she was not afraid, when they tore her from me. She said, 'No; no more than I am now. I could trust God for you, as well as for myself. From the beginning I had a full persuasion that God would deliver you. I knew not how; but I left that to him, and was as sure as if it were already done.' I asked, if the report was true, that she had fought for me. She said, 'No; I knew God would fight for his children.' And shall these souls perish at the last?

When I came back to Francis Ward's, I found many of our brethren waiting upon God. Many also whom I never had seen before, came to rejoice with us. And the next morning, as I rode through the town in my way to Nottingham, every one I met expressed such a cordial affection, that I could scarce believe what I saw and heard . . .

Sat. 22. I rode from Nottingham to Epworth, and on Monday set out for Grimsby; but at Ferry we were at a full stop, the boatmen telling us we could not pass the Trent: It was as much as our lives were worth to put from shore before the storm abated.

We waited an hour; but, being afraid it would do much hurt, if I should disappoint the congregation at Grimsby, I asked the men if they did not think it possible to get to the other shore: They said, they could not tell; but if we would venture our lives, they would venture theirs. So we put off, having six men, two women, and three horses, in the boat. Many stood looking after us on the river-side, in the middle of which we were, when, in an instant, the side of the boat was under water, and the horses and men rolling one over another. We expected the boat to sink every moment; but I did not doubt of being able to swim ashore. The boatmen were amazed as well as the rest; but they quickly recovered, and rowed for life. And soon after, our horses leaping overboard, lightened the boat, and we all came unhurt to land.

They wondered what was the matter I did not rise (for I lay along in the bottom of the boat), and I wondered too, till, upon examination, I found that a large iron crow, which the boatmen sometimes used, was (none knew how) run through the string of my boot, which pinned me down that I could not stir; so that if the boat had sunk, I should have been safe enough from swimming any further.

The same day, and, as near as we could judge, the same hour, the boat in which my brother was crossing the Severn, at the New Passage, was carried away by the wind, and in the utmost danger of splitting upon the rocks. But the same God, when all human hope was past, delivered them as well as us.

In the evening, the house at Grimsby not being able to contain one-fourth of the congregation, I stood in the street, and exhorted every prodigal to 'arise and go to' his 'Father'. One or two endeavoured to interrupt; but they were soon stilled by their own companions. The next day, *Tuesday, 25*, one in the town promised us the use of a large room; but he was prevailed upon to retract his promise before the hour of preaching came. I then designed going to the Cross, but the rain prevented; so that we were a little at a loss, till we were offered a very convenient place, by a 'woman which was a sinner'. I there declared 'Him' (about one o'oclock) whom 'God hath exalted, to give repentance and remission of sins.' And God so confirmed the word of his grace, that I marvelled any one could withstand him.

However, the prodigal held out till the evening, when I enlarged upon *her* sins and faith, who 'washed our Lord's feet with tears, and wiped them with the hairs of her head'. She was then utterly broken in pieces (as, indeed, was well nigh the whole congregation), and came after me to my lodging, crying out, 'O Sir! "What must I do to be saved?" ' Being now informed of her case, I said, 'Escape for your life. Return instantly to your husband.' She said, 'But how can it be? Which way can I go? He is above an hundred miles off. I have just received a letter from him; and he is at Newcastle-upon-Tyne.' I told her, 'I am going for Newcastle in the morning: You may go with me. William Blow shall take you behind him.' And so he did. Glory be to the Friend of sinners! He hath plucked one more brand out of the fire.—Thou poor sinner, thou hast 'received a Prophet in the name of a Prophet': And thou art found of Him that sent him . . .

Wed. 26 . . . William Blow, Mrs. S., and I set out at six. During our whole journey to Newcastle, I scarce observed her to laugh or even smile once. Nor did she ever complain of any thing, or appear moved in the least with those trying circumstances which many times occurred in our way. A steady seriousness, or sadness rather, appeared in her whole behaviour and conversation, as became one that felt the burden of sin and was groaning after salvation. In the same spirit, by all I could observe or learn, she continued during her stay at Newcastle. Not long after, her husband removed from thence, and wrote to her to follow him. She set out in a ship, bound for Hull. A storm met them by the way; the ship sprung a leak; but though it was near the shore, on which many people flocked together, yet the sea ran so exceeding high, that it was impossible to make any help. Mrs. S. was seen standing on the deck, as the ship gradually sunk; and afterwards hanging by her hands on the ropes, till the masts likewise disappeared. Even then, for some moments, they could observe her floating upon the waves, till her clothes, which buoyed her up, being thoroughly wet, she sunk—I trust, into the ocean of God's mercy . . .

Mon. 31. We set out early in the morning, and in the evening came to Newcastle.

Wednesday, November 2. The following advertisement was published:

FOR THE BENEFIT OF MR. ESTE.

By the Edinburgh Company of Comedians, on *Friday, November 4*, will be acted a Comedy, called,

THE CONSCIOUS LOVERS,

To which will be added, a Farce, called,

TRICK UPON TRICK; OR METHODISM DISPLAYED.

On *Friday*, a vast multitude of spectators were assembled in the Moot-Hall to see this. It was believed there could not be less than fifteen hundred people, some hundreds of whom sat on rows of seats built upon the stage. Soon after the Comedians had begun the first act of the play, on a sudden all those seats fell down at once, the supporters of them breaking like a rotten stick. The people were thrown one upon another, about five foot forward, but not one of them hurt. After a short time, the rest of the spectators were quiet, and the actors went on. In the middle of the second act, all the shilling seats gave a crack, and sunk several inches down. A great noise and shrieking followed; and as many as could readily get to the door, went out and returned no more. Notwithstanding this, when the noise was over, the actors went on with the play. In the beginning of the third act the entire stage suddenly sunk about six inches: The players retired with great precipitation; yet in a while they began again. At the latter end of the third act, all the sixpenny seats, without any kind of notice, fell to the ground. There was now a cry on every side; it being supposed that many were crushed in pieces: But, upon inquiry, not a single person (such was the mercy of God!) was either killed or dangerously hurt. Two or three hundred remaining still in the Hall, Mr. Este (who was to act the Methodist) came upon the stage and told them, for all this, he was resolved the farce should be acted. While he was speaking, the stage sunk six inches more; on which he ran back in the utmost confusion, and the people as fast as they could out of the door, none staying to look behind him.

Which is most surprising—that those players acted this farce the next week, or that some hundreds of people came again to see it? . . .

Monday, June 25 [London] and the five following days, we spent in conference with many of our brethren (come from several parts), who desire nothing but to save their own souls, and those that hear them. And surely, as long as they continue thus minded, their labour shall not be in vain in the Lord.

The next week we endeavoured to purge the society of all that did not walk according to the Gospel. By this means we reduced the number of members to less than nineteen hundred. But number is an inconsiderable circumstance. May God increase them in faith and love! ...

Thursday, December 27, 1744. I called on the Solicitor whom I had employed in the suit lately commenced against me in Chancery; and here I first saw that foul monster, *a Chancery Bill!*[21] A scroll it was of forty-two pages, in large folio, to tell a story which needed not to have taken up forty lines! And stuffed with such stupid, senseless, improbable lies (many of them, too, quite foreign to the question) as, I believe, would have cost the compiler his life in any Heathen Court either of Greece or Rome. And this is *equity* in a Christian country! This is the English method of redressing other grievances! ...

Friday, February 22, 1745. There was so much snow about Boroughbridge, that we could go on but very slowly; insomuch, that the night overtook us when we wanted six or seven miles to the place where we designed to lodge. But we pushed on, at a venture, across the moor, and, about eight, came safe to Sandhutton.

Sat. 23. We found the roads abundantly worse than they had been the day before; not only because the snows were deeper, which made the causeways in many places unpassable (and turnpike-roads were not known in these parts of England, till some years after), but likewise because the hard frost, succeeding the thaw, had made all the ground like glass. We were often obliged to walk, it being impossible to ride, and our horses several times fell down while we were leading them, but not once while we were riding them, during the whole journey. It was past eight before we got to Gateshead-Fell, which appeared a great pathless waste of white. The snow filling up and covering all the roads, we were at a loss how to proceed; when an honest man of Newcastle overtook and guided us safe into the town.

Many a rough journey have I had before, but one like this I never had; between wind, and hail, and rain, and ice, and snow, and driving sleet, and piercing cold: But it is past: Those days will return no more, and are, therefore, as though they had never been.

> Pain, disappointment, sickness, strife,
> Whate'er molests or troubles life,
> However grievous in its stay,
> It shakes the tenement of clay,
> When past, as nothing we esteem;
> And pain, like pleasure, is a dream.[22]

On *Monday* and *Tuesday* I diligently inquired who were offended at each other; this being the sin which, of all others, most easily besets the people of Newcastle. And as many of them as had leisure to meet, I heard face to face. It was now an easy thing to remove their offences; for God was in the work; so that they were, one and all, as willing to be reconciled to each other, as I was to have them . . .

Thursday, July 4. I rode to Falmouth. About three in the afternoon I went to see a gentlewoman who had been long indisposed. Almost as soon as I was set down, the house was beset on all sides by an innumerable multitude of people. A louder or more confused noise, could hardly be at the taking of a city by storm. At first Mrs. B. and her daughter endeavoured to quiet them. But it was labour lost. They might as well have attempted to still the raging of the sea. They were soon glad to shift for themselves, and leave K. E. and me to do as well as we could. The rabble roared with all their throats, 'Bring out the Canorum! Where is the Canorum?' (an unmeaning word which the Cornish generally use instead of Methodist). No answer being given, they quickly forced open the outer door, and filled the passage. Only a wainscot-partition was between us, which was not likely to stand long. I immediately took down a large looking-glass which hung against it, supposing the whole side would fall in at once. When they began their work with abundance of bitter imprecations, poor Kitty was utterly astonished, and cried out, 'O Sir, what must we do?' I said, 'We must pray.' Indeed at that time, to all appearance, our lives were not worth an hour's purchase. She asked, 'But, Sir, is it not better for you to hide yourself? To get into the closet?' I answered, 'No. It is best for me to stand just where I am.' Among those without, were the crews of some privateers, which were lately come into the harbour. Some of these, being angry at the slowness of the rest, thrust them away, and, coming up all together, set their shoulders to the inner door, and cried out, 'Avast, lads, avast!' Away went all the hinges at once, and the door fell back into the room. I stepped forward at once into the midst of them, and said, 'Here I am. Which of you has any thing to say to me? To which of you have I done any wrong? To you? Or you? Or you?' I continued speaking till I came, bare-headed as I was (for I purposely left my hat, that they might all see my face), into the middle of the street, and then raising my voice, said, 'Neighbours, countrymen! Do you desire to hear me speak?' They cried vehemently, 'Yes, yes. He shall speak. He shall. Nobody shall hinder him.' But having nothing to stand on, and no advantage of ground, I could be heard by few only. However, I spoke without intermission, and, as far as the sound reached, the people were still; till one or two of their captains turned about and swore, not a man should touch him. Mr. Thomas, a Clergyman, then came up, and asked, 'Are you not ashamed to use a stranger thus?' He was soon seconded by two or three gentlemen of the town, and one of the Aldermen; with whom I walked down the town, speaking all the time, till I came to Mrs. Maddern's house. The gentlemen proposed sending for my horse to the door, and desired me to step in and rest the mean time. But on second thoughts, they judged it not advisable to let me go out among the people again: So they chose to send my horse before me to Penryn, and to send me thither by water; the sea running close by the back-door of the house in which we were.

I never saw before, no, not at Walsal itself, the hand of God so plainly shown as here. There I had many companions who were willing to die with me: Here, not a friend, but one simple girl, who likewise was hurried away from me in an instant, as soon as ever she came out of Mrs. B.'s door. There I received some blows, lost part of my clothes, and was covered over with dirt: Here, although the hands of perhaps some hundreds of people were lifted up to strike or throw, yet they were one and all stopped in the mid-way; so that not a man touched me with one of his fingers; neither was any thing thrown from first to last; so that I had not even a speck of dirt on my clothes. Who can deny that God heareth the prayer, or that he hath all power in heaven and earth?

I took boat at about half an hour past five. Many of the mob waited at the end of the town, who, seeing me escaped out of their hands, could only revenge themselves with their tongues. But a few of the fiercest ran along the shore, to receive me at my landing. I walked up the steep narrow passage from the sea, at the top of which the foremost man stood. I looked him in the face, and said, 'I wish you a good night.' He spake not, nor moved hand or foot till I was on horseback. Then he said, 'I wish you was in hell,' and turned back to his companions.

As soon as I came within sight of Tolcarn (in Wendron parish), where I was to preach in the evening, I was met by many, running as it were for their lives, and begging me to go no further. I asked, 'Why not?' They said, 'The Churchwardens and Constables, and all the heads of the parish, are waiting for you at the top of the hill, and are resolved to have you: They have a special warrant from the Justices met at Helstone, who will stay there till you are brought.' I rode directly up the hill, and observing four or five horsemen, well dressed, went straight to them, and said, 'Gentlemen, has any of you any thing to say to me?—I am John Wesley.' One of them appeared extremely angry at this, that I should presume to say I was 'Mr. John Wesley.' And I know not how I might have fared for advancing so bold an assertion, but that Mr. Collins, the Minister of Redruth (accidentally, as he said) came by. Upon his accosting me, and saying, he knew me at Oxford, my first antagonist was silent, and a dispute of another kind began: Whether this preaching had done any good. I appealed to matter of fact. He allowed (after many words), 'People are the better for the present,' but added, 'To be sure, by and by they will be as bad, if not worse than ever.'

When he rode away, one of the gentlemen said, 'Sir, I would speak with you a little: Let us ride to the gate.' We did so, and he said, 'Sir, I will tell you the ground of this. All the gentlemen of these parts say, that you have been a long time in France and Spain, and are now sent hither by the Pretender; and that these societies are to join him.' Nay, surely, 'all the gentlemen in these parts' will not lie against their own conscience! . . .

Wednesday, September 18. About five we came to Newcastle, in an acceptable time. We found the generality of the inhabitants in the utmost consternation; news being just arrived, that, the morning before, at two o'clock, the Pretender had entered Edinburgh. A great concourse of people were with us in the evening, to whom I expounded the third chapter of Jonah; insisting particularly on that verse, 'Who can tell, if God will return, and repent, and turn away from his fierce anger, that we perish not?'

Thur. 19. The Mayor (Mr. Ridley) summoned all the house-holders of the town to meet him at the Town-Hall; and desired as many of them as were willing, to set their hands to a paper, importing that they would, at the hazard of their goods and lives, defend the town against the common enemy. Fear and darkness were now on every side; but not on those who had seen the light of God's countenance. We rejoiced together in the evening with solemn joy, while God applied those words to many hearts, 'Fear not ye; for I know that ye seek Jesus which was crucified.'

Fri. 20. The Mayor ordered the townsmen to be under arms, and to mount guard in their turns, over and above the guard of soldiers, a few companies of whom had been drawn into the town on the first alarm. Now, also, Pilgrim-Street Gate was ordered to be walled up. Many began to be much concerned for *us*, because our house stood without the walls. Nay, but the Lord is a wall of fire unto all that trust in him.

I had desired all our brethren to join with us this day, in seeking God by fasting and prayer. About one we met, and poured out our souls before him; and we believed he would send an answer of peace.

Sat. 21. The same day the action was, came the news of General Cope's defeat. Orders were now given for the doubling of the guard, and for walling up Pandon and Sally-Port Gates. In the afternoon I wrote the following letter:

'*To the Worshipful, the Mayor of Newcastle.*

'SIR,

'MY not waiting upon you at the Town-Hall was not owing to any want of respect. I reverence you for your office's sake; and much more for your zeal in the execution of it. I would to God every Magistrate in the land would copy after such an example! Much less was it owing to any disaffection to His Majesty King George. But I knew not how far it might be either necessary or proper for me to appear on such an occasion. I have no fortune at Newcastle: I have only the bread I eat, and the use of a little room for a few weeks in the year.

'All I can do for His Majesty, whom I honour and love—I think not less than I did my own father—is this, I cry unto God, day by day, in public and in private, to put all his enemies to confusion: And I exhort all that hear me to do the same; and, in their several stations, to exert themselves as loyal subjects; who, so long as they fear God, cannot but honour the King.

'Permit me, Sir, to add a few words more, out of the fulness of my heart. I am persuaded you fear God, and have a deep sense that His kingdom ruleth over all. Unto whom, then (I may ask you), should we flee for succour, but unto Him whom, by our sins, we have justly displeased? O, Sir, is it not possible to give any check to these overflowings of ungodliness? To the open, flagrant wickedness, the drunkenness and profaneness, which so abound, even in our streets? I just take leave to suggest this. May the God whom you serve direct you in this, and all things! This is the daily prayer of, Sir,

'Your obedient servant, for Christ's sake,

'J.W.'

Sun. 22. The walls were mounted with cannon, and all things prepared for sustaining an assault. Mean time our poor neighbours, on either hand, were busy in removing their goods. And most of the best houses in our street were left without either furniture or inhabitants. Those within the walls were almost equally busy in carrying away their money and goods; and more and more of the Gentry every hour rode southward as fast as they could. At eight I preached at Gateshead, in a broad part of the street, near the Popish chapel, on the wisdom of God in governing the world. How do all things tend to the furtherance of the Gospel!

I never saw before so well-behaved a congregation in any church at Newcastle, as was that at St. Andrew's this morning.

The place appeared as indeed the house of God; and the sermon Mr. Ellison preached was strong and weighty, which he could scarce conclude for tears.

All this week the alarms from the north continued, and the storm seemed nearer every day. Many wondered we would still stay without the walls: Others told us we must remove quickly; for if the cannon began to play from the top of the gates, they would beat all the house about our ears. This made me look how the cannons on the gates were planted; and I could not but adore the providence of God, for it was obvious, 1. They were all planted in such a manner, that no shot could touch our house. 2. The cannon on Newgate so secured us on one side, and those upon Pilgrim-street Gate on the other, that none could come near our house, either way, without being torn in pieces.

On *Friday* and *Saturday* many messengers of lies terrified the poor people of the town, as if the rebels were just coming to swallow them up. Upon this the guards were increased, and abundance of country gentlemen came in, with their servants, horses, and arms. Among those who came from the north was one whom the Mayor ordered to be apprehended, on suspicion of his being a spy. As soon as he was left alone he cut his own throat; but a surgeon coming quickly, sewed up the wound, so that he lived to discover those designs of the rebels, which were thereby effectually prevented.

Sun. 29. Advice came that they were in full march southward, so that it was supposed they would reach Newcastle by Monday evening. At eight I called on a multitude of sinners in Gateshead, to seek the Lord while he might be found. Mr. Ellison preached another earnest sermon, and all the people seemed to bend before the Lord. In the afternoon I expounded part of the Lesson for the day, Jacob wrestling with the angel. The congregation was so moved, that I began again and again, and knew not how to conclude. And we cried mightily to God to send His Majesty King George help from his holy place, and to spare a sinful land yet a little longer, if haply they might know the day of their visitation.

On *Monday* and *Tuesday* I visited some of the societies in the country, and, on *Wednesday, October 2*, returned to Newcastle, where they were just informed that the rebels had left Edinburgh on Monday, and were swiftly marching toward them. But it appeared soon that this also was a false alarm; it being only a party which had moved southward, the main body still remaining in their camp, a mile or two from Edinburgh.

On *Thursday* and *Friday* I visited the rest of the country societies. On *Saturday* a party of the rebels (about a thousand men) came within seventeen miles of Newcastle. This occasioned a fresh alarm in the town; and orders were given by the General that the soldiers should march against them on Monday morning. But these orders were countermanded.

Mr. Nixon (the gentleman who had some days since, upon being apprehended, cut his own throat) being still unable to speak, wrote as well as he could, that the design of the Prince (as they called him) was to seize on Tynemouth Castle, which he knew was well provided both with cannon and ammunition; and thence to march to the hill on the east side of Newcastle, which entirely commands the town. And if this had been done, he would have carried his point, and gained the town without a blow. The Mayor immediately sent to Tynemouth Castle, and lodged the cannon and ammunition in a safer place.

Tues. 8. I wrote to General Husk as follows:

'A SURLY man came to me this evening, as he said, from you. He would not deign to come up stairs to me, nor so much as into the house; but stood in the yard till I came, and then obliged me to go with him into the street, where he said, "You must pull down the battlements of your house, or to-morrow the General will pull them down for you."

'Sir, to me this is nothing. But I humbly conceive it would not be proper for this man, whoever he is, to behave in such a manner to any other of His Majesty's subjects, at so critical a time as this.

'I am ready, if it may be for His Majesty's service, to pull not only the battlements, but the house down; or to give up any part of it, or the whole, into your Excellency's hands.'

Wed. 9 It being supposed that the danger was over for the present, I preached at four in Gateshead (at John Lyddel's), on, 'Stand fast in the faith, quit you like men, be strong'; and then, taking horse with Mr. Shepherd, in the evening reached Sand-button.

Thur. 10. We dined at Ferrybridge, where we were conducted to General Wentworth, who did us the honour to read over all the letters we had about us. We lay at Doncaster, nothing pleased with the drunken, cursing, swearing soldiers, who surrounded us on every side. Can these wretches succeed in any thing they undertake? I fear not, if there be a God that judgeth the earth . . .

Tues. 22. I came to Newcastle in the evening, just as Mr. Trembath was giving out the hymn; and as soon as it was ended began preaching, without feeling any want of strength.

Wed. 23. I found all things calm and quiet; the consternation of the people was over. But the seriousness which it had occasioned in many, continued and increased . . .

Wednesday, December 18 [London]. Being the day of the National Fast,[23] we met at four in the morning. I preached on Joel ii. 12, &c. At nine our service in West-Street began. At five I preached at the Foundery again, on, 'The Lord sitteth above the water-floods.' Abundance of people were at West-Street chapel, and at the Foundery, both morning and evening; as also (we understood) at every place of public worship, throughout London and Westminster. And such a solemnity and seriousness every where appeared as had not been lately seen in England.

We had within a short time given away some thousands of little tracts among the common people. And it pleased God hereby to provoke others to jealousy. Insomuch that the Lord Mayor had ordered a large quantity of papers, dissuading from cursing and swearing, to be printed, and distributed to the Train-bands. And this day, 'An Earnest Exhortation to Serious Repentance' was given at every church-door, in or near London, to every person who came out; and one left at the house of every householder who was absent from church. I doubt not but God gave a blessing therewith. And perhaps then the sentence of desolation was recalled.

It was on this very day that the Duke's army was so remarkably preserved in the midst of the ambuscades at Clifton-Moor. The rebels fired many volleys upon the King's troops, from the hedges and walls, behind which they lay. And yet, from first to last, only ten or twelve men fell, the shot flying over their heads . . .

Friday, May 23, 1746. I made over the houses in Bristol and Kingswood, and the next week, that at Newcastle, to seven Trustees, reserving only to my brother and myself the liberty of preaching and lodging there.

Fri. 30. I light upon a poor, pretty, fluttering thing, lately come from Ireland, and going to be a singer at the play-house. She went in the evening to the chapel, and thence to the watch-night, and was almost persuaded to be a Christian. Her convictions continued strong for a few days; but then her old acquaintance found her, and we saw her no more . . .

Sunday, July 6. After talking largely with both the men and women Leaders, we agreed it would prevent great expense, as well of health as of time and of money, if the poorer people of our society could be persuaded to leave off drinking of tea. We resolved ourselves to begin and set the example. I expected some difficulty in breaking off a custom of six-and-twenty years' standing. And, accordingly, the three first days, my head ached, more or less, all day long, and I was half asleep from morning to night. The third day, on *Wednesday*, in the afternoon, my memory failed, almost entirely. In the evening I sought my remedy in prayer. On *Thursday* morning my head-ache was gone. My memory was as strong as ever. And I have found no inconvenience, but a sensible benefit in several respects, from that very day to this . . .

Thursday, December 4 [London]. I mentioned to the society my design of giving physic to the poor. About thirty came the next day, and in three weeks about three hundred. This we continued for several years, till, the number of patients still increasing, the expense was greater than we could bear: Meantime, through the blessing of God, many who had been ill for months or years, were restored to perfect health . . .

Mon. 29. I resumed my vegetable diet (which I had now discontinued for several years), and found it of use both to my soul and body; but after two years, a violent flux which seized me in Ireland obliged me to return to the use of animal food.

Wed. 31. I heard an amazing instance of the providence of God. About six years ago, Mr Jebner (as he related it himself) and all his family, being eight persons, were in bed, between ten and eleven at night. On a sudden he heard a great crack, and the house instantly fell, all at once, from the top to the bottom. They were all buried in the ruins. Abundance of people gathered together, and in two or three hours dug them out. The beds in which they had lain were mashed in pieces, as was all the furniture of the house; but neither man, woman, nor child was killed or hurt. Only he had a little scratch on his hand.

Saturday, January 3, 1747. I called upon poor Mr. C., who once largely 'tasted of the good word, and the powers of the world to come'. I found him very loving, and very drunk; as he commonly is, day and night. But I could fix nothing upon him. 'He may fall foully, but not finally!'

Sun. 11. In the evening I rode to Brentford; the next day to Newbury; and, *Tuesday, 13*, to the Devizes. The town was in an uproar from end to end, as if the French were just entering; and abundance of swelling words we heard, oaths, curses, and threatenings. The most active man in stirring up the people, we were informed, was Mr J., the C. [Mr. Innys, the curate]. He had been indefatigable in the work, going all the day from house to house. He had also been at the pains of setting up an advertisement in the most public places of the town of 'An Obnubilative. Pantomime Entertainment, to be exhibited at Mr. Clark's' (where I was to preach); the latter part of it contained a kind of *double entendre*, which a modest person cannot well repeat. I began preaching at seven, on 'the grace of our Lord Jesus Christ'. Many of the mob came in, listened a little, and stood still. No one opened his mouth, but attention sat on the face of every hearer.

Wed. 14. I rode on to Bristol, and spent a week in great peace. *Thursday, 22.* About half-hour after twelve I took horse for Wick, where I had appointed to preach at three. I was riding by the wall through St. Nicholas-gate (my horse having been brought to the house where I dined) just as a cart turned short from St. Nicholas-street, and came swiftly down the hill. There was just room to pass between the wheel of it and the wall; but that space was taken up by the carman. I called to him to go back, or I must ride over him; but the man, as if deaf, walked straight forward. This obliged me to hold back my horse. In the mean time the shaft of the cart came full against his shoulder with such a shock as beat him to the ground. He shot me forward over his head as an arrow out of the bow, where I lay, with my arms and legs, I know not how, stretched out in a line close to the wall. The wheel ran by, close to my side, but only dirted my clothes. I found no flutter of spirit, but the same composure as if I had been sitting in my study. When the cart was gone, I rose. Abundance of people gathered round, till a gentleman desired me to step into his shop. After cleaning myself a little, I took horse again, and was at Wick by the time appointed.

I returned to Bristol (where the report of my being killed had spread far and wide) time enough to praise God in the great congregation, and to preach on, 'Thou, Lord, shalt save both man and beast.' My shoulders, and hands, and side, and both my legs, were a little bruised; my knees something more; my right thigh the most, which made it a little difficult to me to walk; but some warm treacle took away all the pain in an hour, and the lameness in a day or two . . .

Monday, February 16. I was wondering, the day before, at the mildness of the weather; such as seldom attends me in my journeys. But my wonder now ceased: The wind was turned full north, and blew so exceeding hard and keen, that when we came to Hatfield, neither my companions nor I had much use of our hands or feet. After resting an hour, we bore up again, through the wind and snow, which drove full in our faces. But this was only a squall. In Baldock-field the storm began in earnest. The large hail drove so vehemently in our faces, that we could not see, nor hardly breathe. However, before two o'clock we reached Baldock, where one met and conducted us safe to Potten.

About six I preached to a serious congregation. *Tuesday, 17.* We set out as soon as it was well light; but it was really hard work to get forward; for the frost would not well bear or break: And the untracked snow covering all the roads, we had much ado to keep our horses on their feet. Meantime the wind rose higher and higher, till it was ready to overturn both man and beast. However, after a short bait at Bugden, we pushed on, and were met in the middle of an open field with so violent a storm of rain and hail, as we had not had before. It drove through our coats, great and small, boots and every thing, and yet froze as it fell, even upon our eye-brows; so that we had scarce either strength or motion left, when we came into our inn at Stilton.

We now gave up our hopes of reaching Grantham, the snow falling faster and faster. However, we took the advantage of a fair blast to set out, and made the best of our way to Stamford-Heath. But here a new difficulty arose, from the snow lying in large drifts. Sometimes horse and man were well nigh swallowed up. Yet in less than an hour we were brought safe to Stamford. Being willing to get as far as we could, we made but a short stop here; and about sunset came, cold and weary, yet well, to a little town called Brig-Casterton.

Wed. 18. Our servant came up and said, 'Sir, there is no travelling to-day. Such a quantity of snow has fallen in the night, that the roads are quite filled up.' I told him, 'At least we can walk twenty miles a day, with our horses in our hands.' So in the name of God we set out. The north-east wind was piercing as a sword, and had driven the snow into such uneven heaps, that the main road was unpassable. However, we kept on, a-foot or on horse-back, till we came to the White Lion at Grantham.

Some from Grimsby had appointed to meet us here; but not hearing any thing of them (for they were at another house, by mistake), after an hour's rest, we set out straight for Epworth. On the road we overtook a Clergyman and his servant; but the tooth-ache quite shut my mouth . . .

Wednesday, March 4. This week I read over with some young men a Compendium of Rhetoric, and a System of Ethics. I see not, why a man of tolerable understanding may not learn in six months' time more of solid philosophy than is commonly learned at Oxford in four (perhaps seven) years.

Sun. 8. I preached at Gateshead, and declared the loving-kindness of the Lord. In the evening, observing abundance of strangers at the Room, I changed my voice, and applied those terrible words, 'I have overthrown some of you as I overthrew Sodom and Gomorrah, and the rest of you were as brands plucked out of the burning; yet have ye not turned unto me, saith the Lord.'

On *Monday, Tuesday,* and *Thursday,* I examined the classes. I had been often told, it was impossible for me to distinguish the precious from the vile, without the miraculous discernment of spirits. But I now saw, more clearly than ever, that this might be done, and without much difficulty, supposing only two things: First, Courage and steadiness in the examiner. Secondly, Common sense and common honesty in the Leader of each class. I visit, for instance, the class in the Close, of which Robert Peacock is Leader. I ask, 'Does this and this person in your class live in drunkenness or any outward sin? Does he go to church, and use the other means of grace? Does he meet you as often as he has opportunity?' Now, if Robert Peacock has common sense, he can answer these questions truly; and if he has common honesty, he will. And if not, some other in the class has both, and can and will answer for him. Where is the difficulty then of finding out if there be any disorderly walker in this class, and, consequently, in any other? The question is not concerning the heart, but the life. And the general tenor of this, I do not say cannot be known, but cannot be hid without a miracle.

Where then is the need of any miraculous discernment in order to purge one of those societies? Nay, where is the use of it? For if I had that discernment, I am to pass sentence only *ex allegatis et probatis* [from things alleged and proved] not according to what I miraculously discern, but according to what is proved in the face of the sun.

The society, which the first year consisted of above eight hundred members, is now reduced to four hundred. But, according to the old proverb, the half is more than the whole. We shall not be ashamed of any of these, when we speak with our enemies in the gate.

Fri. 13. I found Mr. P. and I. almost discouraged at the doctrine of absolute and connotative nouns. I wonder any one has patience to learn Logic, but those who do it on a principle of conscience; unless he learns it as three in four of the young gentlemen in the Universities do: That is, goes about it and about it, without understanding one word of the matter.

In some of the following days I snatched a few hours to read 'The History of the Puritans.'[24] I stand in amaze: First, at the execrable spirit of persecution, which drove those venerable men out of the Church, and with which Queen Elizabeth's Clergy were as deeply tinctured as ever Queen Mary's were. Secondly, at the weakness of those holy Confessors, many of whom spent so much of their time and strength in disputing about surplices and hoods, or kneeling at the Lord's Supper.

Thur. 19. I considered, 'What would I do now, if I was sure I had but two days to live?' All outward things are settled to my wish; the Houses at Bristol, Kingswood, and Newcastle are safe; the deeds whereby they are conveyed to the Trustees took place on the 5th instant; my Will is made; what have I more to do, but to commend my soul to my merciful and faithful Creator? . . .

Thursday, June 4 [London]. I reduced the sixteen Stewards to seven; to whom were given the following instructions:

'1. You are to be men full of the Holy Ghost and wisdom, that you may do all things in a manner acceptable to God.

'2. You are to be present every Tuesday and Thursday morning, in order to transact the temporal affairs of the society.

'3. You are to begin and end every meeting with earnest prayer unto God, for a blessing on all your undertakings.

'4. You are to produce your accounts the first Tuesday in every month, that they may be transcribed into the ledger.

'5. You are to take it in turn, month by month, to be Chairman. The Chairman is to see, that all the rules be punctually observed, and immediately to check him who breaks any of them.

'5. You are to do nothing without the consent of the Minister, either actually had, or reasonably presumed.

'7. You are to consider, whenever you meet, "God is here." Therefore be deeply serious: Utter no trifling word: Speak as in his presence, and to the glory of his great name.

'8. When any thing is debated, let one at once stand up and speak, the rest giving attention. And let him speak just loud enough to be heard, in love and in the spirit of meekness.

'9. You are continually to pray and endeavour that a holy harmony of soul may in all things subsist among you; that in every step you may "keep the unity of the Spirit, in the bond of peace".

'10. In all debates, you are to watch over your spirits; avoiding, as fire, all clamour and contention; being "swift to hear, slow to speak"; in honour, every man preferring another before himself.

'11. If you cannot relieve, do not grieve, the poor: Give them soft words, if nothing else: Abstain from either sour looks, or harsh words. Let them be glad to come, even though they should go empty away. Put yourself in the place of every poor man; and deal with him as you would God should deal with you.

'These instructions, we whose names are under-written (being the present Stewards of the society at London) do heartily receive, and earnestly desire to conform to. In witness whereof we have set our hands.

'N.B. If any Steward shall break any of the preceding rules, after having been thrice admonished by the Chairman, (whereof notice is to be immediately given the Minister), he is no longer Steward.' ...

Tuesday, July 7. I preached at St. Ives; *Wednesday, 8,* at Sithney. On *Thursday* the Stewards of all the societies met. I now diligently inquired what Exhorters there were in each society; whether they had gifts meet for the work; whether their lives were eminently holy; and whether there appeared any fruit of their labour. I found, upon the whole, 1. That there were no less than eighteen Exhorters in the county. 2. That three of these had no gifts at all for the work, neither natural nor supernatural. 3. That a fourth had neither gifts nor grace; but was a dull, empty, self-conceited man. 4. That a fifth had considerable gifts, but had evidently made shipwreck of the grace of God: These therefore I determined immediately to set aside, and advise our societies not to hear them. 5. That J. B., A. L., and J. W. had gifts and grace, and had been much blessed in the work. Lastly, That the rest might be helpful when there was no Preacher in their own or the neighbouring societies, provided they would take no step without the advice of those who had more experience than themselves ...

Wednesday, August 5. Taking horse early in the morning, we rode over the rough mountains of Radnorshire and Montgomeryshire into Merionethshire. In the evening I was surprised with one of the finest prospects, in its kind, that ever I saw in my life. We rode in a green vale, shaded with rows of trees, which made an arbour for several miles. The river laboured along on our left hand, through broken rocks of every size, shape, and colour. On the other side of the river, the mountain rose to an immense height, almost perpendicular: And yet the tall straight oaks stood, rank above rank, from the bottom to the very top; only here and there, where the mountain was not so steep, were interposed pastures or fields of corn. At a distance, as far as the eye could reach, as it were by way of contrast,

> A mountain huge uprear'd
> Its broad bare back,

with vast, rugged rocks hanging over its brow, that seemed to nod portending ruin.

Thur. 6. Between three and four in the afternoon we, with some difficulty, reached Carnarvon. This has the face of a fortified town, having walls (such as they are), and a castle as considerable as that of Cardiff. Here we parted with our guide and interpreter, Mr. Philips. Mr. Tucker and I set out for Holyhead. We intended to cross over into Anglesey, at Baldonferry, four miles from Carnarvon: But not being able to inquire our way (as we spoke no Welsh, and the country people no English), we could not find where the ferry was, till we saw the boat coming over.

We went into the boat about sun-set, and lodged that night at a little inn by the water-side.

Fri. 7. We made a little stop at Llangevenye, seven miles from the ferry. We should have hired a guide to have steered over the sands, but it was quite out of my mind till we came to them; so we went straight across, and came to Holyhead without any stop or hinderance at all.

Sat. 8. Finding one of the packet-boats ready, we went on board about eight o'clock in the morning. It was a dead calm when we rowed out of the harbour: But about two in the afternoon the wind sprung up, and continued till near four on Sunday morning, when we were within sight of the Irish shore.

I could not but observe, 1. That while we were sailing with a fresh gale, there was no wind at all a mile off; but a ship which lay abreast of us was quite becalmed, till we left her out of sight. 2. That a French privateer, which for several days had taken every ship which sailed on that coast, was taken and brought into Dublin Bay, the very morning we arrived there.

Before ten we came to St. George's Quay. Soon after we landed, hearing the bells ringing for church, I went thither directly. Mr.

Lunell came to the Quay just after I was gone, and left word at the house where our things were, he would call again at one. He did so; and took us to his house. About three I wrote a line to the Curate of St. Mary's, who sent me word, he should be glad of my assistance: So I preached there (another gentleman reading Prayers), to as gay and senseless a congregation as ever I saw. After sermon Mr. R. thanked me very affectionately, and desired I would favour him with my company in the morning.

Mon. 10. I met the society at five, and at six preached, on, 'Repent, and believe the Gospel.' The room, large as it was, would not contain the people, who all seemed to taste the good word.

Between eight and nine I went to Mr. R[oquier], the Curate of St. Mary's. He professed abundance of good-will, commended my sermon in strong terms, and begged he might see me again the next morning. But, at the same time, he expressed the most rooted prejudice against Lay-Preachers, or preaching out of a church; and said, the Archbishop of Dublin was resolved to suffer no such irregularities in his diocese.

I went to our brethren, that we might pour out our souls before God. I then went straight to wait on the Archbishop myself; but he was gone out of town.

In the afternoon a gentleman desired to speak with me. He was troubled that it was not with him as in times past, when, at the age of fourteen the power of God came mightily upon him, constraining him to rise out of bed to pour out his prayers and tears from an heart overflowed with love and joy in the Holy Ghost. For some months he scarce knew whether he was in the body—continually walking and talking with God. He has now an abiding peace; but cannot rest till the love of God again fills his heart.

Between six and seven I went to Marlborough-Street. The house wherein we then preached was originally designed for a Lutheran church, and will contain about four hundred people. But four or five times the number may stand in the yard. Many of the rich were there, and many Ministers of every denomination. I preached on, 'The Scripture hath concluded all under sin'; and spoke closely and strongly: But none at all seemed to be offended. If my brother or I could have been here for a few months, I question if there might not have been a larger society here, than even in London itself.

Tues. 11. I waited on the Archbishop at Newbridge, ten miles from Dublin. I had the favour of conversing with him two or three hours; in which I answered abundance of objections. In the evening I returned to Mr. Lunell's. John Trembath preached at Marlborough-Street, to a large congregation both of Laity and Clergy, who behaved with much decency.

Wed. 12. I purposely delayed examining the classes, till I had gone through the Rules of the Society, part of which I explained to them at large, with the reasons of them, every morning.

Thur. 13. We walked in the afternoon to see two persons that were sick near Phœnix-Park. That part of it which joins to the city is sprinkled up and down with trees, not unlike Hyde-Park. But about a mile from the town is a thick grove of old, tall oaks; and in the centre of this, a round, open green (from which are vistas all four ways), with a handsome stone pillar in the midst, having a Phœnix on the top.

I continued preaching, morning and evening, to many more than the house would contain, and had more and more reason to hope they would not all be unfruitful hearers.

Fri. 14. I procured a genuine account of the great Irish massacre in 1641. Surely never was there such a transaction before, from the beginning of the world! More than two hundred thousand men, women, and children, butchered within a few months, in cool blood, and with such circumstances of cruelty as make one's blood run cold! It is well if God has not a controversy with the nation, on this very account, to this day.

Sat. 15. I stayed at home, and spoke to all that came. But I found scarce any Irish among them. At least ninety-nine in an hundred of the native Irish remain in the religion of their forefathers. The Protestants, whether in Dublin or elsewhere, are almost all transplanted lately from England. Nor is it any wonder that those who are born Papists generally live and die such, when the Protestants can find no better ways to convert them than Penal Laws and Acts of Parliament.

Sun. 16. We went to St. James's church in the morning (there being no service at St. Patrick's), and in the afternoon to Christ Church. When I came out of the choir, I could not but observe well nigh the whole congregation drawn up in rows in the body of the church, from the one end to the other. I walked through the midst of them; and they stared their fill: But scarce one spoke either good or bad.

In the evening I had a large number of them in Marlborough-Street, both within doors and without.

Mon. 17. I began examining the society, which I finished the next day. It contained about two hundred and four-score members, many of whom appeared to be strong in faith. The people in general are of a more teachable spirit than in most parts of England. But, on that very account, they must be watched over with the more care, being equally susceptible of good and ill impressions.

Tues. 18. I was informed that Mr. Latrobe, the Moravian Preacher, had read in his pulpit part of the 'Short View of the Difference between the Moravians' and us,[25] with the addition of many bitter words. Herein he did us, unawares, a signal favour; giving an authentic proof that we have nothing to do with them.

Fri. 21. I was desired to see the town and the college. The town has scarce any public building, except the Parliament-house, which is at all remarkable. The churches are poor and mean, both within and without. St. Stephen's Green might be made a beautiful place, being abundantly larger than Lincoln's Inn-Square; but the houses round about it (besides that some are low and bad) are quite irregular, and unlike each other; and little care is taken of the Green itself, which is rough and uneven as a common.

The College contains two little quadrangles; and one about as large as that of New-College in Oxford. There is likewise a bowling-green, a small garden, and a little park; and a new-built handsome library.

I expected we should have sailed on *Saturday, 22*; but no packet-boat was come in. In order to make the best of our time, I preached this day at noon, as well as in the evening. It was not for nothing that our passage was delayed. Who knows what a day may bring forth? . . .

[Wesley returned to Wales on *August 26*.]

Friday, November 16 [London]. I went with two or three friends, to see what are called the Electrical experiments. How must these also confound those poor half-thinkers, who will believe nothing but what they can comprehend? Who can comprehend, how fire lives in water, and passes through it more freely than through air? How flame issues out of my finger, real flame, such as sets fire to spirits of wine? How these, and many more as strange phenomena, arise from the turning round a glass globe? It is all mystery: If haply by any means God may hide pride from man! . . .

Sun. 22. I spent an hour with Mary Cheesebrook, a strange monument of the mercy of God. About six years ago, she was without God in the world, being a kept mistress. An acquaintance brought her one evening to the chapel in West-Street, where God gave her a new heart. She shed abundance of tears, she plucked out the right eye and cast it from her; and from that time procured for herself by hard labour what was needful for life and godliness. She missed no opportunity of coming to the preaching; often after a hard day's work, at May-Fair, she came to the Foundery in the evening, running the greater part of the way. Every Saturday, after paying her little debts, she gave away all the money that remained; leaving the morrow to take thought for the things of itself.

Two years ago she catched a violent cold, which she neglected, till it settled upon her lungs. I knew nothing of her illness till it was past cure, she being then worn to a skeleton. Upon my mentioning her case to Mrs. ——, she sent her half-a-guinea. Molly immediately sent for a poor man, a baker, of whom she had lately taken her bread. She owed him about ten shillings: But an earnest dispute arose between them; for the man would not take the money, saying, she wanted it more than he. But at length she prevailed, saying, she could not die in peace, if she owed any man any thing.

But I found something still lay upon her mind. Upon my pressing her to speak freely, she told me, it was concern for her child, a girl about eight years old, who, after she was gone, would have no friend to take care either of her soul or body. I replied, 'Be at rest in this thing also; I will take care of the child.' From that time she lay (two or three weeks) quietly waiting for the salvation of God ...

Monday, December 21. I went to Newington. Here, in the intervals of writing, I read the deaths of some of the Order *de la Trappe.* I am amazed at the allowance which God makes for invincible ignorance. Notwithstanding the mixture of superstition which appears in every one of these, yet what a strong vein of piety runs through all! What deep experience of the inward work of God; of righteousness, peace, and joy in the Holy Ghost!

Being not convinced, that I had yet delivered my own soul, with regard to that unhappy man, on *Tuesday, 22,* I wrote once more to Mr. H.,[26] as follows:

'DEAR BROTHER,   LONDON, *December 22, 1747*

'1. WHEN you was at Oxford with me, fourteen or fifteen years ago, you was holy and unblamable in all manner of conversation. I greatly rejoiced in the grace of God which was given unto you, which was often a blessing to my own soul. Yet even then you had frequently starts of thought which were not of God, though they at first appeared so to be. But you was humble and teachable; you was easily convinced, and those imaginations vanished away.

'2. More than twelve years ago, you told me, God had revealed it to you, that you should marry my youngest sister. I was much surprised, being well assured that you was able to receive our Lord's saying (so you had continually testified), and to be an "eunuch for the kingdom of heaven's sake". But you vehemently affirmed, the thing was of God; you was certain it was his will. God had made it plain to you that you must marry, and that she was the very person. You asked and gained her consent, and fixed the circumstances relating thereto.

'3. Hence I date your fall. Here were several faults in one. You leaned altogether to your own understanding, not consulting either me, who was then the guide of your soul, or the parents of your intended wife, till you had settled the whole affair. And while you followed the voice of nature, you said it was the voice of God.

'4. In a few days you had a counter-revelation, that you was not to marry her, but her sister. This last error was far worse than the first. But you was now quite above conviction. So, in spite of her poor, astonished parent, of her brothers, of all your vows and promises, you shortly after jilted the younger, and married the elder sister. The other, who had honoured you as an angel from heaven, and still loved you much too well (for you had stole her heart from the God of her youth), refused to be comforted. She fell into a lingering illness, which terminated in her death. And doth not her blood still cry unto God from the earth? Surely it is upon *your* head.

'5. Till this time you was a pattern of lowliness, meekness, seriousness, and continual advertence to the presence of God; and, above all, of self-denial in every kind, and of suffering all things with joyfulness. But there was now a worm at the root of the gourd. Yet it did not presently wither away; but for two years or more, after your marriage, you behaved nearly the same as before.

'Then anger and surliness began to appear, particularly toward your wife. But it was not long before you was sensible of this, and you seemed to have conquered it.

'6. You went up to London ten years ago. After this you began to speak on any head; not with your usual diffidence and self-abasement, but with a kind of confidence in your own judgment, and an air of self-sufficiency. A natural consequence was, the treating with more sharpness and contempt those who opposed either your judgment or practice.

'7. You came to live at London. You then, for a season, appeared to gain ground again. You acted in concert with my brother and me; heard our advice, and sometimes followed it. But this continued only till you contracted a fresh acquaintance with some of the Brethren of Fetter-Lane. Thenceforward you was quite shut up to us; we had no manner of influence over you; you was more and more prejudiced against us, and would receive nothing which we said.

'8. About six years ago you removed to Salisbury, and began a society there. For a year or two you went with them to the church and sacrament, and simply preached faith working by love. God was with you, and they increased both in number, and in the knowledge and love of God.

'About four years since you broke off all friendship with us; you would not so much as make use of our hymns, either in public or private, but laid them quite aside, and took the German hymn-book in their stead.

'You would not willingly suffer any of your people to read anything which we wrote. You angrily caught one of my sermons out of your servant's hand; saying, you would have no such books read in your house. In much the same manner you spoke to Mrs. Whitemarsh, when you found her reading one of the "Appeals". So that as far as in you lay, you fixed a great gulf between us and you, which remains to this day, notwithstanding a few steps lately made towards a re-union.

'About the same time you left off going to church, as well as to the sacrament. Your followers very soon trod in your steps; and not content with neglecting the ordinances of God, they began, after your example, to *despise* them, and all that continued to use them: Speaking with equal contempt of the Public Service, of Private Prayer, of Baptism, and of the Lord's Supper.

'From this time also you began to espouse and teach many uncommon opinions: As, that there is no resurrection of the body; that there is no general judgment to come; and that there is no hell, no worm that never dieth, no fire that never shall be quenched.

'9. Your seriousness, and advertence to the presence of God, now declined daily. You could talk on any thing or nothing, just as others did. You could break a jest, or laugh at it heartily; and as for fasting, abstinence, and self-denial, you, with the Moravians, trampled it under foot.'

In the following paragraphs I recited to him the things he had done with regard to more than one, or two, or three women, concluding thus:

'And now you know not that you have done anything amiss! You can eat and drink and be merry! You are every day engaged with variety of company, and frequent the coffee-houses! Alas, my brother, what is this? How are you above measure hardened by the deceitfulness of sin! Do you remember the story of Santon Barsisa?[27] I pray God your last end may not be like his! O, how have you grieved the Spirit of God! Return to him with weeping, fasting, and mourning. You are in the very belly of hell; only the pit hath not yet shut its mouth upon you. Arise, thou sleeper, and call upon thy God! Perhaps he may yet be found. Because he still bears with me, I cannot despair for you. But you have not a moment to lose. May God this instant strike you to the heart, that you may feel his wrath abiding on you, and have no rest in your bones, by reason of your sin, till all your iniquities are done away!' . . .

Saturday, January 16, 1748 [London]. Upon reviewing the account of the sick, we found great reason to praise God. Within the year, about three hundred persons had received medicines occasionally. About one hundred had regularly taken them, and submitted to a proper regimen. More than ninety of these were entirely cured of diseases they had long laboured under. And the expense of medicines for the entire year amounted to some shillings above forty pounds.

Sun. 17. I made a public collection towards a lending-stock for the poor. Our rule is, to lend only twenty shillings at once, which is repaid weekly within three months. I began this about a year and a half ago: Thirty pounds sixteen shillings were then collected; and out of this, no less than two hundred and fifty-five persons have been relieved in eighteen months. Dr. W., hearing of this design, sent a guinea toward it; as did an eminent Deist the next morning.

Mon. 25. I preached at four; and afterwards set out for Brentford. Thence I rode to Windsor, and preached about noon. We lodged at Morrel-Green, and came to Fisherton on *Tuesday*, about two o'clock.

Mr. Hall, having heard I was coming, had given strict orders that no one should be let in. The inner door he had locked himself, and (I suppose) taken away the key. Yet when I knocked at the outer gate, which was locked also, William Sims opened the wicket. I walked straight in. A girl stood in the gateway, but turned as soon as she saw me. I followed close at her heels, and went in after her, at a back-door. I asked the maid, 'Where is Mr. Hall?' She said, 'In the parlour,' and went in to him. I followed her, and found him sitting with my sister: But he presently rose and went up stairs. He then sent William Sims down, and bid him, 'Tell my brother, he has no business in my house.' After a few minutes, I went to a house in the town, and my sister came to me.

In about an hour, she returned home; but he sent word to the gate, she might go to the place whence she came.

I met a little company, gathered up out of the wreck, both in the evening and at five in the morning, and exhorted them to go on in the Bible way, and not to be wise above that is written ...

Friday, August 12. In riding to Newcastle, I finished the tenth Iliad of Homer. What an amazing genius had this man! To write with such strength of thought, and beauty of expression, when he had none to go before him! And what a vein of piety runs through his whole work, in spite of his Pagan prejudices! Yet one cannot but observe such improprieties intermixed, as are shocking to the last degree.

What excuse can any man of common sense make for

> His scolding heroes and his wounded gods?

Nay, does he not introduce even his 'Father of gods and men', one while shaking heaven with his nod, and soon after using his sister and wife, the empress of heaven, with such language as a carman might be ashamed of? And what can be said for a King, full of days and wisdom, telling Achilles how often he had given him wine when he was a child and sat in his lap, till he had vomited it up on his clothes? Are these some of those 'divine boldnesses which naturally provoke short-sightedness and ignorance to show themselves'?

Tues. 16. We left Newcastle. In riding to Leeds, I read Dr. Hodge's 'Account of the Plague in London'. I was surprised, 1. That he did not learn, even from the symptoms related by himself, that the part first seized by the infection was the stomach; and, 2. That he so obstinately persevered in the hot regimen; though he continually saw the ill success of it,—a majority of the patients dying under his hands ...

Tuesday, July 25, 1749 [Bristol]. I rode over to Kingswood, and inquired particularly into the state of our school there. I was concerned to find that several of the Rules had been habitually neglected: I judged it necessary, therefore, to lessen the family; suffering none to remain therein, who were not clearly satisfied with them, and determined to observe them all.

Thur. 27. I read Mr. Law 'On the Spirit of the Prayer'. There are many masterly strokes therein, and the whole is lively and entertaining; but it is another Gospel. For if God was never angry (as this Tract asserts), he could never be reconciled; and, consequently, the whole Christian doctrine of reconciliation by Christ falls to the ground at once. An excellent method of converting Deists, by giving up the very essence of Christianity! ...

Wednesday, July 19. I finished the translation of 'Martin Luther's Life'. Doubtless he was a man highly favoured of God, and a blessed instrument in his hand. But O! what pity that he had no faithful friend! None that would, at all hazards, rebuke him plainly and sharply, for his rough, untractable spirit, and bitter zeal for opinions, so greatly obstructive of the work of God! ...

Wednesday, October 18. I rode, at the desire of John Bennet, to Rochdale, in Lancashire. As soon as ever we entered the town, we found the streets lined on both sides with multitudes of people, shouting, cursing, blaspheming, and gnashing upon us with their teeth. Perceiving it would not be practicable to preach abroad, I went into a large room, open to the street, and called aloud, 'Let the wicked forsake his way, and the unrighteous man his thoughts.' The word of God prevailed over the fierceness of man. None opposed or interrupted; and there was a very remarkable change in the behaviour of the people, as we afterwards went through the town.

We came to Bolton about five in the evening. We had no sooner entered the main street, than we perceived the lions at Rochdale were lambs in comparison of those at Bolton. Such rage and bitterness I scarce ever saw before, in any creatures that bore the form of men. They followed us in full cry to the house where we went; and as soon as we were gone in, took possession of all the avenues to it, and filled the street from one end to the other. After some time the waves did not roar quite so loud. Mr. P—— [Edward Perronet] thought he might then venture out. They immediately closed in, threw him down, and rolled him in the mire; so that when he scrambled from them, and got into the house again, one could scarce tell what or who he was. When the first stone came among us through the window, I expected a shower to follow; and the rather, because they had now procured a bell to call their whole forces together. But they did not design to carry on the attack at a distance: Presently one ran up and told us the mob had burst into the house: He added, that they had got J[ohn] B[ennet] in the midst of them. They had; and he laid hold on the opportunity to tell them of 'the terrors of the Lord'. Meantime D[avid] T[aylor] engaged another part of them with smoother and softer words. Believing the time was now come, I walked down into the thickest of them. They had now filled all the rooms below. I called for a chair. The winds were hushed, and all was calm and still. My heart was filled with love, my eyes with tears, and my mouth with arguments. They were amazed, they were ashamed, they were melted down, they devoured every word. What a turn was this! O how did God change the counsel of the old Ahithophel into foolishness; and bring all the drunkards, swearers, Sabbath-breakers, and mere sinners in the place, to hear of his plenteous redemption! . . .

Monday, January 22, 1750 [London]. I prayed in the morning at the Foundery, and Howell Harris preached: A powerful orator, both by nature and grace; but owes nothing to art or education.[28]

Wed. 24. I was desired to call on one that was sick, though I had small hopes of doing him any good; he had been so harmless a man for ninety years: Yet he was not out of God's reach. He was quickly convinced that his own righteousness could not recommend him to God. I could then pray for him in confidence of being heard. A few days after he died in peace.

Sun. 28. I read Prayers, and Mr. Whitefield preached. How wise is God in giving different talents to different Preachers! Even the little improprieties both' of his language and manner were a means of profiting many, who would not have been touched by a more correct discourse, or a more calm and regular manner of speaking . . .

Thursday, February 8. It was about a quarter after twelve, that the earthquake began at the skirts of the town. It began in the south-east, went through Southwark, under the river, and then from one end of London to the other. It was observed at Westminster and Grosvenor-Square a quarter before one. (Perhaps, if we allow for the difference of the clocks, about a quarter of an hour after it began in Southwark.) There were three distinct shakes, or wavings to and fro, attended with an hoarse, rumbling noise, like thunder. How gently does God deal with this nation! O that our repentance may prevent heavier marks of his displeasure!

Fri. 9. We had a comfortable watch-night at the chapel. About eleven o'clock it came into my mind, that this was the very day and hour in which, forty years ago, I was taken out of the flames. I stopped, and gave a short account of that wonderful providence. The voice of praise and thanksgiving went up on high, and great was our rejoicing before the Lord ...

Wednesday, March 28 [Holyhead] ... About eleven we were called to go on board, the wind being quite fair: And so it continued till we were just out of the harbour. It then turned west, and blew a storm. There was neither moon nor stars, but rain and wind enough; so that I was soon tired of staying on deck. But we met another storm below: For who should be there, but the famous Mr. Gr[iffith], of Carnarvonshire, a clumsy, overgrown, hard-faced man; whose countenance I could only compare to that (which I saw in Drury-Lane thirty years ago) of one of the ruffians in 'Macbeth'. I was going to lie down, when he tumbled in, and poured out such a volley of ribaldry, obscenity, and blasphemy, every second or third word being an oath, as was scarce ever heard at Billingsgate. Finding there was no room for me to speak, I retired into my cabin, and left him to Mr. Hopper. Soon after, one or two of his own company interposed, and carried him back to his cabin.

Thur. 29. We wrought our way four or five leagues toward Ireland; but were driven back in the afternoon to the very mouth of the harbour: Nevertheless, the wind shifting one or two points, we ventured out again; and by midnight we were got about half seas over; but the wind then turning full against us, and blowing hard, we were driven back again, and were glad, about nine, to get into the bay once more.

In the evening I was surprised to see, instead of some poor, plain people, a room full of men daubed with gold and silver. That I might not go out of their depth, I began expounding the story of Dives and Lazarus. It was more applicable than I was aware; several of them (as I afterwards learned) being eminently wicked men. I delivered my own soul; but they could in nowise bear it. One and another walked away, murmuring sorely. Four stayed till I drew to a close: They then put on their hats, and began talking to one another. I mildly reproved them; on which they rose up and went away, railing and blaspheming. I had then a comfortable hour with a company of plain, honest Welshmen.

In the night there was a vehement storm. Blessed be God that we were safe on shore! *Saturday, 31.* I determined to wait one week longer, and if we could not sail then, to go and wait for a ship at Bristol. At seven in the evening, just as I was going to preach, I heard a huge noise, and took knowledge of the rabble of gentlemen. They had now strengthened themselves with drink and numbers, and placed Captain Gr—— (as they called him) at their head. He soon burst open both the outward and inner door, struck old Robert Griffith, our landlord, several times, kicked his wife, and, with twenty full-mouthed oaths and curses, demanded, 'Where is the Parson?' Robert Griffith came up, and desired me to go into another room, where he locked me in. The Captain followed him quickly, broke open one or two doors, and got on a chair, to look on the top of a bed: But his foot slipping (as he was not a man made for climbing), he fell down backward all his length. He rose leisurely, turned about, and with his troop, walked away.

I then went down to a small company of the poor people, and spent half an hour with them in prayer. About nine, as we were preparing to go to bed, the house was beset again. The Captain burst in first. Robert Griffith's daughter was standing in the passage with a pail of water, with which (whether with design or in her fright, I know not) she covered him from head to foot. He cried as well as he could, 'M—urder! Murder!' and stood very still for some moments. In the mean time Robert Griffith stepped by him, and locked the door. Finding himself alone, he began to change his voice, and cry, 'Let me out! Let me out!' Upon his giving his word and honour, that none of the rest should come in, they opened the door, and all went away together . . .

Friday, May 25 [Bandon, near Cork]. One Roger O'Ferrall fixed up an advertisement at the public Exchange, that he was ready to head any mob, in order to pull down any house that should dare to harbour a swaddler. (A name given to Mr. Cennick first, by a Popish Priest, who heard him speak of a child wrapped in swaddling clothes; and probably did not know the expression was in the Bible, a book he was not much acquainted with.)

All this time God gave us great peace at Bandon, notwithstanding the unwearied labours, both public and private, of good Dr. B[rown, the rector], to stir up the people. But *Saturday, 26*, many were under great apprehensions of what was to be done in the evening. I began preaching in the main street at the usual hour, but to more than twice the usual congregation. After I had spoke about a quarter of an hour, a Clergyman, who had planted himself near me, with a very large stick in his hand, according to agreement, opened the scene. (Indeed his friends assured me he was in drink, or he would not have done it.) But, before he had uttered many words, two or three resolute women, by main strength, pulled him into a house; and, after expostulating a little, sent him away through the garden. But here he fell violently on her that conducted him, not in anger, but love (such as it was); so that she was constrained to repel force by force, and cuff him soundly before he would let her go.

The next champion that appeared was one Mr. M——, a young gentleman of the town. He was attended by two others, with pistols in their hands. But his triumph too was but short; some of the people quickly bore him away, though with much gentleness and civility.

The third came on with greater fury; but he was encountered by a butcher of the town (not one of the Methodists), who used him as he would an ox, bestowing one or two hearty blows upon his head. This cooled his courage, especially as none took his part. So I quietly finished my discourse . . .

Thur. 31. I rode to Rathcormuck. There being a great burying in the afternoon, to which people came from all parts, Mr. Lloyd read part of the Burial Service in the church; after which I preached on, 'The end of all things is at hand.' I was exceedingly shocked at (what I had only heard of before) the Irish howl which followed. It was not a song, as I supposed, but a dismal, inarticulate yell, set up at the grave by four shrill-voiced women, who (we understood) were hired for that purpose. But I saw not one that shed a tear; for that, it seems, was not in their bargain . . .

Friday, June 15. We set out at four, and reached Kilkenny, about twenty-five old Irish miles, about noon. This is by far the most pleasant, as well as most fruitful country, which I have seen in all

Ireland. Our way after dinner lay by Dunmore, the seat of the late Duke of Ormond. We rode through the Park for about two miles, by the side of which the river runs. I never saw either in England, Holland, or Germany, so delightful a place. The walks, each consisting of four rows of ashes, the tufts of trees sprinkled up and down, interspersed with the smoothest and greenest lawns, are beautiful beyond description. And what hath the owner thereof, the Earl of Arran? Not even the beholding it with his eyes.

My horse tired in the afternoon; so I left him behind, and borrowed that of my companion. I came to Aymo about eleven and would very willingly have passed the rest of the night there; but the good woman of the inn was not minded that I should. For some time she would not answer: At last she opened the door just wide enough to let out four dogs upon me. So I rode on to Ballybrittas, expecting a rough salute here too, from a large dog which used to be in the yard. But he never stirred, till the hostler waked and came out. About twelve I laid me down. I think this was the longest day's journey I ever rode; being fifty old Irish, that is, about ninety English miles . . .

[Wesley returned from Ireland on 24 July.]

Wednesday, January 30, 1751. Having received a pressing letter from Dr. Isham, then the Rector of our College, to give my vote at the election for a Member of Parliament, which was to be the next day, I set out early [from London], in a severe frost, with the north-west wind full in my face. The roads were so slippery, that it was scarce possible for our horses to keep their feet: Indeed one of them could not; but fell upon his head, and cut it terribly. Nevertheless, about seven in the evening, God brought us safe to Oxford. A congregation was waiting for me at Mr. Evans's, whom I immediately addressed in those awful words, 'What is a man profited, if he shall gain the whole world, and lose his own soul?'

Thur. 31. I went to the school, where the Convocation was met: But I did not find the decency and order which I expected. The gentleman for whom I came to vote, was not elected: Yet I did not repent of my coming; I owe much more than this to that generous, friendly man, who now rests from his labours.

I was much surprised wherever I went, at the civility of the people—gentlemen as well as others. There was no pointing, no calling of names, as once; no, nor even laughter. What can this mean? Am I become a servant of men? Or is the scandal of the Cross ceased? ...

Saturday, February 2. Having received a full answer from Mr. P—— [Vincent Perronet], I was clearly convinced that I ought to marry. For many years I remained single, because I believed I could be more useful in a single, than in a married state. And I praise God, who enabled me so to do. I now as fully believed, that in my present circumstances, I might be more useful in a married state; into which, upon this clear conviction, and by the advice of my friends, I entered a few days after.

Wed. 6. I met the single men, and showed them on how many accoun s it was good for those who had received that gift from God, to remain 'single for the kingdom of heaven's sake'; unless where a particular case might be an exception to the general rule ...

Friday, June 22. I drew up a short account of the case of Kingswood School.

1. The School began on Midsummer day, 1748. The first Schoolmasters were J[ohn] J[ones], T[homas] R[ichards], W[alter] S[ellon], R[ichard] M[oss], W[illiam] S[pencer], and A[braham] G[rou]. The Rules were printed; and notwithstanding the strictness of them, in two or three months we had twenty-eight scholars: So that the family, including M[ary] D[avey], the housekeeper, R—— T——, our man, and four maid-servants, consisted of forty persons.

2. From the very beginning I met with all sorts of discouragements. Cavillers and prophets of evil were on every side. An hundred objections were made both to the whole design, and every particular branch of it; especially by those from whom I had reason to expect better things: Notwithstanding which, through God's help, I went on; wrote an English, a Latin, a Greek, a Hebrew, and a French Grammar, and printed *Prælectiones Pueriles*, with many other books for the use of the School; and God gave a manifest blessing. Some of the wildest children were struck with

deep conviction; all appeared to have good desires; and two or three began to taste the love of God.

3. Yet I soon observed several things which I did not like. The maids divided into two parties. R—— T—— studiously blew up the coals, by constant whispering and tale-bearing. M[ary] D[avey] did not supply the defects of other servants, being chiefly taken up with thoughts of another kind. And hence the children were not properly attended, nor were things done with due care and exactness.

4. The Masters should have corrected these irregularities; but they added to them. T[homas] R[ichards] was so rough and disobliging, that the children were little profited by him. A[braham] G[rou] was honest and diligent; but his person and manner made him contemptible to the children. R[ichard] M[oss] was grave and weighty in his behaviour, and did much good, till W[alter] S[ellon] set the children against him; and instead of restraining them from play, played with them himself. J[ohn] J[ones] and W[illiam] S[pencer] were weighed down by the rest, who neither observed the Rules in the school nor out of it.

5. The continual breach of that rule, 'Never to let the children work, but in the presence of a Master,' occasioned their growing wilder and wilder, till all their religious impressions were worn off; and the sooner, as four or five of the larger boys were very uncommonly wicked.

6. When I came down in September, 1750, and found the scholars reduced to eighteen, I determined to purge the house thoroughly. Two more of the children (one of them exquisitely wicked) I sent home without delay. M[ary] D[avey], T[homas] R[ichards], R[ichard] M[oss], and three of the maids were gone away already: R—— T——, W[alter] S[ellon], and A[braham] G[rou], went after; so that only two Masters, Mr. J[ones] and S[pencer], remained with Mrs. Hardwick, one maid, and sixteen scholars.

7. I now hoped the time was come for God to revive his work: But we were not low enough yet. So first J[ohn] J[ones], and then W[illiam] S[pencer], grew weary; the Rules were neglected again; and in the following winter, Mr. Page died, and five more scholars

went away. What weakened the hands of the Masters still more, was the bitter evil-speaking of some who continually endeavoured either to drive away the children that remained, or to prevent others from coming.

8. There are now two Masters, the housekeeper, a maid, and eleven children. I believe all in the house are at length of one mind; and trust God will bless us in the latter end, more than in the beginning . . .

Friday, April 24, 1752. [Leaving Grimsby] we rode by a fine seat; the owner of which (not much above fourscore years old) says he desires only to live thirty years longer; ten to hunt, ten to get money (having at present but twenty thousand pounds a year), and ten years to repent. O that God may not say unto him, 'Thou fool, this night shall thy soul be required of thee!'

When I landed at the quay in Hull, it was covered with people, inquiring, 'Which is he? Which is he?' But they only stared and laughed; and we walked unmolested to Mr. A——'s house.

I was quite surprised at the miserable condition of the fortifications; far more ruinous and decayed than those at Newcastle, even before the rebellion. It is well there is no enemy near.

I went to Prayers at three in the old church—a grand and venerable structure. Between five and six the coach called, and took me to Mighton-Car, about half a mile from the town. An huge multitude, rich and poor, horse and foot, with several coaches, were soon gathered together; to whom I cried with a loud voice, and a composed spirit, 'What shall it profit a man, if he shall gain the whole world, and lose his own soul?' Some thousands of the people seriously attended; but many behaved as if possessed by Moloch. Clods and stones flew about on every side; but they neither touched nor disturbed me. When I had finished my discourse, I went to take coach; but the coachman had driven clear away. We were at a loss, till a gentlewoman invited my wife and me to come into her coach. She brought some inconveniences on herself thereby; not only as there were nine of us in the coach, three on each side, and three in the middle; but also as the mob closely attended us, throwing in at the windows (which we did not think it prudent to shut) whatever came next to hand. But a large gentlewoman who sat in my lap, screened me, so that nothing came near me.

The mob, who were increased to several thousands, when I stepped out of the coach into Mr. A——'s house, perceiving I was escaped out of their hands, revenged themselves on the windows with many showers of stones, which they poured in, even into the rooms four stories high. Mr. A—— walked through them to the Mayor's house, who gave him fair words, but no assistance; probably not knowing that himself (the Mayor) might be compelled to make good all the damage which should be done. He then went in quest of Constables, and brought two with him about nine o'clock. With their help he so thoroughly dispersed the mob, that no two of them were left together. But they rallied about twelve, and gave one charge more, with oaths, and curses, and bricks, and stones. After this, all was calm, and I slept sound till near four in the morning.

About five, *Saturday, 25*, we took horse, and made to Pocklington. I was sorry, when I found it was the fair-day, that notice had been given of my preaching; especially when I heard there was no society, and scarce any one awakened in the town. The unusual bitterness of several who met us in the street, made the prospect still more unpromising. However, I went to see the room provided for preaching, but found it was not above five yards square. I then looked at a yard which was proposed; but one circumstance of this I did not like. It was plentifully furnished with stones: Artillery ready at hand for the devil's drunken companions. Just then it began to rain; upon which a gentleman offered a large commodious barn. Thither I went without delay, and began preaching to a few, who increased continually. I have known no such time since we left London. Their tears fell as the rain. None opposed or mocked: So that these made full amends for the behaviour of those at Hull.

The man and his wife at whose house we dined, had been bitterly persecuted both by his and her mother. These were some of the first whose hearts were touched. Immediately after preaching they came up into the room where we were, and confessed, with many tears, how eagerly they had opposed the truth of God, and troubled their children for adhering to it. How wise are all the ways of God! Had it not been fair-day, these had not been there.

Yet some of our company had dreadful forebodings of what was to be at York. A worthy Justice of the Peace (doubtless to quiet the mob there) had just caused to be cried about the streets, stuck up in public places, and even thrown into many houses, part of the 'Comparison between the Papists and Methodists'. Perhaps this might be the occasion of some bitter curses which were given us almost as soon as we entered the gates. But the vain words of those Rabshakehs returned into their own bosoms. I began preaching at six. The chapel was filled with hearers, and with the presence of God. The opposers opened not their mouths. The mourners blessed God for the consolation.

Sun. 26. At seven God was with us as before, and his word brake the rocks in pieces. We left York about nine, as quietly as we came, and rode to Acomb . . .

Sunday, April 15, 1753. I preached in the afternoon at Cocker-mouth, to well nigh all the inhabitants of the town. Intending to go from thence into Scotland, I inquired concerning the road, and was informed I could not pass the arm of the sea which parts the two kingdoms, unless I was at Bonas, about thirty miles from Cockermouth, soon after five in the morning. At first I thought of taking an hour or two's sleep, and setting out at eleven or twelve. But, upon farther consideration, we chose to take our journey first, and rest afterward. So we took horse about seven, and having a calm, moonshiny night, reached Bonas before one. After two or three hours' sleep, we set out again without any faintness or drowsiness.

Our landlord, as he was guiding us over the Frith, very innocently asked, how much a year we got by preaching thus. This gave me an opportunity of explaining to him that kind of gain which he seemed utterly a stranger to. He appeared to be quite amazed; and spake not one word, good or bad, till he took his leave.

Presently after he went, my mare stuck fast in a quagmire, which was in the midst of the high road. But we could well excuse this; for the road all along, for near fifty miles after, was such as I never saw any natural road either in England or Ireland: Nay, far better, notwithstanding the continued rain, than the turnpike road between London and Canterbury.

We dined at Dumfries, a clean, well-built town, having two of the most elegant churches (one at each end of the town) that I have seen. We reached Thorny-Hill in the evening. What miserable accounts pass current in England of the inns in Scotland! Yet here, as well as wherever we called in our whole journey, we had not only everything we wanted, but everything readily and in good order, and as clean as I ever desire.

Tues. 17. We set out about four, and rode over several high, but extremely pleasant, mountains, to Lead-Hill; a village of miners resembling Placey, near Newcastle. We dined at a village called Lesmahaggy, and about eight in the evening reached Glasgow. A gentleman who had overtaken us on the road, sent one with us to Mr. Gillies's house.

Wed. 18. I walked over the city, which I take to be as large as Newcastle-upon-Tyne. The University (like that of Dublin) is only one College, consisting of two small squares; I think not larger, nor at all handsomer, than those of Lincoln College, in Oxford. The habit of the students gave me surprise. They wear scarlet gowns, reaching only to their knees. Most I saw were very dirty, some very ragged, and all of very coarse cloth. The high church is a fine building. The outside is equal to that of most cathedrals in England; but it is miserably defaced within; having no form, beauty, or symmetry left . . .

On *Wednesday, July 25* [Cornwall] the Stewards met at St. Ives, from the western part of Cornwall. The next day I began examining the society; but I was soon obliged to stop short. I found an accursed thing among them; well nigh one and all bought or sold uncustomed goods. I therefore delayed speaking to any more till I had met them all together. This I did in the evening, and told them plain, either they must put this abomination away, or they would see my face no more. *Friday, 27.* They severally promised so to do. So I trust this plague is stayed . . .

Saturday, November 24 [London]. I rode home, and was pretty well till night; but my cough was then worse than ever. My fever returned at the same time, together with the pain in my left breast; so that I should probably have stayed at home on *Sunday, 25,* had it not been advertised in the public papers, that I would preach a charity sermon at the chapel, both morning and afternoon. My cough did not interrupt me while I preached in the morning; but it was extremely troublesome while I administered the sacrament. In the afternoon I consulted my friends, whether I should attempt to preach again or no. They thought I should, as it had been advertised. I did so; but very few could hear. My fever increased much while I was preaching: However, I ventured to meet the society; and for near an hour my voice and strength were restored, so that I felt neither pain nor weakness.

Mon. 26. Dr. F—— told me plain, I must not stay in town a day longer; adding, 'If any thing does thee good, it must be the country air, with rest, asses' milk, and riding daily.' So (not being able to sit an horse) about noon I took coach for Lewisham.

In the evening (not knowing how it might please God to dispose of me), to prevent vile panegyric, I wrote as follows:

Here lieth the Body

OF

JOHN WESLEY,

A BRAND PLUCKED OUT OF THE BURNING:
WHO DIED OF A CONSUMPTION IN THE FIFTY-FIRST YEAR OF HIS AGE,
NOT LEAVING, AFTER HIS DEBTS ARE PAID,
TEN POUNDS BEHIND HIM:
PRAYING,
GOD BE MERCIFUL TO ME, AN UNPROFITABLE SERVANT!

He ordered that this, if any, inscription should be placed on his tombstone.

Wed. 28. I found no change for the better, the medicines which had helped me before, now taking no effect. About noon (the time that some of our brethren in London had set apart for joining in prayer) a thought came into my mind to make an experiment. So I ordered some stone brimstone to be powdered, mixed with the white of an egg, and spread on brown paper, which I applied to my side. The pain ceased in five minutes, the fever in half an hour; and from this hour I began to recover strength. The next day I was able to ride, which I continued to do every day till January 1. Nor did the weather hinder me once; it being always tolerably fair (however it was before) between twelve and one o'clock.

Friday, December 14. Having finished all the books which I designed to insert in the 'Christian Library', I broke through the Doctor's order, not to write, and began transcribing a Journal for the press; and in the evening I went to prayers with the family, without finding any inconvenience.

Thur. 20. I felt a gradual increase of strength, till I took a decoction of the bark, which I do not find (such is the peculiarity of my constitution) will agree with me in any form whatever. This immediately threw me into a purging, which brought me down again in a few days, and quite disappointed me in my design of going out on Christmas-day . . .

Wednesday, October 2, 1754. I walked to Old Sarum, which, in spite of common sense, without house or inhabitant, still sends two members to the Parliament. It is a large, round hill, encompassed with a broad ditch, which, it seems, has been of a considerable depth. At the top of it is a corn-field; in the midst of which is another round hill, about two hundred yards in diameter, encompassed with a wall, and a deep ditch. Probably before the invention of cannon, this city was impregnable. Troy was; but now it is vanished away, and nothing left but 'the stones of emptiness' . . .

Mon. 28. I delivered my own soul, by one more conversation with Sir [James Lowther];[29] the substance of which I wrote to him the next day in the following letter:

'SIR,   *October 28, 1754*

'WHETHER I see you any more in this life or no, I rejoice that I have seen you this once; and that God enabled you to bear with patience, what I spoke in the simplicity of my heart.

'The substance of what I took the liberty to mention to you this morning was, You are on the borders of the grave, as well as I: Shortly we must both appear before God. When it seemed to me, some months since, that my life was near an end, I was troubled that I had not dealt plainly with you. This you will permit me to do now, without any reserve, in the fear and in the presence of God.

'I reverence you for your office as a Magistrate; I believe you to be an honest, upright man; I love you for having protected an innocent people from their cruel and lawless oppressors. But so much the more am I obliged to say (though I judge not; God is the judge), I fear you are covetous; that you love the world: And if you do, as sure as the word of God is true, you are not in a state of salvation.

'The substance of your answer was, "That many people exhort others to charity from self-interest; that men of fortune must mind their fortune; that you cannot go about to look for poor people; that when you have seen them yourself, and relieved them, they were scarce ever satisfied; that many make an ill use of what you give them; that you cannot trust the account people give of themselves by letters; that, nevertheless, you do give to private persons, by the hands of Colonel Hudson and others; that you have also given to several hospitals an hundred pounds at a time; but that you must support your family; that the Lowther family has continued above four hundred years; that you are for great things,—for public charities, and for saving the nation from ruin; and that others may think as they please, but this is your way of thinking, and has been for many years.'

'To this I replied: "1. Sir, I have no self-interest in this matter; I consult your interest, not my own; I want nothing from you; I desire nothing from you; I expect nothing from you: But I am concerned for your immortal spirit, which must so soon launch into eternity. 2. It is true, men of fortune must mind their fortune; but they must not love the world. *If any man love the world, the love of the Father is not in him.* 3. It is true, likewise, you cannot go about to look for poor people; but you may be sufficiently informed of them by those that can. 4. And if some of these are never satisfied, this is no reason for not relieving others. 5. Suppose, too, that some make an ill use of what you give, the loss falls on their own head; you will not lose your reward for their fault: What you laid out, God will pay you again. 6. Yet certainly you do well to have all the assurance you can, that those to whom you give, are likely to make a good use of it; and therefore to expect a stronger recommendation of them than their own, whether by letter or otherwise. 7. I rejoice that you have given to many by so worthy a man as Colonel Hudson, whose word is certainly a sufficient recommendation. 8. I rejoice likewise that you have given some hundreds of pounds to the Hospitals, and wish it had been ten thousand. 9. To the support of the family I did not object; but begged leave to ask, whether this could not be done, without giving ten thousand a year to one who had as much already? And whether you could answer this to God, in the day wherein he shall judge the world? 10. I likewise granted, that the family had continued above four hundred years; but observed, meantime, that God regarded it not a jot the more for this; and that four hundred or one thousand years are but a moment, compared to eternity. 11. I observed likewise that great things may be done, and little things not left undone. 12. And that if this, or any other way of thinking be according to Scripture, then it is sound and good; whereas, if it be contrary to Scripture, it is not good, and the longer we are in it, so much the worse.'

'Upon the whole, I must once more earnestly entreat you to consider yourself, and God, and eternity. As to yourself, you are not the proprietor of any thing; no, not of one shilling in the world. You are only a steward of what another entrusts you with, to be laid out, not according to your will, but his. And what would you think of your steward, if he laid out what is called your money, according to his own will and pleasure? 2. Is not God the sole proprietor of all things? And are not you to give an account to him for every part of his goods? And O how dreadful an account, if you have expended any part of them not according to his will, but your own? 3. Is not death at hand? And are not you and I just stepping into eternity? Are we not just going to appear in the presence of God; and that naked of all worldly goods? Will you then rejoice in the money you have left behind you? Or in that you have given to support a family, as it is called, that is, in truth, to support the pride, and vanity, and luxury, which you have yourself despised all your life long? O, Sir, I beseech you, for the sake of God, for the sake of your own immortal soul, examine yourself, whether you do not love money? If so, you cannot love God. And if we die without the fear of God, what remains? Only to be banished from him for ever and ever! I am, with true respect, Sir,

'Your servant, for Christ's sake.' . . .

Monday, June 2 [1755]. I left Newcastle; and came to Durham, just as Jacob Rowell had done preaching, or rather, attempting to preach; for the mob was so noisy, that he was constrained to break off. I reached Osmotherly in the evening, and found a large congregation waiting. I preached immediately; God renewing my strength, and comforting my heart.

Here I inquired, of eye and ear witnesses, concerning what lately occurred in the neighbourhood. On Tuesday, March 25th last, being the week before Easter, many persons observed a great noise near a ridge of mountains in Yorkshire, called Black-Hamilton. It was observed chiefly in the south-west side of the mountain, about a mile from the course where the Hamilton races are run; near a ridge of rocks, commonly called Whiston-Cliffs, or Whiston-White-Mare; two miles from Sutton, about five from Thirsk.

The same noise was heard on Wednesday, by all who went that way. On Thursday, about seven in the morning, Edward Abbot, weaver, and Adam Bosomworth, bleacher, both of Sutton, riding under Whiston-Cliffs, heard a roaring (so they termed it), like many cannons, or loud and rolling thunder. It seemed to come from the cliffs; looking up to which, they saw a large body of stone, four or five yards broad, split and fly off from the very top of the rocks. They thought it strange, but rode on. Between ten and eleven a larger piece of the rock, about fifteen yards thick, thirty high, and between sixty and seventy broad, was torn off, and thrown into the valley.

About seven in the evening, one who was riding by observed the ground to shake exceedingly; and soon after several large stones or rocks, of some tons weight each, rose out of the ground. Others were thrown on one side, others turned upside down, and many rolled over and over. Being a little surprised, and not very curious, he hasted on his way.

On Friday and Saturday the ground continued to shake, and the rocks to roll over one another. The earth also clave asunder in very many places, and continued so to do till Sunday morning.

Being at Osmotherley, seven miles from the cliffs, on Monday, June 2, and finding Edward Abbot there, I desired him, the next morning, to show me the way thither. I walked, crept, and climbed, round and over great part of the ruins. I could not perceive, by any sign, that there was ever any cavity in the rock at all; but one part of the solid stone is cleft from the rest, in a perpendicular line, and smooth, as if cut with instruments: Nor is it barely thrown down, but split into many hundred pieces; some of which lie four or five hundred yards from the main rock.

The ground nearest the cliff is not raised, but sunk considerably beneath the level: But at some distance it is raised in a ridge of eight or ten yards high, twelve or fifteen broad, and near an hundred long. Adjoining to this lies an oval piece of ground, thirty or forty yards in diameter, which has been removed, whole as it is, from beneath the cliff, without the least fissure, with all its load of rocks; some of which were as large as the hull of a small ship. At a little distance is a second piece of ground, forty or fifty yards across, which has been also transplanted entire, with rocks of various sizes upon it, and a tree growing out of one of them. By the removal of one or both of these, I suppose the hollow near the cliff was made.

All round them lay stones and rocks, great and small; some on the surface of the earth, some half sunk into it, some almost covered, in variety of positions. Between these the ground was cleft asunder in a thousand places: Some of the apertures were nearly closed again; some gaping as at first. Between thirty and forty acres of land, as is commonly supposed (though some reckon above sixty), are in this condition.

On the skirts of these, I observed, in abundance of places, the green turf (for it was pasture land) as it were pared off, two or three inches thick, and wrapped round like sheets of lead. A little farther, it was not cleft or broken at all, but raised in ridges five or six foot long, exactly resembling the graves in a church-yard. Of these there is a vast number.

That part of the cliff from which the rest is torn, lies so high and is now of so bright a colour, that it is plainly visible to all the country round, even at the distance of several miles. We saw it distinctly not only from the street in Thirsk, but for five or six miles, as we rode towards York. So we did likewise in the Great North-Road, between Sandhutton and Northallerton.

But how may we account for this phenomenon? Was it effected by a merely natural cause? If so, that cause must either have been

fire, water, or air. It could not be fire; for then some mark of it
must have appeared, either at the time, or after it. But no such
mark does appear, nor ever did; not so much as the least smoke,
either when the first or second rock was removed, or in the whole
space between Tuesday and Sunday.

It could not be water; for no water issued out when the one or
the other rock was torn off; nor had there been any rains some time
before: It was, in that part of the country, a remarkably dry
season. Neither was there any cavity in that part of the rock,
wherein a sufficient quantity of water might have lodged. On the
contrary, it was one single, solid mass, which was evenly and
smoothly cleft in sunder.

There remains no other natural cause assignable, but imprisoned air. I say imprisoned; for as to the fashionable opinion,
that the exterior air is the grand agent in earthquakes, it is so
senseless, unmechanical, unphilosophical a dream, as deserves not
to be named, but to be exploded. But it is hard to conceive how
even imprisoned air could produce such an effect. It might,
indeed, shake, tear, raise, or sink the earth; but how could it cleave
a solid rock? Here was not room for a quantity of it sufficient to do
anything of this nature; at least, unless it had been suddenly and
violently expanded by fire, which was not the case. Could a small
quantity of air, without that violent expansion, have torn so large
a body of rock from the rest to which it adhered in one solid mass?
Could it have shivered this into pieces, and scattered several of
those pieces some hundred yards round? Could it have transported
those promontories of earth, with their incumbent load, and set
them down, unbroken, unchanged, at a distance? Truly I am not
so great a volunteer in faith as to be able to believe this. He that
supposes this, must suppose air to be not only a very strong (which
we allow), but a very wise agent; while it bore its charge with so
great caution as not to hurt or dislocate any part of it.

What then could be the cause? What, indeed, but God, who
arose to shake terribly the earth; who purposely chose such a place,
where there is so great a concourse of Nobility and Gentry every
year; and wrought in such a manner, that many might see it and
fear; that all who travel one of the most frequented roads in
England, might see it, almost whether they would or no, for many

miles together. It must likewise for many years, maugre all the art of man, be a visible monument of His power; all that ground being now so encumbered with rocks and stones, that it cannot be either ploughed or grazed. Nor will it serve any use, but to tell all that see it, Who can stand before this great God? ...

Mon. 23. I was considering what could be the reasons why the hand of the Lord (who does nothing without a cause) is almost entirely stayed in Scotland, and in great measure in New-England. It does not become us to judge peremptorily; but perhaps some of them may be these: 1. Many of them became 'wise in their own eyes'; they seemed to think they were the men, and there were none like them. And hence they refused God the liberty of sending by whom he would send; and required him to work by men of learning, or not at all. 2. Many of them were bigots, immoderately attached either to their own opinions or mode of worship. Mr. Edwards himself was not clear of this.[30] But the Scotch bigots were beyond all others; placing Arminianism (so called) on a level with Deism, and the Church of England with that of Rome. Hence they not only suffered in themselves and their brethren a bitter zeal, but applauded themselves therein; in showing the same spirit against all who differed from them, as the Papists did against our forefathers. 3. With pride, bitterness, and bigotry, self-indulgence was joined; self-denial was little taught and practised. It is well if some of them did not despise, or even condemn, all self-denial in things indifferent, as in apparel or food, as nearly allied to Popery. No marvel then that the Spirit of God was grieved. Let us profit by their example.

Tues. 24. Observing in that valuable book, Mr. Gillies's 'Historical Collections', the custom of Christian congregations in all ages to set apart seasons of solemn thanksgivings, I was amazed and ashamed that we had never done this, after all the blessings we had received: And many to whom I mentioned it gladly agreed to set apart a day for that purpose.

Mon. 30. I set out for Norwich, and came thither the next evening. As a large congregation was waiting, I could not but preach, though weary enough. The two following days I spoke to each member of the society; and on *Friday, July 4,* took horse again, though how I should ride five miles I knew not. But God so strengthened both man and beast, that I reached Bury the same night, and London the next, far less tired than when I set out from Norwich.

Monday, *7*, was our first day of solemn thanksgiving for the numberless spiritual blessings we have received. And I believe it was a day which will not soon be forgotten.

Thur. *17*. One spent the evening with us who is accounted both a sensible and a religious man. What a proof of the fall! Even with all the advantages of a liberal education, this person, I will be bold to say, knows just as much of heart-religion, of scriptural Christianity, the religion of love, as a child three years old of Algebra. How much then may we suppose a Turk or Heathen to know? Hardly more; perhaps just as much.

Tues. *22*. To oblige a friendly gentlewoman, I was a witness to her will, wherein she bequeathed part of her estate to charitable uses; and part, during his natural life, to her dog Toby. I suppose, though she should die within the year, her legacy to Toby may stand good; but that to the poor is null and void, by the statute of Mortmain![31]

Sun. *27*. I buried the body of Ephraim B[edder], once a pattern to all that believed. But from the time he left off fasting and universal self-denial, in which none was more exemplary for some years, he sunk lower and lower, till he had neither the power, nor the form of religion left. In the beginning of his illness he was in black despair. But much prayer was made for him. Toward the close of it, it pleased God to restore to him the light of his countenance. So, I trust, his backsliding only cost him his life; and he may yet live with God for ever.

I was much affected about this time by a letter sent from a gentleman in Virginia. Part of it runs thus:

'The poor Negro slaves here never heard of Jesus, or his religion, till they arrived at the land of their slavery in America; whom their masters generally neglect, as though immortality was not the privilege of their souls, in common with their own. These poor Africans are the principal objects of my compassion; and, I think, the most proper subject of your charity.

'The inhabitants of Virginia are computed to be about three

hundred thousand; and the one half of them are supposed to be Negroes. The number of these who attend on my ministry, at particular times, is uncertain; but I think there are about three hundred who give a stated attendance. And never have I been so much struck with the appearance of an assembly, as when I have glanced my eye on one part of the House, adorned (so it has appeared to me) with so many black countenances, eagerly attentive to every word they heard, and some of them covered with tears. A considerable number of them, about an hundred, have been baptized, after they had been fully instructed in the great truths of religion, and had evidenced their sense of them by a life of the strictest virtue. As they are not sufficiently polished to dissemble with a good grace, they express the sensations of their hearts so much in the language of simple nature, and with such genuine indications of artless sincerity, that it is impossible to suspect their professions, especially when attended with a suitable behaviour.

'Mr. Todd, Minister of the next congregation, has near the same number under his care; and several of them also, he informs me, discover the same seriousness. Indeed there are multitudes of them in various parts, who are eagerly desirous of instruction. They have generally very little help to read; and yet, to my agreeable surprise, sundry of them, by dint of application, in their very few leisure hours, have made such a progress, that they are able to read their Bible, or a plain author, very intelligibly. But few of their masters will be at the expense of furnishing them with books. I have supplied them to the utmost of my ability. They are exceedingly delighted with Watts's Songs.[32] And I cannot but observe that the Negroes, above all of the human species I ever knew, have the nicest ear for music. They have a kind of ecstatic delight in psalmody: Nor are there any books they so soon learn, or take so much pleasure in, as those used in that heavenly part of divine worship.'

Sunday, August 3. I dined with one who lived for many years with one of the most celebrated beauties in Europe. She was also proud, vain, and nice to a very uncommon degree. But see the end! After a painful and nauseous disease, she rotted away above ground;

and was so offensive for many days before she died, that scarce any could bear to stay in the room ...

Tuesday, December 23 [London]. I was in the robe-chamber, adjoining to the House of Lords, when the King [George II] put on his robes. His brow was much furrowed with age, and quite clouded with care. And is this all the world can give even to a King? All the grandeur it can afford? A blanket of ermine round his shoulders, so heavy and cumbersome he can scarce move under it! An huge heap of borrowed hair, with a few plates of gold and glittering stones upon his head! Alas, what a bauble is human greatness! And even this will not endure. Cover the head with ever so much hair and gold; yet,

> *Scit te Proserpina canum;*
> *Personam capiti detrahet illa tuo ...*

[Death will deprive thee of thy borrowed hair.]

Wednesday, April 14, 1756. I looked over a celebrated book, 'The Fable of the Bees'. Till now I imagined there had never appeared in the world such a book as the works of Machiavel. But Dr. Mandeville goes far beyond it. The Italian only recommends a few vices, as useful to some particular men, and on some particular occasions. But the Englishman loves and cordially recommends vice of every kind; not only as useful now and then, but as absolutely necessary at all times for all communities! Surely Voltaire would hardly have said so much. And even Mr. Sandeman could not have said more ...[33]

[Wesley began a four-month visit to Ireland on 29 March.]

Monday, May 17. Walking up the Red-House Walk (which runs between two rows of meadows, with the river winding through them, and a chain of fruitful hills on the right hand and on the left), I saw the plain reason why strangers usually complain of the unwholesomeness of the water in Cork. Many women were filling vessels with river-water (which is that commonly used in the city for tea and most other purposes) when the tide was at the height.

Now, although, this is not salt, yet it cannot but affect both the stomach and bowels of tender persons ...

Tuesday, July 13. A large congregation was present at five, and stood unmoved, notwithstanding some heavy showers. At noon I preached at Cleg-Hill; at five in the barrack-yard again, where the concourse of people was greater than before. Mr. P[iers], the Minister of a neighbouring parish, and another Clergyman who came with him, received the truth in love: Mrs P[iers] (his wife) found rest to her soul.

But how is it, that almost in every place, even where there is no lasting fruit, there is so great an impression made at first upon a considerable number of people? The fact is this: Everywhere the work of God rises higher and higher, till it comes to a point. Here it seems for a short time to be at a stay. And then it gradually sinks again.

All this may easily be accounted for. At first curiosity brings many hearers: At the same time God draws many by his preventing grace to hear his word, and comforts them in hearing. One then tells another. By this means, on the one hand, curiosity spreads and increases, and, on the other, drawings of God's Spirit touch more hearts; and many of them more powerfully than before. He now offers grace to all that hear; most of whom are in some measure affected, and more or less moved, with approbation of what they hear, desire to please God, and good-will to his messenger: These principles, variously combined and increasing, raise the general work to its highest point. But it cannot stand here; for in the nature of things, curiosity must soon decline. Again, the drawings of God are not followed; and thereby the Spirit of God is grieved. The consequence is, he strives with this and this man no more, and so his drawings end. Thus both the natural and supernatural power declining, most of the hearers will be less and less affected. Add to this, that in the process of the work, 'it must be, that offences will come'. Some of the hearers, if not Preachers also, will act contrary to their profession. Either their follies or faults will be told from one to another, and lose nothing in the telling. Men once curious to hear, will now draw back: Men once drawn, having stifled their good desires, will disapprove what they approved before, and feel dislike, instead of good-will, to the

Preacher. Others, who were more or less convinced, will be afraid or ashamed to acknowledge that conviction. And all these will catch at ill stories (true or false), in order to justify their change. When, by this means, all who do not savingly believe, have quenched the Spirit of God, the little flock goes on from faith to faith; the rest sleep on and take their rest. And thus the number of hearers in every place may be expected first to increase, and then decrease . . .

Mon. 19. No sooner did we enter Ulster than we observed the difference. The ground was cultivated just as in England; and the cottages not only neat, but with doors, chimneys, and windows. Newry, the first town we came to (allowing for the size), is built much after the manner of Liverpool . . .

Monday, September 6. I set out in the machine, and on *Tuesday* evening came to London.

Wednesday, and *Thursday*, I settled my temporal business. It is now about eighteen years since I began writing and printing books; and how much in that time have I gained by printing? Why, on summing up my accounts, I found that on March 1, 1756 (the day I left London last), I had gained by printing and preaching together, a debt of twelve hundred and thirty-six pounds . . .

Monday, October 11. I went to Leigh. Where we dined, a poor woman came to the door with two little children. They seemed to be half-starved, as well as their mother, who was also shivering with an ague. She was extremely thankful for a little food, and still more so for a few pills, which seldom fail to cure that disorder.

In this little journey I read over a curiosity indeed—a French heroic poem, Voltaire's 'Henriade'. He is a very lively writer, of a fine imagination; and allowed, I suppose, by all competent judges, to be a perfect master of the French language: And by him I was more than ever convinced, that the French is the poorest, meanest language in Europe; that it is no more comparable to the German or Spanish, than a bag-pipe is to an organ; and that, with regard to poetry in particular, considering the incorrigible uncouthness of their measure, and their always writing in rhyme (to say nothing of their vile double rhymes, nay, and frequent false rhymes), it is as impossible to write a fine poem in French, as to make fine music upon a Jew's harp.

Tuesday, November 9 [London]. Having procured an apparatus on purpose, I ordered several persons to be electrified, who were ill of various disorders; some of whom found an immediate, some a gradual, cure. From this time I appointed, first some hours in every week, and afterward an hour in every day, wherein any that desired it, might try the virtue of this surprising medicine. Two or three years after, our patients were so numerous that we were obliged to divide them: So part were electrified in Southwark, part at the Foundery, others near St. Paul's, and the rest near the Seven-Dials: The same method we have taken ever since; and to this day, while hundreds, perhaps thousands, have received unspeakable good, I have not known one man, woman, or child, who has received any hurt thereby: So that when I hear any talk of the danger of being electrified (especially if they are medical men who talk so), I cannot but impute it to great want either of sense or honesty . . .

Thursday, July 7, 1757. I rode through one of the pleasantest parts of England to Hornby. Here the zealous landlord turned all the Methodists out of their houses. This proved a singular kindness: For they built some little houses at the end of the town, in which forty or fifty of them live together. Hence with much ado I found my way to Robinhood's Bay, and preached on the quay, to the greatest part of the town: All (except one or two, who were very wise in their own eyes) seemed to receive the truth in love . . .

Tues. 19. Before I left Newcastle I heard a strange relation, which I knew not what to think of. I then desired T. Lee, who was going to the place, to inquire particularly concerning it. He did so, and in consequence of that inquiry wrote me the following account:

'R—— J—— lived about twelve miles from Newcastle.

'His son, some time since, married without his consent. At this he was so enraged, that he wished his right arm might burn off, if ever he gave or left him sixpence.

'However, in March last, being taken ill, he made his will, and left him all his estate. The same evening he died. On Thursday, 10, his widow laying her hand on his back, found it warm. In the evening, those who were with him went into the next room to take a little refreshment. As they were eating, they observed a disagreeable smell, but could find nothing in the room to cause it. Returning into the room where the corpse lay, they found it full of smoke. Removing the sheet which covered the corpse, they saw (to their no small amazement) the body so burnt, that the entrails were bare, and might be seen through the ribs. His right arm was nearly burnt off; his head so burnt that the brains appeared; and a smoke came out of the crown of his head, like the steam of boiling water. When they cast water upon his body, it hissed, just as if cast on red-hot iron. Yet the sheet which was upon him was not singed; but that under him, with the pillow-bier and pillow, and the plank on which he lay, were all burned, and looked as black as charcoal.

'They hastened to put what was left of him into the coffin, leaving some to watch by it. But after it was nailed up, a noise of burning and crackling was heard therein. None was permitted to look into it, till it was carried to Abchester church-yard. It was buried near the steeple. As soon as it was brought to the grave, the steeple was observed to shake. The people hastened away; and it was well they did, for presently part of the steeple fell: So that had they stayed two minutes longer, they must have been crushed in pieces. All these circumstances were related to me and my wife by those who were eye and ear witnesses.' ...

Monday, August 8 [London]. I took a walk in the Charter-House. I wondered that all the squares and buildings, and especially the schoolboys, looked so little. But this is easily accounted for. I was little myself when I was at school, and measured all about me by myself. Accordingly, the upper boys, being then bigger than myself, seemed to me very big and tall; quite contrary to what they appear now when I am taller and bigger than them. I question if this is not the real ground of the common imagination, that our forefathers, and in general men in past ages, were much larger than now: An imagination current in the world eighteen hundred years ago. So Virgil supposes his warrior to throw a stone that could scarce be wielded by twelve men,

Qualia nunc hominum producit corpora tellus.

[Men who are similar in stature to those the earth now bears.]

So Homer, long before:

Οιοι νυν βροτοι εισι.

[Such as are the men of our days.]

Whereas, in reality, men have been, at least ever since the deluge, very nearly the same as we find them now, both for stature and understanding ...

Sunday, September 4 [Cornwall]. I. T. preached at five. I could scarce have believed if I had not heard it, that few men of learning write so correctly as an unlearned tinner speaks extempore. Mr. V[owler] preached two such thundering sermons at church as I have scarce heard these twenty years. O how gracious is God to the poor sinners of St. Agnes! In the church and out of the church they hear the same great truths of the wrath of God against sin, and his love to those that are in Christ Jesus! ...

Tuesday, October 25. In my return [from Bath] a man met me near Hannam, and told me the School-house at Kingswood was burned down. I felt not one moment's pain, knowing that God does all things well. When I came thither, I received a fuller account: About eight on Monday evening, two or three boys went into the gallery, up two pair of stairs. One of them heard a strange crackling in the room above. Opening the stair-case door, he was beat back by smoke, on which he cried out, 'Fire! Murder! Fire!' Mr. Baynes, hearing this, ran immediately down, and brought up a pail of water. But when he went into the room, and saw the blaze, he had not presence of mind to go up to it, but threw the water upon the floor. Meantime one of the boys rung the bell; another called John Maddern from the next house, who ran up, as did James Burges quickly after, and found the room all in a flame. The deal partitions took fire immediately, which spread to the roof of the house. Plenty of water was now brought; but they could not come nigh the place where it was wanted, the room being so filled with flame and smoke, that none could go into it. At last a long ladder, which lay in the garden, was reared up against the wall of the house. But it was then observed, that one of the sides of it was broke in two, and the other quite rotten. However, John How (a young man, who lived next door) run up it, with an axe in his hand. But he then found the ladder was so short, that, as he stood on the top of it, he could but just lay one hand over the battlements. How he got over to the leads none can tell: But he did so, and quickly broke through the roof, on which a vent being made, the smoke and flame issued out as from a furnace: Those who were at the foot of the stairs with water, being able to go no further, then went through the smoke to the door of the leads, and poured it down through the tiling. By this means the fire was quickly quenched, having only consumed a part of the partition, with a box of clothes, and a little damaged the roof, and the floor beneath.

It is amazing that so little hurt was done; for the fire, which began in the middle of the long room (none can imagine how; for no person had been there for several hours before), was so violent, that it broke every pane of glass but two, in the window, both at the east and west end. What was more amazing still, was, that it did not hurt either the beds (which when James Burges came in, seemed all covered with flame), nor the deal partitions on the other side of the room, though it beat against them for a considerable time. What can we say to these things, but that God had fixed the bounds which it could not pass? . . .

Tuesday, March 28, 1758. We went on board, and set sail for Dublin. The wind was fair, and the day extremely fine. Seven or eight miles from the town a small boat overtook us, which brought me letters from London. Some of these earnestly pressed me to return to London, or, however, not to go to Ireland. I consulted my friends, and just as we began our little debate, the wind, which till then was fair and small, turned from east to west, and blew harder and harder. But the point was soon decided. For upon inquiry we found the boat was gone back, and no other was to be had. Presently after the wind returned to the east, and we saw the hand of God.

The Liverpool boat went away in such haste that it left a young man, James Glassbrook, behind; so we were five in all. We had seven more cabin passengers, and many common ones. So good-natured a company I never met with in a ship before. The sea was as smooth as glass, the sun shone without a cloud, and the wind was small and quite fair. So we glided on; till, about nine, I went to prayers with them, and then quietly lay down.

Wed. 29. We were even with the great Welsh mountain,

Penmaen Mawr, at five in the morning. But it then fell calm, so that we were scarce abreast of Holyhead in the evening. This gave us time to speak to all our fellow-passengers. And some fruit quickly appeared; for no oath, no immodest or passionate word, was any more heard in the ship while we were on board.

Thur. 30. Having no wind still, I desired our brethren to come upon the quarter-deck; where we no sooner began singing an hymn, than both passengers and sailors gladly assembled. The wind sprung up almost as soon as I began, and about nine the next day we entered Dublin Bay; after so smooth and pleasant a passage, as the Captain declared, he had not had at that time of year for forty years.

Considering the shortness of the warning, we had a large congregation in the evening; but a very small one in the morning, *April 1.* At this I did not wonder when I was informed, that the preaching at five had been discontinued for near a year and an half. At eight likewise, *Sunday 2,* the congregation was small. I took knowledge that the people of Dublin had neither seen nor heard much of self-denial, since T. Walsh left the kingdom.

All the evenings of the following week we had numerous congregations. Nothing is wanting here but rigorous discipline, which is more needful in this than in any other nation; the people in general being so soft and delicate, that the least slackness utterly destroys them.

Thur. 6. We walked round the College, and saw what was accounted most worthy of observation. The new front is exceeding grand; and the whole square (about as large as Peckwater in Christ Church) would be beautiful, were not the windows too small, as every one will see when the present fashion is out of date . . .

Fri. 21. I dined at Lady ——'s. We need great grace to converse with great people! From which, therefore (unless in some rare instances), I am glad to be excused. *Horæ fugiunt et imputantur!* [The hours fly past and build up on one's account.] Of these two hours I can give no good account.

Tuesday, May 16 . . . This was the hottest day I ever felt in Ireland: Near as hot as any I remember in Georgia. The next morning I was desired to see the house of an eminent scholar near the town [Lurgan]. The door into the yard we found nailed up; but we got in at a gap which was stopped with thorns. I took the house, at first, for a very old barn, but was assured he had built it within five years; not indeed by any old, vulgar model, but purely to his own taste. The walls were part mud, part brick, part stone, and part bones and wood. There were four windows, but no glass in any, lest the pure air should be kept out. The house had two stories, but no stair-case, and no door. Into the upper floor we went by a ladder, through one of the windows; through one of the lower windows, into the lower floor, which was about four foot high. This floor had three rooms—one three square, the second had five sides, the third, I know not how many. I give a particular description of this wonderful edifice, to illustrate that great truth: There is no folly too great even for a man of sense, if he resolve to follow his own imagination! . . .

Tuesday, August 1. The Captain with whom we were to sail was in great haste to have our things on board; but I would not send them while the wind was against us. On *Wednesday*, he sent message after message: So in the evening we went down to the ship, near Passage; but there was nothing ready or near ready for sailing. Hence I learned two or three rules, very needful for those who sail between England and Ireland: 1. Never pay till you set sail: 2. Go not on board till the Captain goes on board: 3. Send not your baggage on board till you go yourself . . . *Thursday, 17* [Bristol]. I went to the cathedral to hear Mr. Handel's 'Messiah'. I doubt if that congregation was ever so serious at a sermon as they were during this performance. In many parts, especially several of the choruses, it exceeded my expectation . . .

Friday, October 6. I designed to go in a wherry to the Isle of Wight; but the watermen were so extravagant in their demands, that I changed my mind, and went in the hoy: And it was well I did; for the sea was so high, it would not have been easy for a small boat to keep above water. We landed at two, and walked on, five little miles, to Newport. The neighbouring camp had filled the town with soldiers, the most abandoned wretches whom I ever yet saw. Their whole glorying was in cursing, swearing, drunkenness, and lewdness. How gracious is God, that he does not yet send these monsters to their own place!

At five I preached in the corn-market, and at six in the morning.

A few even of the soldiers attended. One of these, Benjamin Lawrence, walked with us to Wotton-Bridge; where we intended to take boat. He was in St. Philip's Fort during the whole siege, concerning which I asked him many questions. He said, 1. 'Abundance of cattle was left in the fields, till the French (long expected) came and took them. 2. Abundance of wine was left in the town, even more than the French could use; and there was not enough in the Castle even for the sick men. 3. A large strong, stone house was left standing, within a small distance of the Fort. Behind this the French often formed themselves, particularly before the last assault. 4. This might easily be accounted for. We had few Officers of any experience; and the Governor never came out of his house. 5. The French made two general assaults, and were repulsed; and many blown up by our mines. But the mines having never been looked after till just when we wanted them, most of them were utterly useless; so that only two, out of threescore, did any execution. 6. In their third assault (which they were very hardly persuaded to make) Captain ——, who commanded the guard of an hundred men at the Sally-Port, ran away before he was attacked; and his men, having none to command them, went after. I was left alone, till I retired also; and the French, having none to oppose them, came in. 7. In the morning our men were mad to drive them out, and would have done it in an hour; but that they were told the Fort was given up, and ordered to cease firing. 8. We had, at the approach of the enemy, three thousand eight hundred and thirty-three effective men; and we had very near as many when we surrendered, with plenty of provision and ammunition.' O human justice! One great man is shot, and another is made a Lord! . . .[34]

Thursday, March 29, 1759. I divided the Norwich society into classes, without any distinction between them who had belonged to the Foundery or the Tabernacle.

Sunday, April 1. I met them all at six, requiring every one to show his ticket when he came in: A thing they had never heard of before. I likewise insisted on another strange regulation, That the men and women should sit apart. A third was made the same day. It had been a custom ever since the Tabernacle was built, to have the galleries full of spectators, while the Lord's Supper was administered. This I judged highly improper; and therefore ordered none to be admitted, but those who desired to communicate. And I found far less difficulty than I expected, in bringing them to submit to this also.

The society now contained above five hundred and seventy members; an hundred and three of whom were in no society before, although many of them had found peace with God. I believe they would have increased to a thousand, if I could have stayed a fortnight longer. Which of these will hold fast their profession? The fowls of the air will devour some; the sun will scorch more; and others will be choked by the thorns springing up. I wonder we should ever expect that half of those who 'hear the word with joy' will bring forth fruit unto perfection . . .

Monday, October 15. I walked up to Knowle, a mile from Bristol, to see the French prisoners. Above eleven hundred of them, we were informed, were confined in that little place without any thing to lie on but a little dirty straw, or any thing to cover them but a few foul thin rags, either by day or night, so that they died like rotten sheep. I was much affected, and preached in the evening on (Exodus xxiii. 9), 'Thou shalt not oppress a stranger; for ye know the heart of a stranger, seeing ye were strangers in the land of Egypt.' Eighteen pounds were contributed immediately, which were made up four-and-twenty the next day. With this we bought linen and woollen cloth, which were made up into shirts, waistcoats, and breeches. Some dozen of stockings were added; all which were carefully distributed, where there was the greatest want. Presently after, the Corporation of Bristol sent a large quantity of mattresses and blankets. And it was not long before contributions were set on foot at London, and in various parts of the kingdom; so that I believe from this time they were pretty well provided with all the necessaries of life . . .

Saturday, November 17. I spent an hour agreeably and profitably with Lady G[ertrude] H[otham], and Sir C[harles] H[otham]. It is well a few of the rich and noble are called. O that God would increase their number! But I should rejoice (were it the will of God), if it were done by the ministry of others. If I might choose, I should still (as I have done hitherto) preach the Gospel to the poor . . .

Fri. 23. The roads were so extremely slippery, it was with much difficulty we reached Bedford. We had a pretty large congregation; but the stench from the swine under the Room was scarce supportable. Was ever a preaching-place over a hog-sty before? Surely they love the Gospel, who come to hear it in such a place . . .

Sat. 24. We rode to Everton; Mr. Berridge being gone to preach before the University at Cambridge. Many people came to his house in the evening, and it was a season of great refreshment.

Sun. 25. I was a little afraid my strength would not suffice for reading Prayers and preaching, and administering the Lord's Supper alone, to a large number of communicants; but all was well. Mr. Hicks began his own Service early, and came before I had ended my sermon. So we finished the whole before two, and I had time to breathe before the Evening Service.

In the afternoon God was eminently present with us, though rather to comfort than convince. But I observed a remarkable difference since I was here before, as to the manner of the work. None now were in trances, none cried out, none fell down or were convulsed: Only some trembled exceedingly, a low murmur was heard, and many were refreshed with the multitude of peace.

The danger *was*, to regard extraordinary circumstances too much, such as outcries, convulsions, visions, trances; as if these were essential to the inward work, so that it could not go on without them. Perhaps the danger *is*, to regard them too little, to condemn them altogether; to imagine they had nothing of God in them, and were an hinderance to his work. Whereas the truth is, 1. God suddenly and strongly convinced many that they were lost sinners; the natural consequence whereof were sudden outcries and strong bodily convulsions: 2. To strengthen and encourage them that believed, and to make his work more apparent, he favoured several of them with divine dreams, others with trances and visions: 3. In some of these instances, after a time, nature mixed with grace: 4. Satan likewise mimicked this work of God, in order to discredit the whole work: And yet it is not wise to give up this part, any more than to give up the whole. At first it was, doubtless, wholly from God. It is partly so at this day; and he will enable us to discern how far, in every case, the work is pure, and where it mixes or degenerates.

Let us even suppose that in some few cases there was a mixture of dissimulation; that persons pretended to see or feel what they did not, and imitated the cries or convulsive motions of those who were really overpowered by the Spirit of God: Yet even this should not make us either deny or undervalue the real work of the Spirit. The shadow is no disparagement of the substance, nor the counterfeit of the real diamond.

We may further suppose, that Satan will make these visions an occasion of pride: But what can be inferred from hence? Nothing, but that we should guard against it; that we should diligently exhort all to be little in their own eyes, knowing that nothing avails with God but humble love. But still, to slight or censure visions in general, would be both irrational and unchristian ...

Thursday, March 20, 1760 [Liverpool]. I had a good deal of conversation with Mr. N[ewto]n.[35] His case is very peculiar. Our Church requires that Clergymen should be men of learning, and, to this end, have an University education. But how many have an University education, and yet no learning at all? Yet these men are ordained! Meantime, one of eminent learning, as well as unblamable behaviour, cannot be ordained *because he was not at University*! What a mere farce is this! Who would believe that any Christian Bishop would stoop to so poor an evasion?

[Wesley was in Ireland from 1 April to 24 August.]

Monday, May 5. After preaching in the market-place at Belfast, to a people who care for none of these things, we rode on, with a furious east wind right in our face to Carrickfergus, where I willingly accepted of an invitation from a merchant in the town, Mr. Cobham, to lodge at his house: The rather, when I understood, that Mr. Cavenac, the French Lieutenant-General, was still there. I now received a very particular account of what had been lately transacted here. Mrs. Cobham said, 'My daughter came running in, and said, "Mamma, there are three Indiamen come into the bay, and I suppose my brothers are come in them." (Who had been in the East Indies for some time.) An hour after she came in again, and cried, "O mamma, they say they are Frenchmen; and they are landing; and their guns glitter in the sun."' Mr. Cavenac informed me, that Mr. Thurot[36] had received a thousand men out of the King's Guards, with orders to land in the north of Ireland, at the same time that Monsieur Conflans landed in the south: That a storm drove him up to Bergen, in Norway, from whence he could not get out, till his ships were much damaged, and his provisions consumed; nor could he there procure a supply at any price: That another storm drove him to 66 degrees north latitude; from whence he did not get back to Carrick-Bay till all on board were almost famished, having only an ounce of bread per man daily: That they then landed merely to procure provisions. I asked, 'Is it true, that you had a design to burn the town?' He cried out, 'Jesu, Maria! We never had such a thought! To burn, to destroy, cannot enter into the heart or head of a good man.'

After they had landed (Mrs Cobham and others informed me), they divided into two bodies. One of these marched up to the east gate, the other to the north. Twelve soldiers and a Corporal were there on the wall, who fired upon them when they came near. Immediately General Flaubert fell, having his leg broke by a musket-ball. The next in command, a young Marquis, then led them on. When the English had fired four rounds, having no more ammunition, they retired, and the French entered the town, and at the market-place met those who had come in at the east gate. When they had joined, they marched up to the castle (though the English there, who were an hundred and sixty-two in number, kept a constant fire), the gate of which was not barred, so that the Marquis thrust it open and went in. Just then he was shot dead. Mr. Cavenac immediately took his place, and drew up his men again. The English then desired a parley, and articled to furnish them with provisions in six hours. But they could not perform it, there being little in the town. On this Mr. Cavenac sent for Mr. Cobham, and desired him to go up to Belfast and procure them, leaving his wife with the General, as an hostage for his return. But the poor Frenchmen could not stay for this. At the time prefixed, they began to serve themselves with meat and drink; having been in such want, that they were glad to eat raw oats to sustain nature. They accordingly took all the food they could find, with some linen and wearing-apparel. But they neither hurt nor affronted man, woman, or child, nor did any mischief for mischief's sake;

though they were sufficiently provoked; for many of the inhabitants affronted them without fear or wit, cursed them to their face, and even took up pokers, or other things to strike them.

While Mrs. Cobham was with the General, a little plain-dressed man came in, to whom they all showed a particular respect. It struck into her mind, Is not this Mr. Thurot? Which was soon confirmed. She said to him, 'Sir, you seem much fatigued. Will you step to my house and refresh yourself?' He readily accepted the offer. She prepared a little veal, of which he ate moderately, and drank three glasses of small warm punch; after which he told her, 'I have not taken any food before, nor slept, for eight-and-forty-hours.' She asked, 'Sir, will you please to take a little rest now?' Observing he started, she added, 'I will answer, life for life, that none shall hurt you under my roof.' He said, 'Madam, I believe you: I accept the offer.' He desired that two of his men might lie on the floor by the bed-side, slept about six hours, and then, returning her many thanks, went aboard his ship.

Five days he was kept in the bay by contrary winds. When he sailed, he took the Mayor of Carrick, and another gentleman, as hostages for the delivery of the French prisoners. The next morning, as he was walking the deck, he frequently started, without any visible cause, stepped short, and said, 'I shall die to-day.' A while after he said, to one of the English, 'Sir, I see three ships: Pray take my glass, and tell me freely what you think they are.' He looked some time, and said, 'I think they are English; and I guess they are about forty-gun ships.' He called his Officers, and said, 'Our ships are too foul to fight at a distance: We must board them.' Accordingly, when they came up, after a short fire, he ran up close to Captain Elliot; and Captain Scordeck, with his four-and-twenty hussars, immediately leaped on board. Almost instantly, nine of them lay dead; on which he was so enraged, that he rushed forward with his sabre among the English, who seized his arms and carried him away. Meantime, his men that were left retired into their own ship. Thurot seeing this, cried out, 'Why should we throw away the lives of the poor men?' and ordered to strike the colours. A man going up to do this was shot dead; as was likewise a second; and before a third could do it, Mr. Thurot himself was shot through the heart. So fell a brave man; giving yet another proof, that 'there is no counsel or strength against the Lord' ...

Sunday, August 24. At seven I took leave of my friends, and about noon embarked in the Nonpareil for Chester. We had forty or fifty passengers on board, half of whom were cabin passengers. I was afraid we should have an uneasy time, in the midst of such a crowd of Gentry. We sailed out with a fair wind, but at four in the afternoon it failed, and left us in a dead calm. I then made the gentlemen an offer of preaching, which they thankfully accepted. While I was preaching, the wind sprung up fair; but the next day we were becalmed again. In the afternoon they desired me to give them another sermon; and again the wind sprung up while I was speaking, and continued till, about noon, on *Tuesday,* we landed at Parkgate.

Being in haste, I would not stay for my own horse, which I found could not land till low water. So I bought one, and, having hired another, set forward without delay. We reached Whitchurch that evening.

Wed. 27. We breakfasted at Newport, where, finding our horses begin to fail, we thought it best to take the Birmingham road, that, if they should fail us altogether, we might stay among our friends. But they would go no farther than Wolverhampton; so we hired fresh horses there, and immediately set out for Worcester. But one of them soon after fell, and gave me such a shock (though I did not quit my seat), that I was seized with a violent bleeding at the nose, which nothing we could apply would stop. So we were obliged to go a foot pace for two miles, and then stay at Broadwater.

Thur. 28. Soon after we set out, the other horse fell lame. An honest man, at Worcester, found this was owing to a bad shoe. A smith cured this by a new shoe; but at the same time, by paring the hoof too close, he effectually lamed the other foot, so that we had hard work to reach Gloucester. After resting here awhile, we pushed on to Newport, where I took a chaise, and reached Bristol before eleven.

I spent the two following days with the Preachers, who had been waiting for me all the week: And their love and unanimity was such as soon made me forget all my labour ...

Wednesday, September 17 [Cornwall]. The Room at St. Just was

quite full at five, and God gave us a parting blessing. At noon I
preached on the cliff near Penzance, where no one now gives an
uncivil word. Here I procured an account, from an eye-witness, of
what happened the twenty-seventh of last month. A round pillar,
narrowest at bottom, of a whitish colour, rose out of the sea near
Mousehole, and reached the clouds. One who was riding over the
strand from Marazion to Penzance saw it stand for a short space,
and then move swiftly toward her, till, the skirt of it touching her,
the horse threw her and ran away. It had a strong sulphurous
smell. It dragged with it abundance of sand and pebbles from the
shore; and then went over the land, carrying with it corn, furze, or
whatever it found in its way. It was doubtless a kind of water-
spout; but a water-spout on land, I believe, is seldom seen.

The storm drove us into the House at Newlyn also. *Thursday, 18.*
As we rode from thence, in less than half an hour we were wet to
the skin; but when we came to Penhale, the rain ceased; and, the
people flocking from all parts, we had a comfortable opportunity
together. About six I preached near Helstone. The rain stopped till
I had done, and soon after was as violent as before.

Fri. 19. I rode to Illogan. We had heavy rain before I began, but
scarce any while I was preaching. I learned several other particulars here concerning the water-spout. It was seen near Mousehole
an hour before sunset. About sunset it began travelling over the
land, tearing up all the furze and shrubs it met. Near an hour after
sunset it passed (at the rate of four or five miles an hour) across
Mr. Harris's fields, in Camborne, sweeping the ground as it went,
about twenty yards diameter at bottom, and broader and broader
up to the clouds. It made a noise like thunder, took up eighteen
stacks of corn, with a large hay-stack and the stones whereon it
stood, scattered them all abroad (but it was quite dry), and then
passed over the cliff into the sea . . .

January 2, 1761. I wrote the following letter:

> '*To the Editor of the London Chronicle.*

'SIR,

'OF all the seats of woe on this side hell, few, I suppose, exceed
or even equal Newgate. If any region of horror could exceed it a
few years ago, Newgate in Bristol did; so great was the filth, the

stench, the misery, and wickedness, which shocked all who had a spark of humanity left. How was I surprised then, when I was there a few weeks ago! 1. Every part of it, above stairs and below, even the pit, wherein the felons are confined at night, is as clean and sweet as a gentleman's house; it being now a rule, that every prisoner wash and clean his apartment throughly twice a week. 2. Here is no fighting or brawling. If any thinks himself ill used, the cause is immediately referred to the Keeper, who hears the contending parties face to face, and decides the affair at once. 3. The usual grounds of quarrelling are removed. For it is very rarely that any one cheats or wrongs another, as being sure, if anything of this kind is discovered, to be committed to a closer confinement. 4. Here is no drunkenness suffered, however advantageous it might be to the Keeper, as well as the tapster: 5. Nor any whoredom; the women prisoners being narrowly observed, and kept separate from the men: Nor is any woman of the town now admitted, no, not at any price. 6. All possible care is taken to prevent idleness: Those who are willing to work at their callings are provided with tools and materials, partly by the Keeper, who gives them credit at a very moderate profit, partly by the alms occasionally given, which are divided with the utmost prudence and impartiality Accordingly, at this time, among others, a shoemaker, a tailor, a brazier, and a coachmaker are working at their several trades. 7. Only on the Lord's day they neither work nor play, but dress themselves as clean as they can, to attend the public Service in the chapel, at which every person under the roof is present. None is excused unless sick; in which case he is provided, *gratis*, both with advice and medicines. 8. And in order to assist them in things of the greatest concern, (besides a sermon every Sunday and Thursday,) they have a large Bible chained on one side of the chapel, which any of the prisoners may read. By the blessing of God on these regulations the prison now has a new face: Nothing offends either the eye or ear; and the whole has the appearance of a quiet, serious family. And does not the Keeper of Newgate deserve to be remembered full as well as the Man of Ross? May the Lord remember him in that day! Meantime, will no one follow his example? I am, Sir,

'Your humble servant,

'JOHN WESLEY.' ...

Monday, May 4. About noon I took a walk to the King's College, in Old Aberdeen. It has three sides of a square, handsomely built, not unlike Queen's College in Oxford. Going up to see the Hall, we found a large company of ladies, with several gentlemen. They looked, and spoke to one another, after which one of the gentlemen took courage and came to me. He said, 'We came last night to the College-Close, but could not hear, and should be extremely obliged if you would give us a short discourse here.' I knew not what God might have to do; and so began without delay, on, 'God was in Christ, reconciling the world unto himself.' I believe the word was not lost: It fell as dew on the tender grass.

In the afternoon I was walking in the library of the Marischal College, when the Principal and the Divinity Professor came to me; and the latter invited me to his lodgings, where I spent an hour very agreeably. In the evening, the eagerness of the people made them ready to trample each other under foot. It was some time before they were still enough to hear; but then they devoured every word. After preaching, Sir Archibald Grant (whom business had called to town) sent and desired to speak to me. I could not then, but promised to wait upon him, with God's leave, in my return to Edinburgh.

Tues. 5. I accepted the Principal's invitation, and spent an hour with him at his house. I observed no stiffness at all, but the easy good breeding of a man of sense and learning. I suppose both he and all the Professors, with some of the Magistrates, attended in the evening. I set all the windows open; but the Hall, notwithstanding, was as hot as a bagnio. But this did not hinder either the attention of the people, or the blessing of God.

Wed. 6. We dined at Mr. Ogilvy's, one of the Ministers, between whom the city is divided. A more open-hearted, friendly man, I know not that I ever saw. And indeed I have scarce seen such a set of Ministers in any town of Great Britain or Ireland.

At half-hour after six I stood in the College-Close, and proclaimed Christ crucified. My voice was so strengthened that all could hear; and all were earnestly attentive. I have now 'cast' my 'bread upon the waters': May I 'find it again after many days'!

Thur. 7. Leaving near ninety members in the Society, I rode over to Sir A. Grant's, near Monymusk, about twenty miles northwest from Aberdeen. It lies in a fruitful and pleasant valley, much of which is owing to Sir Archibald's improvements, who has ploughed up abundance of waste ground, and planted some millions of trees. His stately old house is surrounded by gardens, and rows of trees, with a clear river on one side. And about a mile from his house he has laid out a small valley into walks and gardens, on one side of which the river runs. On each side rises a steep mountain; one rocky and bare, the other covered with trees, row above row, to the very top.

About six we went to the church. It was pretty well filled with such persons as we did not look for so near the Highlands. But if we were surprised at their appearance, we were much more so at their singing. Thirty or forty sung an anthem after sermon, with such voices as well as judgment, that I doubt whether they could have been excelled at any cathedral in England.

Fri. 8. We rode to Glammis, about sixty-four measured miles; and on *Saturday, 9,* about sixty-six more, to Edinburgh. I was tired: However, I would not disappoint the congregation; and God gave me strength according to my day.

Sun. 10. I had designed to preach near the Infirmary; but some of the managers would not suffer it. So I preached in our Room, morning and evening, even to the rich and honourable. And I bear them witness, they will endure plain dealing, whether they profit by it or not.

Mon. 11. I took my leave of Edinburgh for the present. The situation of the city, on a hill shelving down on both sides, as well as to the east, with the stately castle upon a craggy rock on the west, is inexpressibly fine. And the main street, so broad and finely paved, with the lofty houses on either hand (many of them seven or eight stories high), is far beyond any in Great Britain. But how can it be suffered, that all manner of filth should still be thrown even into this street continually? Where are the Magistracy, the Gentry, the Nobility of the land? Have they no concern for the honour of their nation? How long shall the capital city of Scotland, yea, and the chief street of it, stink worse than a common-sewer? Will no lover of his country, or of decency and common sense, find a remedy for this?

Holyrood-House, at the entrance of Edinburgh, the ancient Palace of the Scottish Kings, is a noble structure. It was rebuilt and furnished by King Charles the Second. One side of it is a picture-gallery, wherein are pictures of all the Scottish Kings, and an original one of the celebrated Queen Mary: It is scarce possible for any who looks at this to think her such a monster as some have painted her; nor indeed for any who considers the circumstances of her death, equal to that of an ancient martyr . . .

[Wesley began a four-month visit to Ireland on 2 April 1762.]

Monday, April 26. In the evening I preached to a large congregation in the market-house at Lurgan. I now embraced the opportunity which I had long desired, of talking with Mr. Miller, the contriver of that statue which was in Lurgan when I was there before. It was the figure of an old man, standing in a case, with a curtain drawn before him, or over against a clock which stood on the other side of the room. Every time the clock struck, he opened the door with one hand, drew back the curtain with the other, turned his head, as if looking round on the company, and then said, with a clear, loud, articulate voice, 'Past one, two, three,' and so on. But so many came to see this (the like of which all allowed was not to be seen in Europe) that Mr. Miller was in danger of being ruined, not having time to attend his own business; so, as none offered to purchase it, or to reward him for his pains, he took the whole machine in pieces: Nor has he any thought of ever making anything of the kind again . . .

Monday, June 14. I rode to Cork. Here I procured an exact account of the late commotions. About the beginning of December last, a few men met by night near Nenagh, in the county of Limerick, and threw down the fences of some commons, which had been lately inclosed. Near the same time others met in the county of Tipperary, of Waterford, and of Cork. As no one offered to suppress or hinder them, they increased in number continually, and called themselves Whiteboys, wearing white cockades, and white linen frocks. In February there were five or six parties of them, two or three hundred men in each, who moved up and down, chiefly in the night; but for what end did not appear. Only they levelled a few fences, dug up some grounds, and hamstrung some cattle, perhaps fifty or sixty in all. One body of them came into Cloheen, of about five hundred foot, and two hundred horse. They moved as exactly as regular troops, and appeared to be thoroughly disciplined. They now sent letters to several gentlemen, threatening to pull down their houses. They compelled every one they met to take an oath to be true to Queen Sive (whatever that meant) and the Whiteboys; not to reveal their secrets; and to join them when called upon. It was supposed, eight or ten thousand were now actually risen, many of them well armed; and that a far greater number were ready to rise whenever they should be called upon. Those who refused to swear, they threatened to bury alive. Two or three they did bury up to the neck, and left them; where they must quickly have perished, had they not been found in time by some travelling by. At length, toward Easter, a body of troops, chiefly light horse, were sent against them. Many were apprehended and committed to gaol; the rest of them disappeared. This is the plain, naked fact, which has been so variously represented . . .

Saturday, October 1, 1763. I returned to London, and found our house in ruins, great part of it being taken down, in order to a thorough repair. But as much remained as I wanted: Six foot square suffices me by day or by night . . .

Friday, February 24, 1764. I returned to London. *Wednesday, 29.* I heard 'Judith', an Oratorio, performed at the Lock.[37] Some parts of it were exceeding fine; but there are two things in all modern pieces of music, which I could never reconcile to common sense. One is singing the same words ten times over; the other, singing different words by different persons, at one and the same time. And this in the most solemn addresses to God, whether by way of prayer or of thanksgiving. This can never be defended by all the musicians in Europe, till reason is quite out of date . . .

Wednesday, March 21. After riding about two hours and an half from Evesham, we stopped at a little village. We easily perceived by the marks he had left, that the man of the house had been beating his wife. I took occasion from thence to speak strongly to her, concerning the hand of God, and his design in all afflictions. It seemed to be a word in season. She appeared to be not only thankful, but deeply affected.

We had an exceeding large congregation at Birmingham, in what was formerly the playhouse. Happy would it be if all the playhouses in the kingdom were converted to so good an use. After service the mob gathered, and threw some dirt and stones at those who were going out. But it is probable they will soon be calmed, as some of them are in gaol already ...

Saturday, March 31 [Rotherham]. An odd circumstance occurred during the morning preaching. It was well only serious persons were present. An ass walked gravely in at the gate, came up to the door of the House, lifted up his head and stood stock-still, in a posture of deep attention. Might not 'the dumb beast reprove' many who have far less decency, and not much more understanding? ...

Monday, June 11. After Edinburgh, Glasgow, and Aberdeen, I think Inverness is the largest town I have seen in Scotland. The main streets are broad and straight; the houses mostly old, but not very bad, nor very good. It stands in a pleasant and fruitful country, and has all things needful for life and godliness. The people in general speak remarkably good English, and are of a friendly, courteous behaviour.

About eleven we took horse. While we were dining at Nairn, the inn-keeper said, 'Sir, the gentlemen of the town have read the little book you gave me on Saturday, and would be glad if you would please to give them a sermon.' Upon my consenting, the bell was immediately rung, and the congregation was quickly in the kirk. O what a difference is there between South and North Britain! Every one here at least loves to hear the word of God; and none takes it into his head to speak one uncivil word to any, for endeavouring to save their souls.

Doubting whether Mr. Grant was come home, Mr. Kershaw called at the Grange-Green, near Forres, while I rode forward. But Mr. Grant soon called me back. I have seldom seen a more agreeable place. The house is an old castle, which stands on a little hill, with a delightful prospect all four ways; and the hospitable master has left nothing undone to make it still more agreeable. He showed us all his improvements, which are very considerable in every branch of husbandry. In his gardens many things were more forward than at Aberdeen, yea, or Newcastle. And how is it, that none but one Highland gentleman has discovered that we have a tree in Britain, as easily raised as an ash, the wood of which is of full as fine a red as mahogany? namely, the laburnum. I defy any mahogany to exceed the chairs which he has lately made of this . . .

Sunday, August 19. Meeting with a pious and sensible man, who was born in the Isle of Skye, I said, 'Tell me freely, did you yourself ever know a *second-sighted* man?' He answered, after a little pause, 'I have known more than one or two.' I said, 'But were they not deceivers?—How do you know they were really such?' He replied, 'I have been in company with them, when they dropped down as dead. Coming to themselves, they looked utterly amazed, and said, "I have been in such a place, and I saw such and such persons (perhaps fifty miles off) die in such a manner"; and when inquiry was made, I never could find that they were mistaken in one circumstance. But the reason why it is so hard for you to get any information concerning this is, those who have the second sight count it a great misfortune; and it is thought a scandal to their family.' . . .

Monday, December 31. I thought it would be worth while to make an odd experiment. Remembering how surprisingly fond of music the lion at Edinburgh was, I determined to try whether this was the case with all animals of the same kind. I accordingly went to the tower [of London] with one who plays on the German flute. He began playing near four or five lions; only one of these (the rest not seeming to regard it at all) rose up, came to the front of his den, and seemed to be all attention. Meantime, a tiger in the same den started up, leaped over the lion's back, turned and ran under his belly, leaped over him again, and so to and fro incessantly. Can we account for this by any principle of mechanism? Can we account for it at all? . . .

[Wesley visited Ireland between 1 May and 6 August 1765.]

Tuesday, May 14. I wrote the following letter to a friend:

'DEAR SIR,   LONDONDERRY, *May 14, 1765*

'YOUR manner of writing needs no excuse. I hope you will

always write in the same manner. Love is the plainest thing in the world: I know this dictates what you write; and then what need of ceremony?

'You have admirably well expressed what I mean by an opinion, contra-distinguished from an essential doctrine. Whatever is "compatible with love to Christ, and a work of grace", I term an *opinion*. And certainly the holding Particular Election and Final Perseverance is compatible with these.[38] "Yet what fundamental errors", you ask, "have you opposed with half that fervency as you have these opinions?"—I have printed near fifty sermons, and only one of these opposes them at all. I preach about eight hundred sermons in a year; and, taking one year with another, for twenty years past, I have not preached eight sermons in a year upon the subject. But, "how many of your best Preachers have been thrust out because they dissented from you in these particulars"? Not one, best or worst, good or bad, was ever "thrust out" on this account. There has not been a single instance of this kind. Two or three (but far from *the best* of our Preachers) voluntarily left us, after they had embraced those opinions. But it was of their own mere motion: And two I should have expelled for immoral behaviour; but they withdrew, and *pretended* "they did not hold our doctrine". Set a mark, therefore, on him that told you that tale, and let his word for the future go for nothing.

' "Is a man a believer in Jesus Christ, and is his life suitable to his profession?" are not only the *main*, but the *sole* inquiries I make in order to his admission into our society. If he is a Dissenter, he may be a Dissenter still; but if he is a Churchman, I advise him to continue so; and that for many reasons; some of which are mentioned in the tract upon that subject.

'I think on Justification just as I have done any time these seven-and-twenty years; and just as Mr. Calvin does. In this respect I do not differ from him an hair's breadth.

'But the main point between you and me is Perfection. "This", you say, "has no prevalence in these parts; otherwise I should think it my duty to oppose it with my whole strength; not as an opinion, but as a dangerous mistake, which appears to be sub-versive of the very foundation of Christian experience; and which has, in fact, given occasion to the most grievous offences."

Just so my brother and I reasoned thirty years ago, "as thinking it our duty to oppose Predestination with our whole strength; not as an opinion, but as a dangerous mistake, which appears to be subversive of the very foundation of Christian experience; and which has, in fact, given occasion to the most grievous offences".

'That it has given occasion to such offences, I know; I can name time, place, and persons. But still another fact stares me in the face. Mr. H—— and Mr. N—— hold this, and yet I believe these have real Christian experience. But if so, this is only an *opinion*: It is not "subversive" (here is clear proof to the contrary) "of the very foundation of Christian experience". It is "compatible with love to Christ, and a genuine work of grace". Yea, many hold it, at whose feet I desire to be found in the day of the Lord Jesus. If, then, I "oppose this with my whole strength", I am a mere bigot still. I leave *you* in your calm and retired moments to make the application.

'But how came this opinion into my mind? I will tell you with all simplicity. In 1725 I met with Bishop Taylor's "Rules of Holy Living and Dying". I was struck particularly with the chapter upon *intention*, and felt a fixed intention "to give myself up to God". In this I was much confirmed soon after by the "Christian Pattern", and longed to give God all my heart. This is just what I mean by Perfection now: I sought after it from that hour.

'In 1727 I read Mr. Law's "Christian Perfection", and "Serious Call", and more explicitly resolved to be all devoted to God, in body, soul, and spirit. In 1730 I began to be *homo unius libri* [a man of one book] to study (comparatively) no book but the Bible. I then saw, in a stronger light than ever before, that only one thing is needful, even faith that worketh by the love of God and man, all inward and outward holiness; and I groaned to love God with all my heart, and to serve Him with all my strength.

'January 1, 1733, I preached the sermon on the Circumcision of the Heart; which contains all that I now teach concerning salvation from all sin, and loving God with an undivided heart. In the same year I printed (the first time I ventured to print any thing), for the use of my pupils, "A Collection of Forms of Prayer"; and in this I spoke explicitly of giving "the whole heart and the whole life to God". This was then, as it is now, my idea of Perfection, though I should have started at the word.

'In 1735 I preached my farewell sermon at Epworth, in Lincolnshire. In this, likewise, I spoke with the utmost clearness of having one design, one desire, one love, and of pursuing the one end of our life in all our words and actions.

'In January, 1738, I expressed my desire in these words:

> O grant that nothing in my soul
> May dwell but thy pure love alone!
> O may thy love possess me whole,
> My joy, my treasure, and my crown!
> Strange flames far from my heart remove,
> My every act, word, thought be love!

'And I am still persuaded this is what the Lord Jesus hath bought for me with his own blood.

'Now, whether you desire and expect this blessing or not, is it not an astonishing thing that you, or any man living, should be disgusted at me for expecting it; and that they should persuade one another that this hope is "subversive of the very foundations of Christian experience"?'

Why then, whoever retains it cannot possibly have any Christian experience at all. Then my brother, Mr. Fletcher, and I, and twenty thousand more, who seem both to fear and to love God, are in reality children of the devil, and in the road to eternal damnation! . . .

Mon. 27. I took my leave of Londonderry. Mr. Knox sent his servant to conduct me to Sligo, being now as affectionate as Mr. K[nox] of Sligo was the first time I was there. Keeping a steady pace, we rode fifteen miles, so called, in four hours and a half, and came, at noon, to Ballymafay. Here we were shown into a room, where lay a young man, brought near death by a vomiting of blood. Perhaps we were brought into this room, at this time, to save a poor man's life. As we were riding through the mountains, in the afternoon, we overtook one who was just come from Derry, and had heard me preach all the time I was there, both in the evening and the morning. I talked plainly both to her and her husband, and they expressed all possible thankfulness.

At five we reached Donegal, the county-town. What a wonderful set of county-towns are in this kingdom! Donegal and five more would not make up such a town as Islington. Some have twenty houses in them, Mayo three, and Leitrim, I think, not one. Is not this owing in part to the fickleness of the nation, who seldom like anything long, and so are continually seeking new habitations, as well as new fashions, and new trifles of every kind? ...

Saturday, July 13. I read Sir Richard Cox's 'History of Ireland' [1689]. I suppose it is accounted as authentic as any that is extant. But surely never was there the like in the habitable world! Such a series of robberies, murders, and burning of houses, towns, and countries, did I never hear or read of before. I do not now wonder Ireland is thinly inhabited, but that it has any inhabitants at all! Probably it had been wholly desolate before now, had not the English come, and prevented the implacable wretches from going on till they had swept each other from the earth ...

Wednesday, March 12, 1766. I rode over to Kingswood; and having told my whole mind to the Masters and servants, spoke to the children in a far stronger manner than ever I did before. I will kill or cure: I will have one or the other—a Christian school, or none at all ...

Tuesday, July 29 [Lancashire]. In the evening I preached near the preaching-house at Paddiham, and strongly insisted on communion with God, as the only religion that would avail us. At the close of the sermon came Mr. M. His long, white beard showed that his present disorder was of some continuance. In all other respects he was quite sensible; but he told me, with much concern, 'You can have no place in heaven without—a beard! Therefore, I beg, let yours grow immediately.' ...

Sunday, October 5 ... Several evenings this week I preached at Bristol on the Education of Children. Some answered all by that poor, lame, miserable shift, 'O, he has no children of his own!' But many, of a nobler spirit, owned the truth, and pleaded guilty before God ...

Wednesday, November 5. I rode by Shoreham to Sevenoaks. In the little journeys which I have lately taken, I have thought much on the huge encomiums which have been for many ages bestowed on a *country life.* How have all the learned world cried out,

> *O fortunati nimiùm, sua si bona norint*
> *Agricolæ!*

[O too happy country dwellers, if they recognized their own good
fortune!]

But, after all, what a flat contradiction is this to universal
experience! See that little house, under the wood, by the river side!
There is rural life in perfection. How happy then is the farmer that
lives there! Let us take a detail of his happiness. He rises with, or
before, the sun, calls his servants, looks to his swine and cows, then
to his stables and barns. He sees to the ploughing and sowing his
ground, in winter or in spring. In summer and autumn he hurries
and sweats among his mowers and reapers. And where is his
happiness in the mean time? Which of these employments do we
envy? Or do we envy the delicate repast that succeeds, which the
poet so languishes for?

> *O quando faba Pythagoræ cognata, simulque*
> *Uncta satis pingui ponentur oluscula lardo!*

'O the happiness of eating *beans well greased with fat bacon*! Nay, and
cabbage too!'—Was Horace in his senses when he talked thus, or the
servile herd of his imitators? Our eyes and ears may convince us
there is not a less happy body of men in all England than the
country farmers. In general, their life is supremely dull; and it is
usually unhappy too. For of all people in the kingdom, they are
most discontented; seldom satisfied either with God or man ...

Friday, March 20, 1767. I rode on through more storms to
Liverpool: But here too I found no ship to carry my horses: so,
Monday, 23, I set out for Portpatrick. This day we rode but about
forty miles; the next to Kendal, where I preached at six, and spent
a comfortable evening at Serjeant Southwell's. *Wednesday, 25.* The
rain, which began yesterday noon, continued till noon to-day,
without intermission: But though driven against us by a strong
wind, it was nothing so troublesome as the piercing cold, while we
afterwards rode between the snowy mountains, the road also being
covered with snow. However, after a short bait at Keswick, we
reached Cockermouth in the afternoon.

The mare T. Dancer rode being now quite lame, I left him to cross over at Whitehaven; and Mr. Atlay, who came just in time, offered to accompany me to Portpatrick. *Thursday, 26.* We rode through miserable roads to Solway-Frith: But the guides were so deeply engaged in a cock-fight, that none could be procured to show us over. We procured one, however, between three and four: But there was more sea than we expected; so that, notwithstanding all I could do, my legs and the skirts of my coat were in the water. The motion of the waves made me a little giddy; but it had a stranger effect on Mr. Atlay: He lost his sight, and was just dropping off his horse, when one of our fellow-travellers caught hold of him. We rode on nine or ten miles, and lodged at a village called Ruthwell. . . .

About this time [1768] a remarkable work of God broke out among the children at Kingswood School. One of the masters sent me a short account of it as follows:

'REV. AND DEAR SIR,   *April 27, 1768*

'ON Wednesday, the 20th, God broke in upon our boys in a surprising manner. A serious concern has been observable in some of them for some time past; but that night, while they were in their private apartments, the power of God came upon them, even like a mighty, rushing wind, which made them cry aloud for mercy. Last night, I hope, will never be forgotten, when about twenty were in the utmost distress. But God quickly spoke peace to two of them, J[ohn] Gl[asco]t, and T[homas] M[auric]e. A greater display of his love I never saw; they indeed rejoice with joy unspeakable. For my own part, I have not often felt the like power. We have no need to exhort them to pray, for that spirit runs through the whole school; so that this house may well be called, "an house of prayer". While I am writing, the cries of the boys, from their several apartments, are sounding in my ears. There are many still lying at the pool, who wait every moment to be put in. They are come to this, "Lord, I will not, I cannot, rest without thy love". Since I began to write, eight more are set at liberty, and now rejoice in God their Saviour. The names of these are John Coward, John Lion, John Maddern, John Boddily, John Thurgar, Charles Brown, William Higham, and Robert Hindmarsh. Their age is from eight to fourteen. There are but few who withstand the work; nor is it likely they should do it long; for the prayers of those that believe in Christ seem to carry all before them. Among the colliers likewise the work of God increases greatly; two of the colliers' boys were justified this week. The number added to the society since the Conference is an hundred and thirty.

'I had sealed my letter, but have opened it to inform you, that two more of our children have found peace. Several others are under deep conviction. Some of our friends from Bristol are here, who are thunderstruck. This is the day we have wished for so long; the day you have had in view, which has made you go through so much opposition for the good of these poor children.

'JAMES HINDMARSH.' . . .

Friday, May 20. I went on in reading that fine book, Bishop Butler's 'Analogy'. But I doubt it is too hard for most of those for whom it is chiefly intended. *Freethinkers*, so called, are seldom *close thinkers*. They will not be at the pains of reading such a book as this. One that would profit them must dilute his sense, or they will neither swallow nor digest it . . .

Wednesday, 25, and the two following days, being at Sunderland, I took down, from one who had feared God from her infancy, one of the strangest accounts I ever read; and yet I can find no pretence to disbelieve it. The well-known character of the person excludes all suspicion of fraud; and the nature of the circumstances themselves excludes the possibility of a delusion.

It is true there are several of them which I do not comprehend; but this is, with me, a very slender objection: For what is it which I do comprehend, even of the things I see daily? Truly not

The smallest grain of sand, or spire of grass.[39]

I know not how the one grows, or how the particles of the other cohere together. What pretence have I then to deny well-attested facts, because I cannot comprehend them?

It is true, likewise, that the English in general, and indeed most of the men of learning in Europe, have given up all accounts of witches and apparitions, as mere old wives' fables. I am sorry for it; and I willingly take this opportunity of entering my solemn protest against this violent compliment which so many that believe the Bible pay to those who do not believe it. I owe them no such service. I take knowledge, these are at the bottom of the outcry which has been raised; and with such insolence spread throughout the nation, in direct opposition not only to the Bible, but to the suffrage of the wisest and best of men in all ages and nations. They well know (whether Christians know it, or not), that the giving up witchcraft is, in effect, giving up the Bible; and they know, on the other hand, that if but one account of the intercourse of men with separate spirits be admitted, their whole castle in the air (Deism, Atheism, Materialism) falls to the ground. I know no reason, therefore, why we should suffer even this weapon to be wrested out of our hands. Indeed there are numerous arguments besides, which abundantly confute their vain imaginations. But we need not be hooted out of one: Neither reason nor religion require this.

One of the capital objections to all these accounts, which I have known urged over and over, is this, 'Did you ever see an apparition yourself?' No: Nor did I ever see a murder; yet I believe there is such a thing; yea, and that in one place or another murder is committed every day. Therefore I cannot, as a reasonable man, deny the fact; although I never saw it, and perhaps never may. The testimony of unexceptionable witnesses fully convinces me both of the one and the other.

But to set this aside, it has been confidently alleged, that many of these have seen their error, and have been clearly convinced that the supposed preternatural operation was the mere contrivance of artful men. The famous instance of this, which has been spread far and wide, was the drumming in Mr. Mompesson's house at Tedworth; who, it was said, acknowledged it was all a trick, and that he had found out the whole contrivance. Not so: My eldest brother, then at Christ-Church, Oxon, inquired of Mr. Mompesson, his fellow-collegian, whether his father had acknowledged this or not. He answered, 'The resort of gentlemen to my father's house was so great, he could not bear the expense. He therefore took no pains to confute the report that he had found out the cheat; although he, and I, and all the family, knew the account which was published to be punctually true.' . . .[40]

December. In the latter end of the month I took some pains in reading over Dr. Young's 'Night Thoughts', leaving out the indifferent lines, correcting many of the rest, and explaining the hard words, in order to make that noble work more useful to all, and more intelligible to ordinary readers ...

Monday, February 6, 1769. I spent an hour with a venerable woman, near ninety years of age, who retains her health, her senses, her understanding, and even her memory, to a good degree. In the last century she belonged to my grandfather Annesley's congregation, at whose house her father and she used to dine every Thursday; and whom she remembers to have frequently seen in his study, at the top of the house, with his window open, and without any fire, winter or summer. He lived seventy-seven years, and would probably have lived longer, had he not began water drinking at seventy ...

Wednesday, August 23. I went on to Trevecca. Here we found a concourse of people from all parts, come to celebrate the Countess of Huntingdon's birth-day, and the Anniversary of her School, which was opened on the twenty-fourth of August, last year. I preached, in the evening, to as many as her chapel could well contain; which is extremely neat, or rather, elegant; as is the dining-room, the school, and all the house. About nine Howell Harris desired me to give a short exhortation to his family. I did so; and then went back to my Lady's, and laid me down in peace.[41]

Thur. 24. I administered the Lord's Supper to the family. At ten the Public Service began. Mr. Fletcher preached an exceeding lively sermon in the court, the chapel being far too small. After him, Mr. William Williams preached in Welsh, till between one and two o'clock. At two we dined. Meantime, a large number of people had baskets of bread and meat carried to them in the court. At three I took my turn there, then Mr. Fletcher, and, about five, the congregation was dismissed. Between seven and eight the love-feast began, at which I believe many were comforted. In the evening several of us retired into the neighbouring wood, which is exceeding pleasantly laid out in walks; one of which leads to a little mount, raised in the midst of a meadow, that commands a delightful prospect. This is Howell Harris's work, who has likewise greatly enlarged and beautified his house; so that, with the gardens, orchards, walks, and pieces of water that surround it, it is a kind of little paradise . . .

Tuesday, September 5 . . . Last week I read over, as I rode, great part of Homer's Odyssey. I always imagined it was, like Milton's 'Paradise Regained',

> The last faint effort of an expiring Muse.[42]

But how was I mistaken! How far has Homer's latter poem the pre-eminence over the former! It is not, indeed, without its blemishes; among which, perhaps, one might reckon his making Ulysses swim nine days and nine nights without sustenance; the incredible manner of his escape from Polyphemus (unless the goat was as strong as an ox), and the introducing Minerva at every turn, without any *dignus vindice nodus* [difficulty worthy of her intervention]. But his numerous beauties make large amends for these. Was ever man so happy in his descriptions, so exact and consistent in his characters, and so natural in telling a story? He likewise continually inserts the finest strokes of morality (which I cannot find in Virgil); on all occasions recommending the fear of God, with justice, mercy, and truth. In this only he is inconsistent with himself: He makes his hero say,

> Wisdom never lies;

And,

> Him, on whate'er pretence, that lies can tell,
> My soul abhors him as the gates of hell.

Meantime, he himself, on the slightest pretence, tells deliberate lies over and over; nay, and is highly commended for so doing, even by the Goddess of Wisdom! . . .

Tuesday, October 17. We went to Wallingford, a town I never saw before, though I lived so many years at Oxford. How white are the fields here unto the harvest! The whole town seemed flocking together, rich and poor, in the evening, and received the word with joy. But who will endure to the end? Abundance of people came again at five in the morning, and were ready to devour the word. How pleasant it is to see the dawn of a work of grace! But we must not lay too much stress upon it. Abundance of blossoms! But when the sun is up, how many of these will wither away!

Having appointed to preach in Oxford at ten, I was under some difficulty. I did not like to preach in the Dissenting meeting-house; and I did not see how to avoid it. But the proprietors cut the knot for me, by locking up the doors. So I preached in James Mears's garden: And to such a congregation as I had not had in Oxford since I preached in St. Mary's church.

Thence we went to Witney, where we have now a large and commodious House. It was well filled in the evening; and (whoever else did) I found it good to be there; especially at the meeting of the society: The Spirit of glory and of Christ was among them . . .

Tuesday, 24. I preached at Alston, in a large malt-room, where one side of my head was very warm, through the crowd of people, the other very cold, having an open window at my ear. Between six and seven I preached at Northampton; and it was an awful season.

This evening there was such an Aurora Borealis as I never saw before: The colours, both the white, the flame-colour, and the scarlet, were so exceeding strong and beautiful. But they were awful too: So that abundance of people were frighted into many good resolutions . . .

Saturday, February 3 [1770], and at my leisure moments on several of the following days, I read with much expectation, a celebrated book—Rousseau upon Education. But how was I disappointed! Sure a more consummate coxcomb never saw the sun! How amazingly full of himself! Whatever he speaks he pronounces as an oracle. But many of his oracles are as palpably false, as that 'young children never love old people'. No! Do they never love grandfathers and grandmothers? Frequently more than they do their own parents. Indeed they love all that love them, and that with more warmth and sincerity than when they come to riper years.

But I object to his temper more than to his judgment: He is a mere misanthrope; a cynic all over. So indeed is his brother-infidel, Voltaire; and well nigh as great a coxcomb. But he hides both his doggedness and vanity a little better, whereas here it stares us in the face continually.

As to his book, it is whimsical to the last degree; grounded neither upon reason nor experience. To cite particular passages would be endless; but any one may observe concerning the whole, the advices which are good are trite and common, only disguised under new expressions. And those which are new, which are really his own, are lighter than vanity itself. Such discoveries I always expect from those who are too wise to believe their Bibles ...

Wednesday, March 21 ... I now procured an account of two remarkable children, which I think ought not to be buried in oblivion:

'About three weeks before Christmas, 1768, William Cooper, at Walsal, in Staffordshire, then nine years old, was convinced of sin, and would frequently say he should go to hell, and the devil would fetch him. Sometimes he cried out, "I hate him." Being asked, "Whom?" he answered, with great vehemence, "God". This terrified his mother, who, not knowing what was the matter with the child, strove to keep it secret.

'But in about a fortnight, it pleased God to reveal to him his pardoning love. His mouth was then filled with praise, declaring to all what God had done for his soul.

'A few days after Billy was awakened, God was pleased to convince his sister Lucy, then eleven years old. He soon put a song of praise into her mouth also, so that they mightily rejoiced together in God their Saviour. At the same time they were both heavily afflicted in their bodies. But so much the more was the power of God manifested, causing them to continue in the triumph of faith, throughout their sharpest pains.

'On December 30, one of their sisters coming to see them, Billy told her he had been very ill. "But," said he, "I do not mean in my body, but in my soul: I felt my sins so heavy, that I thought I should go to hell; and I saw the devil ready to drag me away. Nay, for a week, I thought myself just in the flames of hell. The sins that troubled me most were, telling lies, and quarrelling with my sister. I saw, if God did not forgive me, I was lost: And I knew quarrelling was as great a sin in Lucy as in me; and if she did not get a pardon, and feel the love of Jesus, she could not go to heaven."

'Lucy said, "When I heard Mr. A. describe two sorts of people, one sort washed in the blood of Christ, and the other not, I found I was not; and therefore, if I died so, must go to hell." Being asked what sin lay most on her conscience, she replied, "Taking his name in vain, by repeating my prayers when I did not think of God."

'When Billy was confessing that he had loved money, Lucy said, "And so did I; and was angry if I had not as much as Billy. I loved money more than God, and he might justly have sent me to hell for it."

'When Billy was asked how he knew his sins were forgiven, he answered, "Christ told me so. I had a great struggle in my heart with the devil and sin, till it pleased Jesus to come into my soul. I now feel his love in my heart, and he tells me he has forgiven my sins."

'Being asked how he did, he replied, "Happy in Jesus: Jesus is sweet to my soul." "Do you choose to live, or die?" He answered, "Neither. I hope, if I live, I shall praise God; and if I die, I am sure I shall go to him; for he has forgiven my sins, and given me his love."

'One asked Lucy, how long she had been in the triumph of faith. She answered, "Only this week: Before I had much to do with Satan; but now Jesus has conquered him for me." While she was speaking, feeling great pain of body, she said, "O I want more of these pains, more of these pains, to bring me nearer to Jesus!"

'One speaking of knowing the voice of Christ, she said, "The voice of Christ is a strange voice to them who do not know their sins forgiven: But I know it; for he has pardoned all my sins, and given me his love. And O what a mercy that such a hell-deserving wretch as me, as *me*, should be made to taste of his love!"

'Billy had frequent fits. When he found one coming, he, with a smile, laid down his head, saying, "O sweet love!" or, "O sweet Jesus!" And as soon as he came to himself, being asked how he did, he would reply, "I am happy in the love of Christ."

'When a gentleman said, "My dear, you could praise God more, if it were not for these ugly fits," he replied, "Sir, they are not ugly; for my dear Jesus sent them; and he has given me patience to bear them; and he bore more for my sins."

'One night, a gentleman and his wife came to see them; and the gentlewoman, looking on Lucy, said, "She looks as if nothing was the matter with her; she is so pleasant with her eyes." She replied, "I have enough to make me look so; for I am full of the love of God." While she spoke, her eyes sparkled exceedingly, and the tears flowed down her cheeks. At this Billy smiled, but could not speak; having been speechless for more than an hour. It seemed he was just going into eternity; but the Lord revived him a little; and as soon as he could speak, he desired to be held up in bed, and looked at the gentleman, who asked him how he did. He answered, "I am happy in Christ, and I hope you are." He said, "I hope I can say I am." Billy replied, "Has Christ pardoned your sins?" He said, "I hope he has." "Sir," said Billy, "hope will not do; for I had this hope, and yet if I had died then, I should surely have gone to hell. But he has forgiven me all my sins, and given me a taste of his love. If you have this love, you will know it, and be sure of it; but you cannot know it without the power of God. You may read as many books about Christ as you please" (he was a great reader); "but if you read all your life, this will only be in your head, and that head will perish: So that, if you have not the love of God in your heart, you will go to hell. But I hope you will not: I will pray to God for you, that he may give you his love."

'Another, coming to see them, inquired how they were. Billy said, "Happier and happier in Christ: Are you so?" He said, "No: I am not so happy as you." "Why," said Billy, "what is the matter? I am afraid you do not pray to Christ; for I am sure he is willing to make you happy."

'One who sat by seemed struck with the discourse, but did not speak. Billy, observing her, said, "And you do not pray as you ought: For if you had the love of Christ in your heart, you would not look down so. I wish you and every one had it." One said, "My dear, would not you give it them, if you might?" He answered, "No; for that would be to take Christ's work out of his hands."

'Many who heard what great things God had done for them, said, "It will be so with you always. If you should live to come into the world again, he would leave you in the dark." They answered, "We do not think so; for our Jesus has promised that he will never leave us."

'A young woman, who had told them so before, speaking in this manner a second time, Billy said to her, "Miss, are you assured of your interest in Christ?" She answered, "I hope I am in Christ; but assurance is no way essential." He replied, "But if you have his love, you will be sure you have it: You will know it in your heart. I am afraid your hope is only in your head. Do you never quarrel with anybody?" She said, "No." "But," says he, "you quarrel with God's word: For he has promised me, none shall pluck me out of his hand; and you say, the world will: So you make God a story-teller." At this she went away displeased.

'There were few came to see them, when either of them was able to speak, but they inquired into the state of their souls; and, without fear, told them the danger of dying without an assurance of the love of God.

'One coming to see them, was talked to very closely by Billy, till she could bear no more. She turned to Lucy, and said, "You were always good children, and never told stories." "Yes, Madam," said Lucy, "but I did, when I was afraid of being beat; and when I said my prayers; for I did not think of God; and I called him, My Father, when I was a child of wrath: And as to praying, I could not pray till it pleased him by his Spirit to show me my sins. And he showed me, we might say as many prayers as we would, and go to church or meeting; yet all this, if we had not Christ for our foundation, would not do."

'When they were asked, if they were afraid to die, they always answered, "No; for what can death do? He can only lay his cold hand upon our bodies."

'One told Lucy, "Now you may live as you please, since you are sure of going to heaven." She replied, "No, I would not sin against my dear Saviour if you would give me this room full of gold."

'On the Monday before he died, Billy repeated that hymn with the most triumphant joy,

> Come, let us join our cheerful songs
> With angels round the throne!

Afterwards he repeated the Lord's Prayer. The last words he spoke intelligibly were, "How pleasant is it to be with Christ, for ever and ever—for ever and ever! Amen! Amen! Amen!"

'While he lay speechless, there came into the room some who he feared knew not God. He seemed much affected, wept and moaned much, waved his hand, and put it on his sister's mouth; intimating, as she supposed, that she could speak to them. On Wednesday evening, February 1, his happy spirit returned to God.' She died soon after.

In the following days I went on slowly, through Staffordshire and Cheshire, to Manchester. In this journey, as well as in many others, I observed a mistake that almost universally prevails; and I desire all travellers to take good notice of it, which may save them both from trouble and danger. Near thirty years ago, I was thinking, 'How is it that no horse ever stumbles while I am reading?' (History, poetry, and philosophy I commonly read on horseback, having other employment at other times.) No account can possibly be given but this: Because then I throw the reins on his neck. I then set myself to observe; and I aver, that in riding above an hundred thousand miles, I scare ever remember any horse (except two, that would fall head over heels any way) to fall, or make a considerable stumble, while I rode *with a slack rein*. To fancy, therefore, that a *tight rein* prevents stumbling is a capital blunder. I have repeated the trial more frequently than most men in the kingdom can do. A slack rein will prevent stumbling, if any thing will. But in some horses nothing can . . .

Monday, May 14. After ten years' inquiry, I have learned what are the Highlands of Scotland. Some told me, 'The Highlands begin when you cross the Tay'; others, 'when you cross the North Esk'; and others, 'when you cross the river Spey': But all of them missed the mark. For the truth of the matter is, the Highlands are bounded by no river at all, but by Carns, or heaps of stones laid in a row, south-west and north-east, from sea to sea. These formerly divided the kingdom of the Picts from that of the Caledonians, which included all the country north of the Carns; several whereof are still remaining. It takes in Argyleshire, most of Perthshire, Murrayshire, with all the north-west counties. This is called the Highlands, because a considerable part of it (though not the whole) is mountainous. But it is not more mountainous than North-Wales, nor than many parts of England and Ireland: Nor do I believe it has any mountain higher than Snowdon hill, or the Skiddaw in Cumberland. Talking Erse, therefore, is not the thing that distinguishes these from the Lowlands. Neither is this or that river; both the Tay, the Esk, and the Spey running through the Highlands, not south of them . . .

Thursday, June 28. I rode to Mr. Sutcliffe's at Hoohole; a lovely valley encompassed with high mountains. I stood on the smooth grass before his house (which stands on a gently-rising ground) and all the people on the slope before me. It was a glorious opportunity. I trust many 'came boldly to the throne', and found 'grace to help in time of need'.

I can hardly believe that I am this day entered into the sixty-eighth year of my age. How marvellous are the ways of God! How has he kept me even from a child! From ten to thirteen or fourteen, I had little but bread to eat, and not great plenty of that. I believe this was so far from hurting me, that it laid the foundation of lasting health. When I grew up, in consequence of reading Dr. Cheyne,[43] chose to eat sparingly, and drink water. This was another great means of continuing my health, till I was about seven-and-twenty. I then began spitting blood, which continued several years. A warm climate cured this. I was afterwards brought to the brink of death by a fever; but it left me healthier than before. Eleven years after, I was in the third stage of a consumption; in three months it pleased God to remove this also. Since that time I have known neither pain nor sickness, and am now healthier than I was forty years ago. This hath God wrought! . . .

It was the day before [Saturday 15 September] that I first observed a very uncommon concern in the children at Kingswood School, while I was explaining, and enforcing upon them, the first principles of religion.

Tues. 18. Most of them went to see the body of Francis Evans, one of our neighbours, who died two or three days before. About seven Mr. Hindmarsh met them all in the school, and gave an exhortation suited to the occasion. He then gave out that hymn,

> And am I born to die,
> To lay this body down?
> And must my trembling spirit fly
> Into a world unknown?[44]

This increased their concern; so that it was with great difficulty they contained themselves till he began to pray. Then Al[exander] M[athe]r, and R[ichar]d N[obl]e, cried aloud for mercy; and quickly another and another, till all but two or three were constrained to do the same; and as long as he continued to pray, they continued the same loud and bitter cry. One of the maids, Elizabeth Nutt, was as deeply convinced as any of them. After prayer, Mr. H. said, 'Those of you who are resolved to serve God may go and pray together.' Fifteen of them did so, and continued wrestling with God, with strong cries and tears, till about nine o'clock.

Wed. 19. At the morning prayer many of them cried out again, though not so violently. From this time their whole spirit and behaviour were changed: They were all serious and loving to each other. The same seriousness and mildness continued on *Thursday*; and they walked together, talking only of the things of God. On *Friday* evening their concern greatly increased, and caused them to break out again into strong cries. *Saturday, 22.* They seemed to lose none of their concern, and spent all their spare time in prayer.

Sun. 23. Fifteen of them gave me their names; being resolved, they said, to serve God. In the afternoon I gave them a strong exhortation, and afterward Mr. Rankin. Their very countenances were entirely changed. They drank in every word.

Tues. 25. During the time of prayer in the evening, they were affected just as the Tuesday before. The two other maids were then present, and were both cut to the heart ...

Wednesday, January 23, 1771. For what cause I know not to this day, —— set out for Newcastle, purposing 'never to return'. *Non eam reliqui: Non dimissi: Non revocabo* [I did not desert her: I did not send her away: I will not ask her to return].

Fri. 25. I revised and transcribed my Will, declaring as simply, as plainly, and as briefly as I could, nothing more nor nothing else, but 'what I would have done with the worldly goods which I leave behind me'. ...

Thursday, March 14. I went through both the upper and lower rooms of the London Workhouse. It contains about an hundred children, who are in as good order as any private family. And the whole house is as clean, from top to bottom, as any gentleman's needs be. And why is not every workhouse in London, yea, through the kingdom, in the same order? Purely for want either of sense, or of honesty and activity, in them that superintend it . . .

[Wesley was in Ireland from 24 March to 22 July.]

Sunday, March 24. I immediately set myself to inquire into the state of the society in Dublin. It was plain there had been a continual jar, for at least two years last past, which had stumbled the people, weakened the hands of the Preachers, and greatly hindered [the work of God]. I wanted to know the ground of this; and, that I might do nothing rashly, determined to hear the parties, separately first, and then face to face. Having already talked with the Preachers, I talked this evening with the Leaders at large; and from the spirit which appeared in all, I had a good hope that all hinderances would be removed. On *Wednesday* evening I met the Leaders again, and gave them an opportunity of explaining themselves further; and on *Friday* I appointed an extraordinary meeting, at which some spoke with much warmth. But I tempered them on each side, so that they parted in peace.

Sat. 30. I preached at the new preaching-house, near the barracks, about six in the evening. Many attended here who cannot, and many who will not, come to the other end of the town. So that I am persuaded the preaching here twice or thrice a week, will be much for the Glory of God.

Sun. 31. The Leaders, Stewards, and Preachers, spoke their minds freely to each other. I now saw the whole evil might be removed, all parties being desirous of peace.

On *Monday, Tuesday,* and *Wednesday,* I visited the classes, and found a general faintness had run through the society. Yet for several days God has given a general blessing, and strengthened many of the feeble-minded. On *Tuesday* I preached again at the new House, and many were greatly comforted.

On *Wednesday* evening I read over to the Leaders the following paper:

1. That it may be more easily discerned whether the members of our societies are working out their own salvation, they are divided into little companies, called classes. One person in each of these is

styled the Leader: It is his business, 1. To see each person in his class once a week; to inquire how their souls prosper; to advise, reprove, comfort, or exhort them: 2. To receive what they are willing to give toward the expense of the society: And, 3. To meet the Assistant and the Stewards once a week.

2. This is the whole and sole business of a Leader, or any number of Leaders. But it is common for the Assistant in any place when several Leaders are met together, to ask their advice, as to anything that concerns either the temporal or spiritual welfare of the society. This he may, or he may not do, as he sees best. I frequently do it in the larger societies; and on many occasions I have found, that in a multitude of counsellors there is safety.

3. From this short view of the original design of Leaders, it is easy to answer the following questions:

Q. 1. What authority has a single Leader?

He has authority to meet his class, to receive their contributions, and to visit the sick in his class.

Q. 2. What authority have all the Leaders of a society met together?

They have authority to show their class-papers to the Assistant; to deliver the money they have received to the Stewards, and to bring in the names of the sick.

Q. 3. But have they not authority to restrain the Assistant, if they think he acts improperly?

No more than any member of the society has. After mildly speaking to him, they are to refer the thing to Mr. W.

Q. 4. Have they not authority to hinder a person from preaching?

None but the Assistant has this authority.

Q. 5. Have they not authority to displace a particular Leader?

No more than the door-keeper has. To place and to displace Leaders belongs to the Assistant alone.

Q. 6. Have they not authority to expel a particular member of the society?

No: The Assistant only can do this.

Q. 7. But have they not authority to regulate the temporal and spiritual affairs of the society?

Neither the one nor the other. Temporal affairs belong to the Stewards; spiritual to the Assistant.

Q. 8. Have they authority to make any collection of a public nature?

No: The Assistant only can do this.

Q. 9. Have they authority to receive the yearly subscription?

No: This also belongs to the Assistant.

4. Considering these things, can we wonder at the confusion which has been here for some years?

If one wheel of a machine gets out of its place, what disorder must ensue!

In the Methodist discipline, the wheels regularly stand thus: The Assistant, the Preachers, the Stewards, the Leaders, the people.

But here the Leaders, who are the lowest wheel but one, were got quite out of their place. They were got at the top of all, above the Stewards, the Preachers, yea, and above the Assistant himself.

5. To this, chiefly, I impute the gradual decay of the work of God in Dublin.

There has been a jar throughout the whole machine. Most of the wheels were hindered in their motion. The Stewards, the Preachers, the Assistant, all moved heavily. They felt all was not right. But if they saw where the fault lay, they had not strength to remedy it.

But it may be effectually remedied now. Without rehearsing former grievances (which may all die and be forgotten), for the time to come, let each wheel keep its own place. Let the Assistant, the Preachers, the Stewards, the Leaders, know and execute their several offices. Let none encroach upon another, but all move together in harmony and love. So shall the work of God flourish among you, perhaps as it never did before; while you all hold the unity of the Spirit in the bond of peace. DUBLIN, *March 29, 1771* ...

* * *

Wednesday, May 22. After preaching at Balligarane, I rode to Ashkayton. There are no ruins, I believe, in the kingdom of Ireland to be compared to these. The old Earl of Desmond's castle is very large, and has been exceeding strong. Not far from this, and formerly communicating with it by a gallery, is his great hall or banqueting-room. The walls are still firm and entire; and these with the fine carvings of the window-frames (all of polished marble) give some idea of what it was once. Its last master lived like a Prince for many years, and rebelled over and over against Queen Elizabeth. After his last rebellion, his army being totally routed, he fled into the woods with two or three hundred men. But the pursuit was so hot, that these were soon scattered from him, and he crept alone into a small cabin. He was sitting there, when a soldier came in and struck him. He rose and said, 'I am the Earl of Desmond.' The wretch, rejoicing that he had found so great a prize, cut off his head at once. Queen Elizabeth and King James allowed a pension to his relict for many years. I have seen a striking picture of her, in her widow's weeds, said to be taken when she was an hundred and forty years old.

At a small distance from the castle stands the old Abbey, the finest ruin of the kind in the kingdom. Not only the walls of the church, and many of the apartments, but the whole cloisters, are entire. They are built of black marble exquisitely polished, and vaulted over with the same. So that they are as firm now as when they were built, perhaps seven or eight hundred years ago; and if not purposely destroyed, (as most of the ancient buildings in Ireland have been), may last these thousand years. But add these to the years they have stood already, and what is it to eternity? A moment! . . .

Sunday, June 9. I seldom look at the old castle at Augher, without thinking of the famous Sir Phelim O'Neale. In the beginning of the Irish Rebellion, he called one night at Mr. Kennedy's, an intimate acquaintance and foster-brother (a very sacred relation among the Irish), and said, 'Rise, come away with me, that I may protect you, for fear some of my straggling parties should hurt you.' Mrs. Kennedy, being very near her time, said, 'Nay, gossip, consider my condition, and do not take my husband from me.' He replied, 'You fool, it is for his own good.' But soon after they were gone, Mrs. K. said, 'My heart misgives me; whatever comes of it, I must follow them.' So, as well as she could, she walked between her man-servant and her maid, an Irish girl. About sunrise they came near Augher castle, where Sir Phelim was standing with his men. Just by him was her husband, hanged on a tree. Sir Phelim, seeing her, sent and ordered the man and maid to stand from her. The man did so: The maid replied, 'No; I will die with my mistress.' On this he ordered his men to fire. She fell, and two infants fell out of her. Such was the mercy of the Irish at that time! Such the spirit which their good Priests infused into them! ...

Friday, August 23. I preached at noon, to a lovely congregation of plain, artless people, at Houghton; and in the Town-Hall at Pembroke, in the evening, to many rich and elegant hearers. *Sunday, 25.* At ten I began the Service at St. Daniel's. The church, as usual, would ill contain the congregation. In the afternoon I preached in Monk-Town church (one of the three belonging to Pembroke), a large, old, ruinous building. I suppose it has scarce had such a congregation in it during this century. Many of them were gay, genteel people: So I spake on the first elements of the Gospel. But I was still out of their depth. O how hard it is to be shallow enough for a polite audience! ...

Tuesday, November 5. In our way to Bury we called at Felsham, near which is the seat of the late Mr. Reynolds. The house is, I think, the best contrived and the most beautiful I ever saw. It has four fronts, and five rooms on a floor, elegantly, though not sumptuously, furnished. At a small distance stands a delightful grove. On every side of this, the poor, rich man, who had no hope beyond the grave, placed seats, to enjoy life as long as he could. But being resolved none of his family should be 'put into the ground', he built a structure in the midst of the grove, vaulted above and beneath, with niches for coffins, strong enough to stand for ages. In one of these he had soon the satisfaction of laying the remains of his only child; and, two years after, those of his wife. After two years more, in the year 1759, having eat, and drank, and forgotten God, for eighty-four years, he went himself to give an account of his stewardship ...

Fri. 29. We viewed the improvements of that active and useful man, the late Duke of Cumberland. The most remarkable work is the triangular tower which he built on the edge of Windsor-Park. It is surrounded with shrubberies and woods, having some straight, some serpentine, walks in them, and commands a beautiful prospect all three ways: A very extensive one to the south-west. In the lower part is an alcove, which must be extremely pleasant in a summer evening. There is a little circular projection at each corner, one of which is filled by a geometrical staircase: The other two contain little apartments, one of which is a study. I was agreeably surprised to find many of the books not only religious, but admirably well chosen. Perhaps the great man spent many hours here, with only Him that seeth in secret; and who can say how deep that change went, which was so discernible in the latter part of his life?[45]

Hence we went to Mr. Bateman's house, the oddest I ever saw with my eyes. Every thing breathes antiquity; scarce a bedstead is to be seen that is not an hundred and fifty years old; and everything is quite out of the common way: He scorns to have any thing like his neighbours. For six hours, I suppose, these elegant oddities would much delight a curious man; but after six months they would probably give him no more pleasure than a collection of feathers . . .

Tuesday, January 14, 1772. I spent an agreeable hour with Dr. S——, the oldest acquaintance I now have. He is the greatest genius in little things, that ever fell under my notice. Almost every thing about him is of his own invention, either in whole or in part. Even his fire-screen, his lamps of various sorts, his ink-horn, his very save-all. I really believe, were he seriously to set about it, he could invent the best mouse-trap that ever was in the world . . .

Friday, February 7. I called on a friend at Hampton-Court, who went with me through the house. It struck me more than any thing of the kind I have seen in England; more than Blenheim House itself. One great difference is, every thing there appears designedly grand and splendid; here every thing is quite, as it were, natural, and one thinks it cannot be otherwise. If the expression may be allowed, there is a kind of stiffness runs through the one, and an easiness through the other. Of pictures I do not pretend to be a judge; but there is one, by Paul Rubens, which particularly struck me, both with the design and the execution of it. It is Zacharias and Elizabeth, with John the Baptist, two or three years old, coming to visit Mary, and our Lord sitting upon her knee. The passions are surprisingly expressed, even in the children; but I could not see either the decency or common sense of painting them stark naked: Nothing can defend or excuse this: It is shockingly absurd, even an Indian being the judge. I allow, a man who paints thus may have a good hand, but certainly *cerebrum non habet* [he has no brains] . . .

Tues. 11. I casually took a volume of what is called, 'A Sentimental Journey through France and Italy'.[46] *Sentimental*! what is that? It is not English: He might as well say, *Continental*. It is not sense. It conveys no determinate idea; yet one fool makes many. And this nonsensical word (who would believe it?) is become a fashionable one! However, the book agrees full well with the title; for one is as queer as the other. For oddity, uncouthness, and unlikeness to all the world beside, I suppose, the writer is without a rival . . .

Friday, March 21. I met several of my friends, who had begun a subscription to prevent my riding on horseback; which I cannot do quite so well, since a hurt which I got some months ago. If they continue it, well; if not, I shall have strength according to my need . . .

Monday, April 6. In the afternoon I drank tea at Am. O.[47] But how was I shocked! The children that used to cling about me, and drink in every word, had been at a boarding-school. There they had unlearned all religion, and even seriousness; and had learned pride, vanity, affectation, and whatever could guard them against the knowledge and love of God. Methodist parents, who would send your girls headlong to hell, send them to a fashionable boarding school! . . .

Wed. 15 . . . In the afternoon we had a furious storm of rain and snow: However, we reached Selkirk safe. Here I observed a little piece of stateliness which was quite new to me: The maid came in, and said, 'Sir, *the lord of the stable* waits to know if he should feed your horses.' We call him *ostler* in England. After supper all the family seemed glad to join with us in prayer . . .

Tues. 28. We walked through the Duke of Athol's gardens, in which was one thing I never saw before—a summer-house in the middle of a green-house, by means of which one might in the depth of winter enjoy the warmth of May, and sit surrounded with greens and flowers on every side.

In the evening I preached once more at Perth, to a large and serious congregation. Afterwards they did me an honour I never thought of—presented me with the freedom of the city ...

Wednesday, May 20 ... In the evening I preached at Dunbar. *Thursday, 21.* I went to the Bass, seven miles from it, which, in the horrid reign of Charles the Second, was the prison of those venerable men who suffered the loss of all things for a good conscience. It is a high rock surrounded by the sea, two or three miles in circumference, and about two miles from the shore. The strong east wind made the water so rough, that the boat could hardly live: And when we came to the only landing-place (the other sides being quite perpendicular), it was with much difficulty that we got up, climbing on our hands and knees. The castle, as one may judge by what remains, was utterly inaccessible. The walls of the chapel, and of the Governor's house, are tolerably entire. The garden-walls are still seen near the top of the rock, with the well in the midst of it. And round the walls there are spots of grass, that feed eighteen or twenty sheep. But the proper natives of the island are Solund-geese, a bird about the size of a Muscovy-duck, which breed by thousands, from generation to generation, on the sides of the rock. It is peculiar to these, that they lay but one egg, which they do not sit upon at all, but keep it under one foot (as we saw with our eyes), till it is hatched. How many prayers did the holy men confined here offer up, in that evil day! And how many thanksgivings should we return, for all the liberty, civil and religious, which we enjoy!

At our return, we walked over the ruins of Tantallon Castle, once the seat of the great Earls of Douglas. The front walls (it was four square) are still standing, and by their vast height and huge thickness, gives us a little idea of what it once was. Such is human greatness! ...

Monday, October 26. At twelve I set out in the stage coach, and in the evening came to Norwich. *Tuesday, 27.* Finding abundance of people were out of work, and, consequently, in the utmost want (such a general decay of trade having hardly been known in the memory of man), I enforced, in the evening, 'Seek ye first the kingdom of God, and his righteousness; and all these things shall be added unto you.' For many years I have not seen so large a congregation here, in the mornings as well as evenings. One reason of which may be this: Thousands of people, who, when they had fulness of bread, never considered whether they had any souls or not, now they are in want begin to think of God . . .

Monday, January 4, 1773 [London]. I began revising my letters and papers. One of them was wrote above an hundred and fifty years ago (in 1619), I suppose by my grandfather's father, to her he was to marry in a few days. Several were wrote by my brothers and me when at school, many while we were at the University; abundantly testifying (if it be worth knowing) what was our aim from our youth up.

Thur. 7. I called where a child was dying of the smallpox, and rescued her from death and the Doctors, who were giving her saffron, &c., to drive them out! Can any one be so ignorant still?

We observed *Friday, the 8th*, as a day of fasting and prayer, on account of the general want of trade and scarcity of provisions. The next week I made an end of revising my letters; and from those I had both wrote and received, I could not but make one remark—that for above these forty years, of all the friends who were once the most closely united, and afterwards separated from me, every one had separated himself! He left me, not I him. And from both mine and their own letters, the steps whereby they did this are clear and undeniable . . .

Thur. 28. I buried the remains of poor E. T., of whom, *ever since she died*, her husband speaks as a most excellent woman, and a most affectionate wife! I have known many such instances: Many couples, who while they lived together spoke of each other as mere sinners; but as soon as either was dead, the survivor spake of the deceased as the best creature in the world . . .

[Wesley began a three-month visit to Ireland on 26 March.]

Wednesday, May 12. Took my leave of this affectionate people, and in the evening preached at Clare. What a contrast between Clare and Limerick!—A little ruinous town; no inn that could afford us either meat, or drink, or comfortable lodging; no society, and next to no congregation, till the soldiers came. After preaching,

I spent an agreeable hour with the Commanding Officer; and, having procured a tolerable lodging in the barracks, slept in peace.

Thur. 13. We went on, through a most dreary country, to Galway; where, at the late survey, there were twenty thousand Papists, and five hundred Protestants. But which of them are Christians, have the mind that was in Christ, and walk as he walked? And without this, how little does it avail, whether they are called Protestants or Papists! At six I preached in the Court-House, to a large congregation, who all behaved well. *Friday, 14.* In the evening I preached at Ballinrobe; and on *Saturday* went on to Castlebar. Entering the town, I was struck with the sight of the Charter-School;—no gate to the court-yard, a large chasm in the wall, heaps of rubbish before the house-door, broken windows in abundance; the whole a picture of slothfulness, nastiness, and desolation! I did not dream there were any inhabitants, till, the next day, I saw about forty boys and girls walking from church. As I was just behind them, I could not but observe, 1. That there was neither Master nor Mistress, though, it seems, they were both well: 2. That both boys and girls were completely dirty: 3. That none of them seemed to have any garters on, their stockings hanging about their heels: 4. That in the heels, even of many of the girls' stockings, were holes larger than a crown-piece. I gave a plain account of these things to the Trustees of the Charter-School in Dublin: Whether they are altered or no, I cannot tell . . .

Mon. 24 . . . One of my horses having a shoe loose, I borrowed Mr. Watson's horse, and left him with the chaise. When we came near Enniskillen, I desired two only to ride with me, and the rest of our friends to keep at a distance. Some masons were at work on the first bridge, who gave us some coarse words. We had abundance more as we rode through the town; but many soldiers being in the street, and taking knowledge of me in a respectful manner, the mob shrunk back. An hour after, Mr. Watson came in the chaise. Before he came to the bridge, many ran together, and began to throw whatever came next to hand. The bridge itself they had blocked up with large stones, so that a carriage could not pass; but an old man cried out, 'Is this the way you use strangers?' and rolled away the stones. The mob quickly rewarded him by plastering him over with mortar from head to foot. They then fell upon the carriage, which they cut with stones in several places, and well nigh covered with dirt and mortar. From one end of the town to the other, the stones flew thick about the coachman's head. Some of them were two or three pounds' weight, which they threw with all their might. If but one of them had struck him, it would have effectually prevented him from driving any farther; and then, doubtless, they would have given an account of the chaise and horses.

I preached at Sydore in the evening and morning, and then set out for Roosky. The road lay not far from Enniskillen. When we came pretty near the town, both men and women saluted us, first with bad words, and then with dirt and stones. My horses soon left them behind; but not till they had broke one of the windows, the glass of which came pouring in upon me; but did me no further hurt.

About an hour after, John Smith came to Enniskillen. The masons on the bridge preparing for battle, he was afraid his horse would leap with him into the river; and therefore chose to alight. Immediately they poured in upon him a whole shower of dirt and stones. However, he made his way through the town, though pretty much daubed and bruised . . .

Thur. 27. I went on to Londonderry. *Friday, 28.* I was invited to see the Bishop's palace (a grand and beautiful structure), and his garden, newly laid, and exceeding pleasant. Here I innocently gave some offence to the gardener, by mentioning the English of a Greek word. But he set us right, warmly assuring us that the English name of the flower is not Crane's bill, but Geranium! . . .

Monday, June 14. After preaching at Lurgan, I inquired of Mr. Miller, whether he had any thoughts of perfecting his speaking statue, which had so long lain by. He said he had altered his design; that he intended, if he had life and health, to make two, which would not only speak, but sing hymns alternately with an articulate voice; that he had made a trial, and it answered well. But he could not tell when he should finish it, as he had much business of other kinds, and could only give his leisure hours to this. How amazing is it that no man of fortune enables him to give all his time to the work!

I preached in the evening at Lisburn. All the time I could spare here was taken up by poor patients. I generally asked, 'What remedies have you used?' and was not a little surprised. What has fashion to do with physic? Why (in Ireland, at least), almost as much as with head-dress. Blisters, for anything or nothing, were all the fashion when I was in Ireland last. Now the grand fashionable medicine for twenty diseases (who would imagine it?) is mercury sublimate! Why is it not an halter, or a pistol? They would cure *a little* more speedily.

Tues. 15. I went to dreary Newtown[ards]. This place always makes me pensive. Even in Ireland I hardly see anywhere such heaps of ruins as here; and they are considerably increased since I was here before. What a shadow is human greatness!

The evening congregation in the new market-house appeared deeply attentive, especially the backsliders; several of whom determined to set out afresh.

When I came to Belfast, I learned the real cause of the late insurrections in this neighbourhood. Lord Donegal, the proprietor of almost the whole country, came hither to give his tenants new leases. But when they came, they found two merchants of the town had taken their farms over their heads; so that multitudes of them, with their wives and children, were turned out to the wide world. It is no wonder that, as their lives were now bitter to them, they should fly out as they did. It is rather a wonder that they did not go much farther. And if they had, who would have been most in fault? Those who were without home, without money, without food for themselves and families? Or those who drove them to this extremity? . . .

Monday, July 5. About eleven we crossed Dublin bar, and were at Hoy-Lake the next afternoon. This was the first night I ever lay awake in my life, though I was at ease in body and mind. I believe few can say this: In seventy years I never lost one night's sleep! . . .

Wed. 21. We had our Quarterly Meeting at London; at which I was surprised to find, that our income does not yet answer our expense. We were again near two hundred pounds bad. My private account I find still worse. I have laboured as much as many writers; and all my labour has gained me, in seventy years, a debt of five or six hundred pounds . . .

Tuesday, August 3. Our Conference began. I preached mornings as well as evenings; and it was all one. I found myself just as strong as if I had preached but once a day.

Sun. 8. At night I set out in the machine, and on *Monday* reached Bristol. In the way I looked over Mr. ———'s Dissertations. I was surprised to find him a thorough convert of Mr. Stonehouse's, both as to the pre-existence of souls, and the non-eternity of hell. But he is far more merciful than Mr. Stonehouse. He allows it to last (not five millions, but) only thirty thousand years!

It would be excusable, if these menders of the Bible would offer their hypotheses modestly. But one cannot excuse them when they not only obtrude their novel scheme with the utmost confidence, but even ridicule that scriptural one which always was, and is now, held by men of the greatest learning and piety in the world. Hereby they promote the cause of infidelity more effectually than either Hume or Voltaire.

Thur. 12. I set out for Cornwall; and the next day we came to Collumpton. For five or six days, I think, the weather has been as hot as it is in Georgia. After preaching, I went on to Exeter with Ralph Mather, then an humble, scriptural Christian. *Saturday, 14.* I went on to Plymouth-Dock, and in the evening preached in the Square. *Sunday, 15.* As I could not sleep (an uncommon thing with me) till near two in the morning, my companion was afraid I should not be able to go through the labour of the day; but I knew I did not go a warfare at my own cost. At seven I preached in Mr. Kinsman's preaching-house, on, 'Strive to enter in at the strait gate'; and I think many received the truth in the love thereof. Between one and two I preached in the Tabernacle at Plymouth; and in the evening declared in the Square, to a multitude of people, the nature of that love, without which all we say, know, believe, do, and suffer, profits nothing.

Mon. 16. In the evening I preached at St. Austle; *Tuesday, 17,* in the Coinage-Hall at Truro; at six, in the main street at Helstone. How changed is this town, since a Methodist Preacher could not ride through it without hazard of his life!

Wed. 18. I preached in the Town-Hall in Penzance. It was soon filled from end to end; and it was filled with the power of God. One would have thought every soul must have bowed down before Him. In the evening I preached at St. Just; *Friday, 20,* in Penzance and Marazion; and in the evening in the market-place at St. Ives, to the largest congregation I have yet seen in Cornwall.

Sat. 21. I preached in Illogan and at Redruth; *Sunday, 22,* in St. Agnes Church-town, at eight; about one at Redruth; and at five, in the amphitheatre at Gwennap. The people both filled it, and covered the ground round about, to a considerable distance. So that, supposing the space to be four-score yards square, and to contain five persons in a square yard, there must be above two-and-thirty thousand people; the largest assembly I ever preached to. Yet I found, upon inquiry, all could hear, even to the skirts of the congregation! Perhaps the first time that a man of seventy had been heard by thirty thousand persons at once! ...

Wednesday, October 6. Taking chaise at two in the morning, in the evening I came well to London. The rest of the week I made what inquiry I could into the state of my accounts. Some confusion had arisen from the sudden death of my book-keeper; but it was less than might have been expected.

Monday, 11, and the following days, I took a little tour through Bedfordshire and Northamptonshire. Between Northampton and Towcester we met with a great natural curiosity, the largest elm I ever saw; it was twenty-eight feet in circumference; six feet more than that which was some years ago in Magdalen-College walks at Oxford.

Friday, December 17. Meeting with a celebrated book, a volume of Captain Cook's Voyages, I sat down to read it with huge expectation. But how was I disappointed! I observed, 1. Things absolutely incredible: 'A nation without any curiosity'; and, what is stranger still (I fear related with no good design), 'without any sense of shame! Men and women coupling together in the face of the sun, and in the sight of scores of people! Men whose skin, cheeks, and lips are white as milk.' Hume or Voltaire might believe this; but I cannot. I observed, 2. Things absolutely impossible. To instance in one, for a specimen. A native of Otaheite is said to understand the language of an island eleven hundred degrees [? miles] distant from it in latitude; besides I know not how many hundreds in longitude! So that I cannot but rank this narrative with that of Robinson Crusoe; and account Tupia to be, in several respects, akin to his man Friday.

Saturday, 25, and on the following days, we had many happy opportunities of celebrating the solemn Feast-days, according to the design of their institution. We concluded the year with a Fast-day, closed with a solemn watch-night.

Tuesday, January 4, 1774. Three or four years ago, a stumbling horse threw me forward on the pommel of the saddle. I felt a good deal of pain; but it soon went off, and I thought of it no more. Some months after I observed, *testiculum alterum altero duplo majorem esse.* I consulted a Physician: He told me it was a common case, and did not imply any disease at all. In May twelvemonth it was grown near as large as a hen's egg. Being then at Edinburgh, Dr. Hamilton insisted on my having the advice of Drs. Gregory and Munro. They immediately saw it was a Hydrocele, and advised me, as soon as I came to London, to aim at a radical cure, which they judged might be effected in about sixteen days: When I came to London, I consulted Mr. Wathen. He advised me, 1. Not to think of a radical cure, which could not be hoped for, without my lying in one posture fifteen or sixteen days. And he did not know whether this might not give a wound to my constitution, which I should never recover. 2. To do nothing while I continued easy. And this advice I was determined to take.

Last month the swelling was often painful. So on this day, Mr. Wathen performed the operation, and drew off something more than half a pint of a thin, yellow, transparent water. With this came out (to his no small surprise) a pearl of the size of a small shot; which he supposed might be one cause of the disorder, by occasioning a conflux of humours to the part. *Wednesday, 5.* I was as perfectly easy, as if no operation had been performed.

Tues. 11. I began at the east end of the town to visit the society from house to house. I know no branch of the pastoral office, which is of greater importance than this. But it is so grievous to flesh and blood, that I can prevail on few, even of our Preachers, to undertake it.

Sun. 23. Mr. Pentycross assisted me at the chapel. O what a curse upon the poor sons of men is the confusion of opinions! Worse by many degrees than the curse of Babel, the confusion of tongues. What but this could prevent this amiable young man from joining heart and hand with us?

Mon. 24. I was desired by Mrs. Wright, of New-York, to let her take my effigy in wax-work. She has that of Mr. Whitefield and many others; but none of them, I think, comes up to a well-drawn picture . . .

Tuesday, May 17, I preached on the Green at Glasgow once more, although the north wind was piercing cold. At five in the morning I commended our friends to God.

How is it that there is no increase in this society? It is exceeding easy to answer. One Preacher stays here two or three months at a time, preaching on Sunday mornings, and three or four evenings in a week. Can a Methodist preacher preserve either bodily health, or spiritual life, with this exercise? And if he is but half alive, what will the people be? Just so it is at Greenock too.

Wed. 18. I went to Edinburgh, and on *Thursday* to Perth. Here likewise the morning preaching had been given up: Consequently the people were few, dead, and cold. These things must be remedied, or we must quit the ground.

In the way to Perth, I read that ingenious tract, Dr. Gregory's 'Advice to his Daughters'. Although I cannot agree with him in all things (particularly as to dancing, decent pride, and both a reserve and a delicacy which I think are quite unnatural); yet I allow there are many fine strokes therein, and abundance of common sense: And if a young woman followed this plan in little things, in such things as daily occur, and in great things copied after Miranda, she would form an accomplished character.

Fri. 20. I rode over to Mr. Fraser's, at Monedie, whose mother-in-law was to be buried that day. O what a difference is there between the English and the Scotch method of burial! The English does honour to human nature; and even to the poor remains, that were once a temple of the Holy Ghost! But when I see in Scotland a coffin put into the earth, and covered up without a word spoken, it reminds me of what was spoken concerning Jehoiakim, 'He shall be buried with the burial of an ass!' . . .

Mon. 23 . . . In the evening I preached at Dundee, and on *Tuesday, 24,* went on to Arbroath. In the way I read Lord K[ame]'s plausible 'Essays on Morality and Natural Religion'. Did ever man take so much pains to so little purpose, as he does in his Essay on Liberty and Necessity? *Cui bono?* What good would it do to mankind, if he could convince them that they are a mere piece of clock-work? that they have no more share in directing their own actions, than in directing the sea or the north wind? He owns, that 'if men saw themselves in this light, all sense of moral obligation, of right and wrong, of good or ill desert, would immediately cease'. Well, my Lord sees himself in this light; consequently, if his own doctrine is true, he has no 'sense of moral obligation, of right and wrong, of good or ill desert'. Is he not then excellently well-qualified for a Judge? Will he condemn a man for not 'holding the wind in his fist'? . . .[48]

Saturday, June 11, set out for the Dales. About noon I preached at Wolsingham, and in the evening near the preaching-house in Weardale.

Sun. 12. The rain drove us into the House, both morning and afternoon. Afterwards I met the poor remains of the select society; but neither of my two lovely children, neither Peggy Spence nor Sally Blackburn, were there. Indeed a whole row of such I had seen before; but three in four of them were now as careless as ever. In the evening I sent for Peggy Spence and Sally Blackburn. Peggy came, and I found she had well nigh regained her ground, walking in the light, and having a lively hope of recovering all that she had lost. Sally flatly refused to come, and then ran out of doors. Being found at length, after a flood of tears, she was brought almost by force. But I could not get one look, and hardly a word, from her. She seemed to have no hope left: Yet she is not out of God's reach.

I now inquired into the causes of the grievous decay in the vast work of God, which was here two years since; and I found several causes had concurred: 1. Not one of the Preachers that succeeded was capable of being a nursing-father to the new-born children: 2. Jane Salkeld, one great instrument of the work, marrying, was debarred from meeting the young ones; and there being none left who so naturally cared for them, they fell heaps upon heaps: 3. Most of the liveliest in the society were the single men and women; and several of these in a little time contracted an inordinate affection for each other; whereby they so grieved the Holy Spirit of God, that he in great measure departed from them: 4. Men arose among ourselves, who undervalued the work of God, and called the great work of sanctification a delusion. By this they grieved some, and angered others; so that both the one and the other were much weakened: 5. Hence, the love of many waxing cold, the Preachers were discouraged; and jealousies, heart-burnings, evil-surmisings, were multiplied more and more. There is now a little revival: God grant it may increase! ...

Mon. 20. About nine I set out for Horsley, with Mr. Hopper and Mr. Smith, I took Mrs. Smith and her two little girls, in the chaise with me. About two miles from the town just on the brow of the hill, on a sudden both the horses set out, without any visible cause, and flew down the hill, like an arrow out of a bow. In a minute John fell off the coach-box. The horses then went on full speed, sometimes to the edge of the ditch on the right, sometimes on the left. A cart came up against them: They avoided it as exactly as if the man had been on the box. A narrow bridge was at the foot of the hill. They went directly over the middle of it. They ran up the next hill with the same speed; many persons meeting us, but getting out of the way. Near the top of the hill was a gate, which led into a farmer's yard. It stood open. They turned short, and run through it, without touching the gate on one side, or the post on the other. I thought, 'However, the gate which is on the other side of the yard, and is shut, will stop them': But they rushed through it as if it had been a cobweb, and galloped on through the corn-field. The little girls cried out, 'Grandpapa, save us!' I told them, 'Nothing will hurt you: Do not be afraid'; feeling no more fear or care, (blessed be God!) than if I had been sitting in my study. The horses ran on, till they came to the edge of a steep precipice. Just then Mr. Smith, who could not overtake us before, galloped in between. They stopped in a moment. Had they gone on ever so little, he and we must have gone down together!

I am persuaded both evil and good angels had a large share in this transaction: How large we do not know now; but we shall know hereafter.

I think some of the most remarkable circumstances were, 1. Both the horses, which were tame and quiet as could be, starting out in a moment just at the top of the hill, and running down full speed. 2. The coachman's being thrown on his head with such violence, and yet not hurt at all. 3. The chaise running again and again to the edge of each ditch, and yet not into it. 4. The avoiding the cart. 5. The keeping just the middle of the bridge. 6. The turning short through the first gate, in a manner that no coachman in England could have turned them, when in full gallop. 7. The going through the second gate as if it had been but smoke, without slackening their pace at all. This would have been impossible, had not the end of the chariot-pole struck exactly on the centre of the gate; whence the whole, by the sudden impetuous shock, was broke into small pieces. 8. That the little girl, who used to have fits, on my saying, 'Nothing will hurt you,' ceased crying, and was quite composed. Lastly, That Mr. Smith struck in just then: In a minute more we had been down the precipice; and had not the horses then stopped at once, they must have carried him and us down together. 'Let those give thanks whom the Lord hath redeemed, and delivered from the hand of the enemy!'

Fri 24. I read over Dr. Wilson's tract on the Circulation of the Blood. What are we sure of but the Bible? I thought nothing had been more sure, than that the heart is the grand moving power, which both begins and continues the circulation. But I think the Doctor has clearly proved, that it does not begin at the heart; and that the heart has quite another office, only *receiving* the blood, which then moves on through its channels, on the mere principle of suction, assisted by the ethereal fire, which is connected with every particle of it.

Sun. 26. In the morning I preached at the Ballast-Hills, among the glassmen, keelmen, and sailors. As these had nothing to pay, I exhorted them 'to buy wine and milk without money and without price'.

Mon. 27. I took my leave of this lovely place and people, and about ten preached to a serious congregation at Durham. About six I preached at Stockton-upon-Tees, on a text suited to the congregation, 'Where their worm dieth not, and the fire is not quenched.'

Tues. 28. This being my birth-day, the first day of my seventy-second year, I was considering, How is this, that I find just the same strength as I did thirty years ago? That my sight is considerably better now, and my nerves firmer, than they were then? That I have none of the infirmities of old age, and have lost several I had in my youth? The grand cause is, the good pleasure of God, who doeth whatsoever pleaseth Him. The chief means are, 1. My constantly rising at four, for about fifty years. 2. My generally preaching at five in the morning; one of the most healthy exercises in the world. 3. My never travelling less, by sea or land, than four thousand five hundred miles in a year . . .

At ten, on *Wednesday, July 20*, I preached at Wimberton. None of the hearers was more attentive than an old acquaintance of my father's—Mr. George Stovin, formerly a Justice of the peace near Epworth, now as teachable as a little child, and determined to know nothing save Christ crucified. About two I preached in an open place at Scotter, and in the evening at Owston. One of my audience here was Mr. Pinder, a contemporary of mine at Oxford. But any that observed so feeble, decrepit an old man, tottering over the grave, would imagine there was a difference of *forty*, rather than *two*, years between us! . . .

Thursday, August 25. At eleven I preached within the walls of the old church at the Hay. Here and everywhere I heard the same account of the proceedings at [Llancroyes]. The Jumpers[49] (all who were there informed me) were first in the court, and afterwards in the house. Some of them leaped up many times, men and women, several feet from the ground: They clapped their hands with the utmost violence; they shook their heads; they distorted all their features; they threw their arms and legs to and fro, in all variety of postures; they sung, roared, shouted, screamed with all their might, to the no small terror of those that were near them. One gentlewoman told me, she had not been herself since, and she did not know when she should. Meantime the person of the house was delighted above measure, and said, 'Now the power of God is come indeed.' . . .

Thursday, October 6 [Bristol]. I met those of our society who had votes in the ensuing election, and advised them, 1. To vote, without fee or reward, for the person they judged most worthy: 2. To speak no evil of the person they voted against: And, 3. To take care their spirits were not sharpened against those that voted on the other side . . .

Monday, 31, and the following days, I visited the societies near London. *Friday, November 4*. In the afternoon John Downes (who had preached with us many years) was saying 'I feel such a love to the people at West-Street, that I could be content to die with them.

I do not find myself very well; but I must be with them this evening.' He went thither, and began preaching, on, 'Come unto me, ye that are weary and heavy-laden.' After speaking ten or twelve minutes, he sunk down, and spake no more, till his spirit returned to God.

I suppose he was by nature full as great a genius as Sir Isaac Newton. I will mention but two or three instances of it: When he was at school, learning Algebra, he came one day to his master, and said, 'Sir, I can prove this proposition a better way than it is proved in the book.' His master thought it could not be; but upon trial, acknowledged it to be so. Some time after, his father sent him to Newcastle with a clock, which was to be mended. He observed the clockmaker's tools, and the manner how he took it in pieces, and put it together again; and when he came home, first made himself tools, and then made a clock, which went as true as any in the town. I suppose such strength of genius as this, has scarce been known in Europe before.

Another proof of it was this: Thirty years ago, while I was shaving, he was whittling the top of a stick: I asked, 'What are you doing?' He answered, 'I am taking your face, which I intend to engrave on a copper-plate.' Accordingly, without any instruction, he first made himself tools, and then engraved the plate. The second picture which he engraved, was that which was prefixed to the 'Notes upon the New Testament'. Such another instance, I suppose, not all England, or perhaps Europe, can produce.

For several months past, he had far deeper communion with God, than ever he had in his life; and for some days he had been frequently saying, 'I am so happy, that I scarce know how to live. I enjoy such fellowship with God, as I thought could not be had on this side heaven.' And having now finished his course of fifty-two years, after a long conflict with pain, sickness, and poverty, he gloriously rested from his labours, and entered into the joy of his Lord.

Tues. 8. I baptized two young women; one of whom found a deep sense of the presence of God in his ordinance; the other received a full assurance of his pardoning love, and was filled with joy unspeakable.

Sun. 13. After a day of much labour, at my usual time, (half-hour past nine), I lay down to rest. I told my servants, 'I must rise at three, the Norwich coach setting out at four.' Hearing one of them knock, though sooner than I expected, I rose and dressed myself; but afterwards, looking at my watch, I found it was but half-hour past ten. While I was considering what to do, I heard a confused sound of many voices below; and looking out at the window towards the yard, I saw it was light as day. Meantime, many large flakes of fire were continually flying about the house; all the upper part of which was built of wood, which was near as dry as tinder. A large deal-yard, at a very small distance from us, was all in a light fire; from which the north-west wind drove the flames directly upon the Foundery; and there was no probability of help, for no water could be found. Perceiving I could be of no use, I took my Diary and my papers, and retired to a friend's house. I had no fear; committing the matter into God's hands, and knowing He would do whatever was best. Immediately the wind turned about from north-west to south-east; and our pump supplied the engines with abundance of water; so that in a little more than two hours, all the danger was over . . .

Thur. 17. About noon I preached at Lowestoft, where the little flock are remarkably lively. The evening congregation at Yarmouth was all attention; and truly the power of God was present to heal them.

In the evening I returned to Norwich. Never was a poor society so neglected as this has been for the year past. The morning preaching was at an end; the bands suffered all to fall in pieces; and no care at all taken of the classes, so that whether they met or not, it was all one; going to church and sacrament were forgotten; and the people rambled hither and thither as they listed.

On *Friday* evening I met the society, and told them plain, I was resolved to have a regular society or none. I then read the Rules, and desired every one to consider whether he was willing to walk by these Rules or no. Those in particular, of meeting their class every week, unless hindered by distance or sickness (the only reasons for not meeting which I could allow), and being constant at church and sacrament. I desired those who were so minded to meet me the next night, and the rest to stay away. The next night we had far the greater part; on whom I strongly enforced the same thing. *Sunday, 20.* I spoke to every Leader, concerning every one under his care; and put out every person whom they could not recommend to me. After this was done, out of two hundred and four members, one hundred and seventy-four remained. And these points shall be carried, if only fifty remain in the society . . .

Wednesday, February 22, 1775. I had an opportunity of seeing Mr. Gordon's curious garden at Mile-end, the like of which I suppose is hardly to be found in England, if in Europe. One thing in particular I learned here, the real nature of the tea-tree. I was informed, 1. That the Green and the Bohea are of quite different species. 2. That the Bohea is much tenderer than the Green. 3. That the Green is an evergreen; and bears, not only in the open air, but in the frost, perfectly well. 4. That the herb of Paraguay likewise bears the frost, and is a species of tea. 5. And I observed that they are all species of bay or laurel. The leaf of Green tea is both of the colour, shape, and size of a bay leaf: That of Bohea is smaller, softer, and of a darker colour. So is the herb of Paraguay, which is of a dirty green; and no larger than our common red sage . . .

[Wesley began a four-month visit to Ireland on 2 April.]

Tuesday, June 13. I was not very well in the morning, but supposed it would soon go off. In the afternoon, the weather being extremely hot, I lay down on the grass, in Mr. Lark's orchard, at Cock-Hill. This I had been accustomed to do for forty years, and never remember to have been hurt by it: Only I never before lay on my face; in which posture I fell asleep. I waked a little, and but a little, out of order, and preached with ease to a multitude of people. Afterwards I was a good deal worse. However, the next day I went on a few miles to the Grange. The table was placed here in such a manner, that, all the time I was preaching, a strong and sharp wind blew full on the left side of my head; and it was not without a good deal of difficulty that I made an end of my sermon. I now found a deep obstruction in my breast: My pulse was exceeding weak and low; I shivered with cold, though the air was sultry hot; only now and then burning for a few minutes. I went early to bed, drank a draught of treacle-and-water, and applied treacle to the soles of my feet. I lay till seven on *Thursday, 15*, and then felt considerably better. But I found near the same obstruction in my breast: I had a low, weak pulse; I burned and shivered by turns; and, if I ventured to cough, it jarred my head exceedingly. In going on to Derry-Anvil, I wondered what was the matter, that I could not attend to what I was reading; no, not for three minutes together; but my thoughts were perpetually shifting. Yet, all the time I was preaching in the evening (although I stood in the open air, with the wind whistling round my head), my mind was as composed as ever. *Friday, 16*. In going to Lurgan, I was again surprised that I could not fix my attention on what I read: Yet, while I was preaching in the evening, on the Parade, I found my mind perfectly composed; although it rained a great part of the time, which did not well agree with my head. *Saturday, 17*. I was persuaded to send for Dr. Laws, a sensible and skilful Physician. He told me I was in a high fever, and advised me to lay by. But I told him that could not be done; as I had appointed to preach at several places, and must preach as long as I could speak. He then prescribed a cooling draught, with a grain or two of camphor, as my nerves were universally agitated. This I took with me to Tanderagee: But when I came there, I was not able to preach; my understanding being quite confused, and my strength entirely gone. Yet I breathed freely, and had not the least thirst, nor any pain, from head to foot.

I was now at a full stand, whether to aim at Lisburn, or to push forward for Dublin. But my friends doubting whether I could bear so long a journey, I went straight to Derry-Aghy; a gentleman's seat, on the side of a hill, three miles beyond Lisburn. Here nature sunk, and I took my bed. But I could no more turn myself therein, than a new-born child. My memory failed, as well as my strength, and well nigh my understanding. Only those words ran in my mind, when I saw Miss Gayer on one side of the bed, looking at her mother on the other:

> She sat, like Patience on a monument,
> Smiling at grief.

But still I had no thirst, no difficulty of breathing, no pain, from head to foot.

I can give no account of what followed for two or three days, being more dead than alive. Only I remember it was difficult for me to speak, my throat being exceeding dry. But Joseph Bradford tells me I said on *Wednesday*, 'It will be determined before this time to-morrow'; that my tongue was much swollen, and as black as a coal; that I was convulsed all over; and that for some time my heart did not beat perceptibly, neither was any pulse discernible.

In the night of *Thursday, 22,* Joseph Bradford came to me with a cup, and said, 'Sir, you must take this.' I thought, 'I will, if I can swallow, to please him; for it will do me neither harm nor good.' Immediately it set me a vomiting; my heart began to beat and my pulse to play again; and from that hour the extremity of the symptoms abated. The next day I sat up several hours, and walked four or five times across the room. On *Saturday*, I sat up all day, and walked across the room many times, without any weariness; on *Sunday*, I came down stairs, and sat several hours in the parlour; on *Monday*, I walked out before the house; on *Tuesday*, I took an airing in the chaise; and on *Wednesday*, trusting in God, to the astonishment of my friends, I set out for Dublin.

I did not determine how far to go that day, not knowing how my strength would hold. But finding myself no worse at Bann-bridge, I ventured to Newry; and, after travelling thirty (English) miles, I was stronger than in the morning.

Thur. 29. I went on to the Man-of-war, forty (Irish) miles from the Globe, at Newry. *Friday, 30.* We met Mr. Simpson (with several other friends), coming to meet us at Drogheda; who took us to his country seat at James-Town, about two miles from Dublin.

Tuesday, July 4. Finding myself a little stronger, I preached for the first time; and I believe most could hear. I preached on *Thursday* again; and my voice was clear, though weak. So on *Sunday* I ventured to preach twice, and found no weariness at all. *Monday, 10.* I began my regular course of preaching, morning and evening.

While I was in Dublin, I read two extraordinary books, but of very different kinds—Mr. Sheridan's 'Lectures on Elocution', and 'The Life of Count Marsay'; and was disappointed in both. There is more matter in the penny tract, 'On Action and Utterance', abundantly more, than in all Mr. S.'s book; though he seems to think himself a mere Phenix. Count Marsay was doubtless a pious man, but a thorough enthusiast; guided, in all his steps, not by the written word, but by his own imagination; which he calls the Spirit.

Sun. 23. I again assisted at St. Patrick's in delivering the elements of the Lord's Supper. In the evening I embarked in the Nonpareil; and, about ten on *Tuesday* morning, landed at Park-Gate. *Wednesday, 26.* I found one relic of my illness,—my hand shook, so that I could hardly write my name. But after I had been well electrified, by driving four or five hours, over very rugged, broken pavement, my complaint was removed, and my hand was as steady as when I was ten years old ...

Thursday, October 12. About noon I preached at Watlington; and in the evening at Oxford, in a large House formerly belonging to the Presbyterians. But it was not large enough: Many could not get in. Such a congregation I have not seen at Oxford, either for seriousness, or number, for more than twenty years.

I borrowed here a volume of Lord Chesterfield's Letters, which I had heard very strongly commended. And what did I learn?— That he was a man of much wit, middling sense, and some learning; but as absolutely void of virtue, as any Jew, Turk, or Heathen that ever lived. I say, not only void of all religion (for I doubt whether he believed there is a God, though he tags most of his letters with the name, for better sound sake), but even of virtue, of justice, and mercy, which he never once recommended to his son. And truth he sets at open defiance: He continually guards him against it. Half his letters inculcate deep dissimulation, as the most necessary of all accomplishments. Add to this, his studiously instilling into the young man all the principles of debauchery, when himself was between seventy and eighty years old. Add his cruel censure of that amiable man, the Archbishop of Cambray (*quantum dispar illi*) [what a vast disparity between the two], as a mere time-serving hypocrite! And this is the favourite of the age! Whereas, if justice and truth take place, if he is rewarded according to his desert, his name will stink to all generations ...

Friday, 27. I preached about noon at Hanslop. In my way I looked over a volume of Dr. Swift's Letters. I was amazed! Was ever such trash palmed upon the world, under the name of a great man? More than half of what is contained in those sixteen volumes, would be dear at twopence a volume; being all, and more than all, the dull things which that witty man ever said ...

Wednesday, November 29. About this time I published the following letter in Lloyd's 'Evening Post':

'SIR,

'I HAVE been seriously asked, "From what motive did you publish your *Calm Address to the American Colonies?*"[50]

'I seriously answer, Not to get money. Had that been my motive, I should have swelled it into a shilling pamphlet, and have entered it at Stationers' Hall.

'Not to get preferment for myself, or my brother's children. I am a little too old to gape after it for myself: And if my brother or I sought it for them, we have only to show them to the world.

'Not to please any man living, high or low. I know mankind too well. I know they that love you for political service, love you less than their dinner; and they that hate you, hate you worse than the devil.

'Least of all did I write with a view to inflame any: Just the contrary. I contributed my mite toward putting out the flame which rages all over the land. This I have more opportunity of observing than any other man in England. I see with pain to what an height this already rises, in every part of the nation. And I see many pouring oil into the flame, by crying out, "How unjustly, how cruelly, the King is using the poor Americans; who are only contending for their liberty, and for their legal privileges!"

'Now there is no possible way to put out this flame, or hinder its rising higher and higher, but to show that the Americans are not used either cruelly or unjustly; that they are not injured at all, seeing they are not contending for liberty (this they had, even in its full extent, both civil and religious); neither for any legal privileges; for they enjoy all that their charters grant. But what they contend for, is, the illegal privilege of being exempt from parliamentary taxation. A privilege this, which no charter ever gave to any American colony yet; which no charter can give, unless it be confirmed both by King, Lords, and Commons; which, in fact, our colonies never had; which they never claimed till the present reign: And probably they would not have claimed it now, had they not been incited thereto by letters from England. One of these was read, according to the desire of the writer, not only at the continental Congress, but likewise in many congregations throughout the Combined Provinces. It advised them to seize upon all the King's Officers; and exhorted them, "Stand valiantly, only for six months, and in that time there will be such commotions in England that you may have your own terms."

'This being the real state of the question, without any colouring or aggravation, what impartial man can either blame the King, or commend the Americans?

'With this view, to quench the fire, by laying the blame where it was due, the "Calm Address" was written. I am, Sir,

'Your humble servant,

'JOHN WESLEY.

'As to reviewers, newswriters, London Magazines, and all that kind of gentlemen, they behave just as I expected they would. And let them lick up Mr. Toplady's spittle still: A champion worthy of their cause.' . . .[51]

Saturday, December 9. In answer to a very angry letter, lately published in 'the Gazetteer', I published the following:

'TO THE REV. MR. CALEB EVANS.

'REV. SIR,

'YOU affirm, 1. That I once "doubted whether the measures taken with respect to America could be defended either on the foot of law, equity, or prudence". I did doubt of these five years, nay indeed five months, ago.

'You affirm, 2. That I "declared", (last year), "the Americans were an oppressed, injured people". I do not remember that I did; but very possibly I might.

'You affirm, 3. That I then "strongly recommended an argument for the exclusive right of the colonies to tax themselves". I believe I did; but I am now of another mind.

'You affirm, 4. "You say in the Preface, *I never saw that book.*" I did say so. The plain case was, I had so entirely forgotten it, that even when I saw it again, I recollected nothing of it, till I had read several pages. If I had, I might have observed that you borrowed more from Mr. P. than I did from Dr. Johnson. Though I know not whether I should have observed it, as it does not affect the merits of the cause.

'You affirm, 5. "You say, *But I really believe he was told so*"; and add, "Supposing what I asserted was false, it is not easy to conceive what reason you could have for believing I was told so." My reason was, I believed you feared God, and therefore would not tell a wilful untruth; so I made the best excuse for you which I thought the nature of the thing would admit of. Had you not some reasons to believe this of me; and therefore to say (at least), "I hope he forgot it?"

' "But at this time I was perfectly unknown to you." No, at this time I knew you wrote that tract; but had I not, charity would have induced me to hope this, even of an entire stranger.

'You now have my "feeble reply"; and if you please to advance any new argument (personal reflections I let go), you may perhaps receive a farther reply from

> 'Your humble servant,
> 'JOHN WESLEY ...

Tuesday, January 2, 1776. Being pressed to pay a visit to our brethren at Bristol, some of whom had been a little unsettled by the patriots, so called, I set out early; but the roads were so heavy, that I could not get thither till night. I came just time enough, not to see, but to bury, poor Mr. Hall, my brother-in-law, who died on Wednesday morning; I trust, in peace; for God had given him deep repentance. Such another monument of divine mercy, considering how low he had fallen, and from what height of holiness, I have not seen, no, not in seventy years! I had designed to visit him in the morning; but he did not stay for my coming. It is enough, if, after all his wanderings, we meet again in Abraham's bosom.

Wednesday, May 1. I set out early, and the next afternoon reached Whitehaven; and my chaise-horses were no worse for travelling near a hundred and ten miles in two days.

In travelling through Berkshire, Oxfordshire, Bristol, Gloucestershire, Worcestershire, Warwickshire, Staffordshire, Cheshire, Lancashire, Yorkshire, Westmoreland, and Cumberland, I diligently made two inquiries: The first was, concerning the increase or decrease of the people; the second, concerning the increase or decrease of trade. As to the latter, it is, within these two last years, amazingly increased; in several branches in such a manner as has not been known in the memory of man: Such is the fruit of the entire civil and religious liberty which all England now enjoys! And as to the former, not only in every city and large town, but in every village and hamlet, there is no decrease, but a very large and swift increase. One sign of this is the swarms of little children which we see in every place. Which, then, shall we most admire, the ignorance or confidence of those that affirm, population decreases in England? I doubt not but it increases full as fast here, as in any province of North America.

Mon. 6. After preaching at Cockermouth and Wigton, I went on to Carlisle, and preached to a very serious congregation. Here I saw a very extraordinary genius, a man blind from four years of age, who could wind worsted, weave flowered plush on an engine and loom of his own making; who wove his own name in plush, and made his own clothes, and his own tools of every sort. Some years ago, being shut up in the organ-loft at church, he felt every part of it, and afterwards made an organ for himself, which, judges say, is an exceeding good one. He then taught himself to play upon it psalm-tunes, anthems, voluntaries, or anything which he heard. I heard him play several tunes with great accuracy, and a complex voluntary: I suppose all Europe can hardly produce such another instance. His name is Joseph Strong. But what is he the better for all this, if he is still 'without God in the world?'

Tues. 7. I went on to Selkirk. The family came to prayer in the evening, after which the mistress of it said, 'Sir, my daughter Jenny would be very fond of having a little talk with you. She is a strange lass; she will not come down on the Lord's day but to public worship, and spends all the rest of the day in her own chamber.' I desired she would come up; and found one that earnestly longed to be altogether a Christian. I satisfied her mother that she was not mad; and spent a little time in advice, exhortation, and prayer . . . *Saturday, 18.* I read over Dr. Johnson's 'Tour to the Western Isles'. It is a very curious book, wrote with admirable sense, and, I think, great fidelity; although, in some respects, he is thought to bear hard on the nation, which I am satisfied he never intended . . .

Mon. 20. I preached about eleven at Old Meldrum, but could not reach Banff till near seven in the evening. I went directly to the Parade, and proclaimed, to a listening multitude, 'the grace of our Lord Jesus Christ'. All behaved well but a few Gentry, whom I rebuked openly; and they stood corrected.

After preaching, Mrs. Gordon, the Admiral's widow, invited me to supper. There I found five or six as agreeable women as I have seen in the kingdom; and I know not when I have spent two or three hours with greater satisfaction. In the morning I was going to preach in the assembly-room, when the Episcopal Minister sent and offered me the use of his chapel. It was quickly filled. After reading prayers, I preached on those words in the Second Lesson, 'What lack I yet?' and strongly applied them to those in particular who supposed themselves to be 'rich and increased in goods, and lacked nothing'. I then set out for Keith.

Banff is one of the neatest and most elegant towns that I have seen in Scotland. It is pleasantly situated on the side of a hill, sloping from the sea, though close to it; so that it is sufficiently sheltered from the sharpest winds. The streets are straight and broad. I believe it may be esteemed the fifth, if not the fourth, town in the kingdom. The county quite from Banff to Keith is the best peopled of any I have seen in Scotland. This is chiefly, if not entirely, owing to the late Earl of Findlater. He was indefatigable in doing good, took pains to procure industrious men from all parts, and to provide such little settlements for them as enabled them to live with comfort.

About noon I preached at the New-Mills, nine miles from Banff, to a large congregation of plain, simple people. As we rode in the afternoon the heat overcame me, so that I was weary and faint before we came to Keith; but I no sooner stood up in the market-place than I forgot my weariness; such were the seriousness and attention of the whole congregation, though as numerous as that at Banff. Mr. Gordon, the Minister of the parish, invited me to supper, and told me his kirk was at my service. A little society is formed here already; and is in a fair way of increasing. But they were just now in danger of losing their preaching-house, the owner being determined to sell it. I saw but one way to secure it for them, which was to buy it myself. So (who would have thought it?) I bought an estate, consisting of two houses, a yard, a garden, with three acres of good land. But he told me flat, 'Sir, I will take no less for it than sixteen pounds ten shillings, to be paid, part now, part at Michaelmas, and the residue next May.'

Here Mr. Gordon showed me a great curiosity. Near the top of the opposite hill, a new town is built, containing, I suppose, a hundred houses, which is *a town of beggars*. This, he informed me, was the professed, regular occupation of *all* the inhabitants. Early in spring they all go out, and spread themselves over the kingdom; and in autumn they return, and do what is requisite for their wives and children . . .

Mon. 27. I paid a visit to St. Andrew's, once the largest city in the kingdom. It was eight times as large as it is now, and a place of very great trade: But the sea rushing from the north-east, gradually destroyed the harbour and trade together: In consequence of which, whole streets (that were) are now meadows and gardens. Three broad, straight, handsome streets remain, all pointing at the old cathedral; which, by the ruins, appears to have been above three hundred feet long, and proportionably broad and high: So that it seems to have exceeded York Minster, and to have at least equalled any cathedral in England. Another church, afterwards used in its stead, bears date 1124. A steeple, standing near the cathedral, is thought to have stood thirteen hundred years.

What is left of St. Leonard's College is only a heap of ruins. Two Colleges remain. One of them has a tolerable Square; but all the windows are broke, like those of a brothel. We were informed, the students do this before they leave the College. Where are their blessed Governors in the mean time? Are they all fast asleep? The other College is a mean building, but has a handsome library newly erected. In the two Colleges, we learned, were about seventy students; near the same number as at Old-Aberdeen. Those at New-Aberdeen are not more numerous: Neither those at Glasgow. In Edinburgh, I suppose there are a hundred. So four Universities contain three hundred and ten students! These all come to their several Colleges in November, and return home in May! So they *may* study five months in the year, and lounge all the rest! O where was the common sense of those who instituted such Colleges? In the English Colleges, every one *may* reside all the year, as all my pupils did: And I should have thought myself little better than a highwayman, if I had not lectured them every day in the year, but Sundays ...

Saturday, August 17 [Cornwall]. We found Mr. Hoskins, at Cubert, alive; but just tottering over the grave. I preached in the evening, on 2 Cor. v. 1–4, probably the last sermon he will hear from me. I was afterwards inquiring, if that scandal of Cornwall, the plundering of wrecked vessels, still subsisted. He said, 'As much as ever; only the Methodists will have nothing to do with it. But three months since a vessel was wrecked on the south coast, and the tinners presently seized on all the goods; and even broke in pieces a new coach which was on board, and carried every scrap of it away.' But is there no way to prevent this shameful breach of all the laws both of religion and humanity? Indeed there is. The Gentry of Cornwall may totally prevent it whenever they please. Let them only see that the laws be strictly executed upon the next plunderers; and after an example is made of ten of these, the next wreck will be unmolested. Nay, there is a milder way. Let them only agree together, to discharge any tinner or labourer that is concerned in the plundering of a wreck, and advertise his name, that no Cornish gentleman my employ him any more; and neither tinner nor labourer will any more be concerned in that bad work ...

Saturday, September 7. Went on to Bristol.

Mon. 9. I began, what I had long intended, visiting the society from house to house, setting apart at least two hours in a day for that purpose. I was surprised to find the simplicity with which one and all spoke, both of their temporal and spiritual state. Nor could I easily have known, by any other means, how great a work God has wrought among them. I found exceeding little to reprove; but much to praise God for. And I observed one thing which I did not expect: In visiting all the families, without Lawford-Gate, by far the poorest about the city, I did not find so much as one person who was out of work.

Another circumstance I critically inquired into, What is the real number of the people? Dr. Price says (doubtless to encourage our good friends, the French and Spaniards), 'The people of England are between four and five millions; supposing them to be four, or four and a half, on an average, in one house.'[52] I found, in the families which I visited, about six in a house. But one who has lately made a more general inquiry, informs me, there are, without Lawford-Gate, seven in a house. The same information I received from one who has lately made the inquiry, concerning the inhabitants of Redcliff. Now, if at four in a house, we are four millions, must we not, at seven in a house, be seven millions?

But even this is far short of the truth; for a plain reason, the houses are miscomputed. To give one instance: The houses without Lawford-Gate are computed to be a thousand. Now, at the sitting of the Justices, some years since, there were two hundred public-houses. Was then one house in five a public-house? No, surely; one in ten at the utmost. If so, there were two thousand houses; and, consequently, fourteen thousand persons. I believe, there are now full twenty thousand. And these are nothing near a quarter of the present inhabitants of Bristol.

Wed. 11. I preached about one at Bath; and about six, in a meadow, near the preaching-house, in Frome, besought a listening multitude 'not to receive the grace of God in vain'.

Thur. 12. I spent about two hours in Mr. Hoare's gardens, at Stourton. I have seen the most celebrated gardens in England; but these far exceed them all: 1. In the situation; being laid out on the sloping sides of a semicircular mountain: 2. In the vast basin of water inclosed between them, covering, I suppose, sixty acres of ground: 3. In the delightful interchange of shady groves and sunny glades, curiously mixed together. Above all, in the lovely grottoes, two of which excel everything of the kind which I ever saw; the fountain-grotto, made entirely of rock-work, admirably well imitating nature; and the castle-grotto, into which you enter unawares, beneath a heap of ruins. This is within totally built of roots of trees, wonderfully interwoven. On one side of it is a little hermitage, with a lamp, a chair, a table, and bones upon it.

Others were delighted with the temples, but I was not: 1. Because several of the statues about them were mean: 2. Because I cannot admire the images of devils; and we know the gods of the Heathens are but devils: 3. Because I defy all mankind to reconcile statues with nudities, either to common sense or common decency.

Returning from thence through Maiden-Bradley, we saw the

clumsy house of the Duke of Somerset; and afterwards the grand and elegant one of Lord Weymouth, beautifully situated in a lovely park ...[53]

Thursday, December 5. Returned to London.

In the way, I read over Mr. Gray's Works, and his Life wrote by Mr. Mason. He is an admirable poet, not much inferior to either Prior or Pope; but he does not appear, upon the whole, to have been an amiable man. His picture, I apprehend, expresses his character;—sharp, sensible, ingenious; but, at the same time, proud, morose, envious, passionate, and resentful. I was quite shocked at the contempt with which he more than once speaks of Mr. Mason; one full as ingenious as himself, yea, full as good a poet (as even 'Elfrida' shows, as much as Mr. Gray despises, or affects to despise it); and, over and above, possessed of that modesty and humanity, wherein Mr. Gray was so greatly deficient ...

Wednesday, January 15, 1777. I began visiting those of our society who lived in Bethnal-Green hamlet. Many of them I found in such poverty as few can conceive without seeing it. O why do not all the rich that fear God constantly visit the poor? Can they spend part of their spare time better? Certainly not. So they will find in that day when 'every man shall receive his own reward according to his own labour'.

Such another scene I saw the next day, in visiting another part of the society. I have not found any such distress, no, not in the prison of Newgate. One poor man was just creeping out of his sick-bed, to his ragged wife and three little children; who were more than half naked, and the very picture of famine; when one bringing in a loaf of bread, they all ran, seized upon it, and tore it in pieces in an instant. Who would not rejoice that there is another world? ...

Sunday, March 2. To-day I received from an eye-witness a particular account of a late remarkable occurrence. Captain Bell, a most amiable man, beloved of all that knew him, and just engaged to one which he tenderly loved, sailed from England last autumn. On September 20 he was hailed by the Hawke, a small sloop, Captain Arthur Crawford, Commander, who told him he came from Halifax, in His Majesty's service, cruising for American privateers. Captain Bell invited him to breakfast, entertained him with all kindness, and made him some little presents: But on his cursing and swearing at the Americans, mildly reproved him, and he desisted. Mr. M'Aness, the Supercargo, seeing him walk round the ship, and diligently observe everything in it, told Captain Bell, 'Be upon your guard, this is certainly an enemy!' But the Captain answered, 'It cannot be; no man can act so base a part.'

Captain Crawford returned to his own ship, and sailing under the stern of the other, while Captain Bell and some others were standing on the quarter-deck, ordered his men to fire at him. They did so, and shot him in the belly, so that his bowels came out. But he did not fall. He ordered them to fire again: He fell; and while his men were carrying him away, Crawford took the vessel.

Captain Bell being conveyed into the cabin, sent and desired to speak with Captain Crawford: But he would not come. He then desired to speak with his own sailors, one by one. One of them saying, 'Sir, you have been basely murdered,' he replied, 'Love your enemies; pray for them that despitefully use you. What are our sufferings to those which our Lord endured for us?' He then desired the account which St. John gives of our Lord's sufferings to be read to him. He desired his love to all that loved the Lord Jesus; particularly to her he was about to marry. Then bidding them all farewell, he died in peace, about two hours after he received the second shot.

But what did Captain Crawford do amiss? Have not the English also taken American ships by surprise? Yes; but not with such circumstances. For, 1. He hoisted no colours, nor ever summoned the ship to yield: 2. He fired on men who thought nothing of the matter, and pointed the men to Captain Bell in particular. So it was a deliberate murder. Such is the mercy, such the gratitude, of American rebels! . . .

Friday, July 18. The more I converse with the society at Haverford, the more I am united to them. *Saturday, 19.* About eleven I preached at Howton, two miles short of the Ferry. There was an uncommon blessing among the simple-hearted people. At Pembroke, in the evening, we had the most elegant congregation I have seen since we came into Wales. Some of them came in dancing, and laughing, as into a theatre; but their mood was quickly changed, and in a few minutes they were as serious as my subject—Death. I believe, if they do not take great care, they will remember it—for a week!

Tuesday, August 5 [Bristol]. Our yearly Conference began. I now particularly inquired (as that report had been spread far and wide) of every Assistant, 'Have you reason to believe, from your own observation, that the Methodists are a fallen people? Is there a decay or an increase in the work of God where you have been? Are the societies in general more dead, or more alive to God, than they were some years ago?' The almost universal answer was, 'If we must "know them by their fruits", there is no decay in the work of God, among the people in general. The societies are not dead to God: They are as much alive as they have been for many years. And we look on this report as a mere device of Satan, to make our hands hang down.'

'But how can this question be decided?' You, and you, can judge no farther than you see. You cannot judge of one part by another; of the people of London, suppose, by those of Bristol. And none but myself has an opportunity of seeing them throughout the three kingdoms.

But to come to a short issue. In most places, the Methodists are still a poor, despised people, labouring under reproach, and many inconveniences; therefore, wherever the power of God is not, they decrease. By this, then, you may form a sure judgment. Do the Methodists in general decrease in number? Then they decrease in grace; they are a fallen, or, at least, a falling people. But they do not decrease in number; they continually increase: Therefore they are not a fallen people.

The Conference concluded on *Friday*, as it began, in much love. But there was one jarring string: John Hilton told us, he must withdraw from our Connexion, because he saw the Methodists were a fallen people. Some would have reasoned with him, but it was lost labour; so we let him go in peace ...

Monday, November 17. I went to Norwich, and preached there in the evening. The House was far too small, the congregation being lately increased very considerably. But I place no dependence in this people; they wave to and fro, like the waves of the sea ...

Monday, February 2, 1778. I had the satisfaction of spending an hour with that real patriot, Lord ———.[54] What an unheard-of thing it is, that even in a Court, he should retain all his sincerity! He is, indeed (what I doubt Secretary Craggs never was),

> Statesman, yet friend to truth.

Perhaps no Prince in Europe, besides King George, is served by two of the honestest, and two of the most sensible, men in his kingdom.

This week I visited the society, and found a surprising difference in their worldly circumstances. Five or six years ago, one in three, among the lower ranks of people, was out of employment; and the case was supposed to be nearly the same through all London and Westminster. I did not now, after all the tragical outcries of want of trade that fill the nation, find one in ten out of business; nay, scarce one in twenty, even in Spitalfields . . .

Tuesday, September 1. I went to Tiverton. I was musing here on what I heard a good man say long since—'Once in seven years I burn all my sermons; for it is a shame if I cannot write better sermons now than I could seven years ago.' Whatever others can do, I really cannot. I cannot write a better sermon on the Good Steward, than I did seven years ago: I cannot write a better on the Great Assize, than I did twenty years ago: I cannot write a better on the Use of Money, than I did near thirty years ago: Nay, I know not that I can write a better on the Circumcision of the Heart, than I did five-and-forty years ago. Perhaps, indeed I may have read five or six hundred books more than I had then, and may know a little more History, or Natural Philosophy, than I did; but I am not sensible that this has made any essential addition to my knowledge in Divinity. Forty years ago I knew and preached every Christian doctrine which I preach now . . .

Wednesday, April 28, 1779. I preached at Wakefield in the evening; *Thursday, 29,* at Rothwell and Leeds; and on *Friday* noon, at Harewood. In the afternoon we walked to Mr. Lascelles's house. It is finely situated on a little eminence, commanding a most delightful prospect of hill and dale, and wood and water. It is built of a fine white stone, with two grand and beautiful fronts. I was not much struck with anything within. There is too much sameness in all the great houses I have seen in England; two rows of large, square rooms, with costly beds, glasses, chairs, and tables. But here is a profusion of wealth; every pane of glass, we were informed, cost six-and-twenty shillings. One looking-glass cost five hundred pounds, and one bed, six hundred. The whole floor was just on the plan of Montague-House; now the British Museum. The grounds round the house are pleasant indeed, particularly the walks on the river-side, and through the woods. But what has the owner thereof, save the beholding them with his eyes? . . .

Saturday, July 3. I reached Grimsby, and found a little trial. In this, and many other parts of the kingdom, those striplings, who call themselves Lady Huntingdon's Preachers, have greatly hindered the work of God. They have neither sense, courage, nor grace, to go and beat up the devil's quarters, in any place where Christ has not been named; but wherever we have entered as by storm, and gathered a few souls, often at the peril of our lives, they creep in, and, by doubtful disputations, set every one's sword against his brother. One of these has just crept into Grimsby, and is striving to divide the poor little flock; but I hope his labour will be in vain, and they will still hold 'the unity of the Spirit in the bond of peace' . . .

Thursday, September 23 . . . In the evening one sat behind me in the pulpit at Bristol, who was one of our first Masters at Kingswood. A little after he left the school, he likewise left the society. Riches then flowed in upon him; with which, having no relations, Mr. Spencer designed to do much good—after his death. 'But God said unto him, Thou fool!' Two hours after, he died intestate, and left all his money to—be scrambled for!

Reader! if you have not done it already, make your Will before you sleep! . . .

Friday, October 8. We took chaise, as usual, at two, and about eleven came to Cobham. Having a little leisure, I thought I could not employ it better than in taking a walk through the gardens. They are said to take up four hundred acres, and are admirably well laid out. They far exceed the celebrated gardens at Stow; and that in several respects: 1. In situation; lying on a much higher hill, and having a finer prospect from the house. 2. In having a natural river, clear as crystal, running beneath and through them. 3. In the buildings therein; which are fewer indeed, but far more elegant; yea, and far better kept, being nicely clean, which is sadly wanting at Stow. And, lastly, In the rock-work; to which nothing of the kind at Stow is to be compared.

This night I lodged in the new house at London. How many more nights have I to spend there?

Mon. 11. I began my little tour into Northamptonshire. In the evening I preached at Stony-Stratford; the next day at Honslip, and at Morton, a little mile from Buckingham. *Wednesday, 13.* Having so lately seen Stourhead and Cobham gardens, I was now desired to take a view of the much more celebrated gardens at Stow. The first thing I observed was the beautiful water which runs through the gardens, to the front of the house. The tufts of trees, placed on each side of this, are wonderfully pleasant; and so are many of the walks and glades through the woods, which are disposed with a fine variety. The large pieces of water interspersed give a fresh beauty to the whole. Yet there are several things which must give disgust to any person of common sense: 1. The buildings, called Temples, are most miserable, many of them both within and without. Sir John Vanbrugh's is an ugly, clumsy, lump, hardly fit for a gentleman's stable. 2. The temples of Venus and Bacchus, though large, have nothing elegant in the structure; and the paintings in the former, representing a lewd story, are neither well designed nor executed. Those in the latter are quite faded, and most of the inscriptions vanished away. 3. The statues are full as coarse as the paintings, particularly those of Apollo and the Muses, whom a person, not otherwise informed, might take to be nine cook-maids. 4. Most of the water in the ponds is dirty, and thick as puddle. 5. It is childish affectation to call things here by Greek or Latin names, as Styx, and the Elysian Fields. 6. It was ominous for My Lord to entertain himself and his noble company in a grotto built on the bank of Styx; that is, on the brink of hell. 7. The river on which it stands is a black, filthy puddle, exactly resembling a common sewer. 8. One of the stateliest monuments is taken down—the Egyptian Pyramid; and no wonder, considering the two inscriptions, which are still legible; the one,

> *Linquenda tellus, et domus, et placens*
> *Uxor: Neque harum, quas colis, arborum*
> *Te præter invisas cupressos,*
> *Ulla brevem dominum sequetur!*

[You must leave behind you these grounds, this house and your charming wife, and, of these trees which you are cultivating, none but the baleful cypresses will accompany you their short-lived owner to the tomb.]

The other,

Lusisti satis, edisti satis, atque bibisti:
Tempus abire tibi est: Ne potum largius æquo
Rideat, et pulset lasciva decentius ætas.

[You have had a good time and had your fill of food and drink; now it is time for you to be off, lest an age which takes its pleasures in more civilized fashion should mock your over-indulgence in drink and ostracize you.]

Upon the whole, I cannot but prefer Cobham gardens to those at Stow: For, 1. The river at Cobham shames all the ponds at Stow. 2. There is nothing at Stow comparable to the walk near the wheel which runs up the side of a steep hill, quite grotesque and wild. 3. Nothing in Stow gardens is to be compared to the large temple, the pavilion, the antique temple, the grotto, or the building at the head of the garden; nor to the neatness which runs through the whole.

But there is nothing even at Cobham to be compared, 1. To the beautiful cross at the entrance of Stourhead gardens. 2. To the vast body of water. 3. The rock-work grotto. 4. The temple of the sun. 5. The hermitage. Here too every thing is nicely clean, as well as in full preservation. Add to this, that all the gardens hang on the sides of a semicircular mountain. And there is nothing either at Cobham or Stow which can balance the advantage of such a situation ...

Monday, July 24, 1780. I went to Bristol. While I was at Bath, I narrowly observed and considered the celebrated Cartoons;[55] the three first in particular. What a poor *designer* was one of the finest painters in the world! 1. Here are two men in a boat; each of them more than half as long as the boat itself. 2. Our Lord, saying to Peter, 'Feed my sheep,' points to three or four sheep standing by him. 3. While Peter and John heal the lame man, two naked boys stand by them. For what? O pity that so fine a painter should be utterly without common sense!

In the evening I saw one of the greatest curiosities in the vegetable creation—the Nightly Cereus. About four in the afternoon, the dry stem began to swell; about six, it gradually opened; and about eight, it was in its full glory. I think the inner part of this flower, which was snow-white, was about five inches diameter; the yellow rays which surrounded it, I judged, were in diameter nine or ten inches. About twelve it began to droop, being covered with a cold sweat; at four it died away ...

Friday, August 25 [Cornwall]. I preached in the market-place at St. Ives, to most of the inhabitants of the town. Here is no opposer now. Rich and poor see, and very many feel, the truth.

I now looked over a volume of Mr. K—'s Essays.[56] He is a lively writer, of middling understanding. But I cannot admire his style at all. It is prim, affected, and highly Frenchified. I object to the beginning so many sentences with participles. This does well in French, but not in English. I cannot admire his judgment in many particulars. To instance in one or two: He depresses Cowley beyond all reason; who was far from being a mean poet. Full as unreasonably does he depress modern eloquence. I believe I have heard speakers at Oxford, to say nothing of Westminster, who were not inferior to either Demosthenes or Cicero ...

Friday, December 22 [London]. At the desire of some of my friends, I accompanied them to the British Museum. What an immense field is here for curiosity to range in! One large room is filled from top to bottom with things brought from Otaheite; two or three more with things dug out of the ruins of Herculaneum! Seven huge apartments are filled with curious books; five with manuscripts; two with fossils of all sorts, and the rest with various animals. But what account will a man give to the Judge of quick and dead for a life spent in collecting all these? ...

Thursday, January 25, 1781. I spent an agreeable hour at a concert of my nephews. But I was a little out of my element among lords and ladies. I love plain music and plain company best ...

Sunday, April 8 [Warrington]. The service was at the usual hours. I came just in time to put a stop to a bad custom, which was creeping in here: A few men, who had fine voices, sang a Psalm

which no one knew, in a tune fit for an opera, wherein three, four,
or five persons, sung different words at the same time! What an
insult upon common sense! What a burlesque upon public worship! No custom can excuse such a mixture of profaneness and
absurdity.

Mon. 9. Desiring to be in Ireland as soon as possible, I hastened
to Liverpool, and found a ship ready to sail; but the wind was
contrary, till on *Thursday* morning, the Captain came in haste, and
told us, the wind was come quite fair. So Mr. Floyd, Snowden,
Joseph Bradford, and I, with two of our sisters, went on board. But
scarce were we out at sea, when the wind turned quite foul, and
rose higher and higher. In an hour I was so affected, as I had not
been for forty years before. For two days I could not swallow the
quantity of a pea of any thing solid, and very little of any liquid. I
was bruised and sore from head to foot, and ill able to turn me on
the bed. All *Friday*, the storm increasing, the sea of consequence
was rougher and rougher. Early on *Saturday* morning, the hatches
were closed, which, together with the violent motion, made our
horses so turbulent, that I was afraid we must have killed them,
lest they should damage the ship. Mrs. S. now crept to me, threw
her arms over me, and said, 'O Sir, we will die together!' We had
by this time three feet water in the hold, though it was an
exceeding light vessel. Meantime we were furiously driving on a
lee-shore; and when the Captain cried, 'Helm a lee' she would not
obey the helm. I called our brethren to prayers; and we found free
access to the throne of grace. Soon after we got, I know not how,
into Holyhead harbour, after being sufficiently buffeted by the
winds and waves, for two days and two nights.

The more I considered, the more I was convinced, it was not the
will of God I should go to Ireland at this time. So we went into the
stage-coach without delay, and the next evening came to Chester.

I now considered in what place I could spend a few days to the
greatest advantage. I soon thought of the Isle of Man, and those
parts of Wales which I could not well see in my ordinary course. I
judged it would be best to begin with the latter. So, after a day or
two's rest, on *Wednesday, 18,* I set out for Brecon, purposing to take
Whitchurch (where I had not been for many years) and Shrewsbury in my way. At noon I preached in Whitchurch, to a

numerous and very serious audience; in the evening at Shrewsbury; where, seeing the earnestness of the people, I agreed to stay another day.

Here I read over Sir Richard Hill's Letter to Mr. Madan, on his Defence of Polygamy. I think it is home to the point; and wish always to write (if I must write controversy) in just such a spirit.

Not knowing the best way from hence to Brecon, I thought well to go round by Worcester. I took Broseley in my way, and thereby had a view of the iron bridge over the Severn: I suppose the first and the only one in Europe. It will not soon be imitated.

In the evening I preached at Broseley; and on *Saturday, 21*, went on to Worcester. I found one of our Preachers, Joseph Cole, there; but unable to preach through his ague. So that I could not have come more opportunely . . .

Friday, June 8 [Isle of Man]. Having now visited the island round, east, south, north, and west, I was thoroughly convinced that we have no such Circuit as this, either in England, Scotland, or Ireland. It is shut up from the world; and, having little trade, is visited by scarce any strangers. Here are no Papists, no Dissenters of any kind, no Calvinists, no disputers. Here is no opposition, either from the Governor (a mild humane man), from the Bishop (a good man), or from the bulk of the Clergy. One or two of them did oppose for a time; but they seem now to understand better. So that we have now rather too little, than too much, reproach; the scandal of the cross being, for the present, ceased. The natives are a plain, artless, simple people; unpolished, that is, unpolluted; few of them are rich or genteel; the far greater part, moderately poor; and most of the strangers that settle among them are men that have seen affliction. The Local Preachers are men of faith and love, knit together in one mind and one judgment. They speak either Manx or English, and follow a regular plan, which the Assistant gives them monthly.

The isle is supposed to have thirty thousand inhabitants. Allowing half of them to be adults, and our societies to contain one or two and twenty hundred members, what a fair proportion is this! What has been seen like this, in any part either of Great Britain or Ireland? . . .

Friday, July 6. To-day I finished the second volume of Dr.

Robertson's 'History of America'. His language is always clear and strong, and frequently elegant; and I suppose his history is preferable to any history of America which has appeared in the English tongue. But I cannot admire, First, His intolerable prolixity in this history, as well as his 'History of Charles the Fifth'. He promises eight books of the History of America, and fills four of them with critical dissertations. True, the dissertations are sensible, but they have lost their way; they are not history: And they are swelled beyond all proportion; doubtless, for the benefit of the author and the bookseller, rather than the reader. I cannot admire, Secondly, A Christian Divine writing a history, with so very little of Christianity in it. Nay, he seems studiously to avoid saying any thing which might imply that he believes the Bible. I can still less admire, Thirdly, His speaking so honourably of a professed Infidel; yea, and referring to his masterpiece of Infidelity, 'Sketches of the History of Man';[57] as artful, as unfair, as disingenuous a book, as even Toland's 'Nazarenus'.[58] Least of all can I admire, Fourthly, His copying after Dr. Hawkesworth (who once professed better things), in totally excluding the Creator from governing the world.[59] Was it not enough, never to mention the Providence of God, where there was the fairest occasion, without saying expressly, 'The *fortune* of Certiz', or '*chance*', did thus or thus? So far as fortune or chance governs the world, God has no place in it.

The poor American, though not pretending to be a Christian, knew better than this. When the Indian was asked, 'Why do you think the beloved ones take care of *you*?' he answered, 'When I was in the battle, the bullet went on this side, and on that side; and this man died, and that man died; and I am alive! So I know, the beloved ones take care of *me*.'[60]

It is true, the doctrine of a particular Providence (and any but a *particular* Providence is no Providence at all) is absolutely out of fashion in England: And a prudent author might write this to gain the favour of his gentle readers. Yet I will not say, this is real prudence; because he may lose hereby more than he gains; as the majority, even of Britons, to this day, retain some sort of respect for the Bible . . .

Tuesday, October 9. I preached at Winchester, where I went with great expectation to see that celebrated painting in the cathedral, the raising of Lazarus.[61] But I was disappointed. I observed, 1. There was such a huddle of figures, that, had I not been told, I should not ever have guessed what they meant. 2. The colours in general were far too glaring, such as neither Christ nor his followers ever wore. When will painters have common sense?

Wed. 10. I opened the new preaching-house just finished at Newport in the Isle of Wight. After preaching, I explained the nature of a Methodist society; of which few had before the least conception. *Friday, 12.* I came to London, and was informed that my wife died on Monday. This evening she was buried, though I was not informed of it till a day or two after . . .

March 29, 1782. (Being *Good-Friday.*) I came to Macclesfield just time enough to assist Mr. Simpson in the laborious service of the day. I preached for him morning and afternoon; and we administered the sacrament to about thirteen hundred persons. While we were administering, I heard a low, soft, solemn sound, just like that of an Æolian harp. It continued five or six minutes, and so affected many, that they could not refrain from tears. It then gradually died away. Strange that no other organist (that I know) should think of this. In the evening, I preached at our Room. Here was that harmony which art cannot imitate . . .

Saturday, July 13. I spent an hour in Hagley-Park; I suppose inferior to few, if any, in England. But we were straitened for time. To take a proper view of it, would require five or six hours. Afterwards I went to the Leasowes, a farm so called, four or five miles from Hagley. I never was so surprised. I have seen nothing in all England to be compared with it. It is beautiful and elegant all over. There is nothing grand, nothing costly; no temples, so called; no statues; (except two or three, which had better have been spared); but such walks, such shades, such hills and dales, such lawns, such artless cascades, such waving woods, with water intermixed, as exceed all imagination! On the upper side, from the openings of a shady walk, is a most beautiful and extensive prospect. And all this is comprised in the compass of three miles! I doubt if it be exceeded by any thing in Europe.

The father of Mr. Shenstone was a gentleman-farmer, who bred him at the University, and left him a small estate. This he wholly laid out in improving the Leasowes, living in hopes of great preferment, grounded on the promises of many rich and great friends. But nothing was performed, till he died at forty-eight; probably of a broken heart! . . . *Wednesday, 24.* My brother and I paid our last visit to Lewisham, and spent a few pensive hours with the relict of our good friend, Mr. Blackwell. We took one more walk round the garden and meadow, which he took so much pains to improve. Upwards of forty years this has been my place of retirement, when I could spare two or three days from London. In that time, first Mrs. Sparrow went to rest; then Mrs. Dewall; then good Mrs. Blackwell; now Mr. Blackwell himself. Who can tell how soon we may follow them? . . .

Wednesday, October 23. I visited the house of mourning at Shoreham, and read the strange account at first hand. Not long after his former wife died, Mr. H. paid his addresses to Miss B. He had been intimately acquainted with her for some years. By immense assiduity, and innumerable professions of the tenderest affection, he, by slow degrees, gained hers. The time of marriage was fixed: The ring was bought: The wedding clothes were sent to her. He came one Thursday, a few days before the wedding-day, and showed the most eager affection; so he did on Saturday. He came again on the Wednesday following, sat down very carelessly on a chair, and told her with great composure, that he did not love her at all, and therefore could not think of marrying her. He talked a full hour in the same strain, and then walked away!

Her brother sent a full account of this to Miss Perronet, who read it with perfect calmness, comforted her niece, and strongly exhorted her to continue steadfast in the faith. But the grief which did not outwardly appear, preyed the more upon her spirits, till, three or four days after, she felt a pain in her breast, lay down, and in four minutes died. One of the ventricles of her heart burst; so she literally died of a broken heart.

When old Mr. Perronet heard that his favourite child, the stay of his old age, was dead, he broke into praise and thanksgiving to God, who had 'taken another of his children out of this evil world'!

But Mr. H., meantime has done nothing amiss. So both himself and his friends say! . . .

Monday, June 2 [1783], and the following days, I employed in settling my business, and preparing for my little excursion. *Wednesday, 11.* I took coach with Mr. Brackenbury, Broadbent, and Whitfield; and in the evening we reached Harwich. I went immediately to Dr. Jones, who received me in the most affectionate manner. About nine in the morning we sailed; and at nine on *Friday, 13,* landed at Helvoetsluys. Here we hired a coach for Briel, but were forced to hire a wagon also, to carry a box which one of us could have carried on his shoulders. At Briel we took a boat to Rotterdam. We had not been long there, when Mr. Bennet, a bookseller, who had invited me to his house, called upon me. But as Mr. Loyal, the Minister of the Scotch congregation, had invited me, he gave up his claim, and went with us to Mr. Loyal's. I found a friendly, sensible, hospitable, and, I am persuaded, a pious man. We took a walk together round the town, all as clean as a gentleman's parlour. Many of the houses are as high as those in the main street at Edinburgh; and the canals, running through the chief streets, make them convenient, as well as pleasant; bringing the merchants' goods up to their doors. Stately trees grow on all their banks. The whole town is encompassed with a double row of elms; so that one may walk all round it in the shade.

Sat. 14. I had much conversation with the two English Ministers, sensible, well-bred, serious men. These, as well as Mr. Loyal, were very willing I should preach in their churches; but they thought it would be best for me to preach in the Episcopal church. By our conversing freely together, many prejudices were removed, and all our hearts seemed to be united together.

In the evening we again took a walk round the town, and I observed, 1. Many of the houses are higher than most in Edinburgh. It is true they have not so many stories; but each story is far loftier. 2. The streets, the outside and inside of their houses in every part, doors, windows, well-staircases, furniture, even floors, are kept so nicely clean that you cannot find a speck of dirt. 3. There is such a grandeur and elegance in the fronts of the large houses, as I never saw elsewhere; and such a profusion of marble within, particularly in their lower floors and staircases, as I wonder other nations do not imitate. 4. The women and children (which I least of all expected) were in general the most beautiful I ever saw. They were surprisingly fair, and had an inexpressible air of innocence in their countenance. 5. This was wonderfully set off by their dress, which was *simplex munditiis*, plain and neat in the highest degree. 6. It has lately been observed, that growing vegetables greatly resist putridity; so there is an use in their numerous rows of trees which was not thought of at first. The elms balance the canals, preventing the putrefaction which those otherwise might produce.

One little circumstance I observed, which I suppose is peculiar to Holland: To most chamber-windows a looking-glass is placed on the outside of the sash, so as to show the whole street, with all the passengers. There is something very pleasing in these moving pictures. Are they found in no other country? ...

Mon. 16. We set out in a track-skuit[62] for the Hague. By the way we saw a curiosity: The gallows near the canal, surrounded with a knot of beautiful trees! So the dying man will have one pleasant prospect here, whatever befalls him hereafter! At eleven we came to Delft, a large, handsome town, where we spent an hour at a merchant's house, who, as well as his wife, a very agreeable woman, seemed both to fear and to love God. Afterwards we saw the great church; I think nearly, if not quite, as long as York Minster. It is exceedingly light and elegant within, and every part is kept exquisitely clean. The tomb of William the First is much admired; particularly his statue, which has more life than one would think could be expressed in brass.

When we came to the Hague, though we had heard much of it, we were not disappointed. It is, indeed, beautiful beyond expression. Many of the houses are exceeding grand, and are finely intermixed with water and wood; yet not too close, but so as to be sufficiently ventilated by the air ...

Fri. 20. We breakfasted at Mr. Ferguson's, near the heart of the city. At eleven we drank coffee (the custom in Holland) at Mr. J——'s, a merchant, whose dining-room is covered, both walls and ceiling, with the most beautiful paintings. He and his lady walked with us in the afternoon to the Stadt-House; perhaps the grandest buildings of the kind in Europe. The great hall is a noble room indeed, near as large as that of Christ-Church in Oxford. But I have neither time nor inclination to describe particularly this amazing structure ...

At eleven I spent an hour with a woman of large fortune, who appeared to be as much devoted to God as her. We were immediately as well acquainted with each other, as if we had known each other for many years. But indeed an easy good-breeding (such as I never expected to see here) runs through all the genteeler people of Amsterdam. And there is such a child-like simplicity in all that love God, as does honour to the religion they profess.

About two we called upon Mr. V——n, and immediately fell into close conversation. There seems to be in him a peculiar softness and sweetness of temper; and a peculiar liveliness in Mrs. V——n. Our loving dispute, concerning deliverance from sin, was concluded within an hour: And we parted, if that could be, better friends than we met. Afterwards we walked to Mr. J——'s house in the Plantations, a large tract of ground, laid out in shady walks. These lie within the city walls: But there are other walks, equally pleasant, without the gates. Indeed nothing is wanting but the power of religion, to make Amsterdam a paradise ...

Fri. 27. I walked over to Mr. L[oten]'s country-house, about three miles from the city. It is a lovely place, surrounded with delightful gardens, laid out with wonderful variety. Mr. L[oten] is of an easy genteel behaviour, speaks Latin correctly, and is no stranger to philosophy. Mrs. L[oten] is the picture of friendliness and hospitality; and young Mr. L[oten] seems to be cast in the same mould. We spent a few hours very agreeably. Then Mr. L[oten] would send me back in his coach.

Being sick of inns (our bill at Amsterdam alone amounting to near a hundred florins), I willingly accepted of an invitation to lodge with the sons-in-law of James Oddie ...

Tuesday, July 1. I called on as many as I could of my friends, and we parted with much affection. We then hired a yacht, which brought us to Helvoetsluys, about eleven the next day. At two we went on board; but the wind turning against us, we did not reach Harwich till about nine on *Friday* morning. After a little rest we procured a carriage, and reached London about eleven at night.

I can by no means regret either the trouble or expense which attended this little journey. It opened me a way into, as it were, a new world; where the land, the buildings, the people, the customs, were all such as I had never seen before. But as those with whom I conversed were of the same spirit with my friends in England, I was as much at home in Utrecht and Amsterdam, as in Bristol and London . . .

Mon. 14. I took a little journey into Oxfordshire, and found the good effects of the late storms. The thunder had been uncommonly dreadful; and the lightning had tore up a field near High-Wycomb, and turned the potatoes into ashes. In the evening I preached in the new preaching-house at Oxford, a lightsome, cheerful place, and well filled with rich and poor, scholars as well as townsmen. *Tuesday, 15.* Walking through the city, I observed it swiftly improving in everything but religion. Observing narrowly the Hall at Christ-Church, I was convinced it is both loftier and larger than that of the Stadt-House in Amsterdam. I observed also, the gardens and walks in Holland, although extremely pleasant, were not to be compared with St. John's, or Trinity gardens; much less with the parks, Magdalen water-walks, &c., Christ-Church meadow, or the White Walk.

Wed. 16. I went on to Witney. There were uncommon thunder and lightning here last Thursday; but nothing to that which were there on Friday night. About ten the storm was just over the town; and both the bursts of thunder and lightning, or rather sheets of flame, were without intermission. Those that were asleep in the town were waked, and many thought the day of judgment was come. Men, women, and children, flocked out of their houses, and kneeled down together in the streets. With the flames, the grace of God came down also in a manner never known before; and as the impression was general, so it was lasting: It did not pass away with the storm; but the spirit of seriousness, with that of grace and supplication, continued . . .

Monday, October 27. I talked at large with M. F. Such a case I have not known before. She has been in the society nearly from the beginning. She found peace with God five-and-thirty years ago; and the pure love of God a few years after. Above twenty years she has been a Class and a Band Leader, and of very eminent use. Ten months since she was accused of drunkenness, and of revealing the secret of her friend. Being informed of this, I wrote to Norwich (as I then believed the charge), that she must be no longer a Leader, either of a band or a class. The Preacher told her further, that, in his judgment, she was unfit to be a member of the society. Upon this she gave up her ticket, together with the band and her class-papers. Immediately all her friends (of whom she seemed to have a large number) forsook her at once. No one knew her, or spoke to her. She was as a dead thing out of mind!

On making a more particular inquiry, I found that Mrs. W——— (formerly a common woman) had revealed her own secret, to Dr. Hunt, and twenty people besides. So the first accusation vanished into air. As to the second, I verily believe, the drunkenness with which she was charged, was, in reality, the falling down in a fit. So we have thrown away one of the most useful Leaders we ever had, for these wonderful reasons! . . .

Thursday, December 18. I spent two hours with that great man, Dr. Johnson, who is sinking into the grave by a gentle decay . . .

Saturday, February 14, 1784. I desired all our Preachers to meet, and consider thoroughly the proposal of sending Missionaries to the East Indies. After the matter had been fully considered, we were unanimous in our judgment, that we have no call thither yet, no invitation, no providential opening of any kind.

Thur. 19. I spent an agreeable hour with the modern Hannibal, Pascal Paoli; probably the most accomplished General that is now in the world.[63] He is of a middle size, thin, well-shaped, genteel, and has something extremely striking in his countenance. How much happier is he now, with his moderate pension, than he was in the midst of his victories!

On *Saturday*, having a leisure hour, I made an end of that strange book, 'Orlando Furioso'. Ariosto had doubtless an uncommon genius, and subsequent poets have been greatly indebted to him: Yet it is hard to say, which was the most out of his senses, the hero or the poet. He has not the least regard even to probability; his marvellous transcends all conception. Astolpho's shield and horn, and voyage to the moon, the lance that unhorses every one, the all-penetrating sword, and I know not how many impenetrable helmets and coats of mail—leaves transformed into ships, and into leaves again—stones turned into horses, and again into stones—are such monstrous fictions as never appeared in the world before, and, one would hope, never will again. O who, that is not himself out of his senses, can compare Ariosto with Tasso! . . .

Tuesday, May 4. I reached Aberdeen between four and five in the afternoon. *Wednesday, 5.* I found the morning preaching had been long discontinued: Yet the bands and the select society were kept up. But many were faint and weak for want of morning preaching and prayer-meetings, of which I found scarce any traces in Scotland.

In the evening I talked largely with the Preachers, and showed them the hurt it did both to them and the people, for any one Preacher to stay six or eight weeks together in one place. Neither can he find matter for preaching every morning and evening, nor will the people come to hear him. Hence he grows cold by lying in bed, and so do the people. Whereas, if he never stays more than a fortnight together in one place, he may find matter enough, and the people will gladly hear him. They immediately drew up such a plan for this Circuit, which they determined to pursue . . .

Sat. 15. We set out early, and dined at Aberdeen. On the road I read Ewen Cameron's Translation of Fingal. I think he has proved the authenticity of it beyond all reasonable contradiction: But what a poet was Ossian! Little inferior to either Homer or Virgil; in some respects superior to both. And what an hero was Fingal! Far more humane than Hector himself, whom we cannot excuse for murdering one that lay upon the ground; and with whom Achilles, or even pious Æneas, is not worthy to be named. But who is this excellent translator, Ewen Cameron? Is not his other name Hugh Blair? . . .[64]

Sunday, June 27. I preached at Misterton, at eight; and at Overthorpe about one. At four I took my stand in Epworth market-place, and preached on those words in the Gospel for the day, 'There is joy in heaven over one sinner that repenteth, more than over ninety and nine just persons that need no repentance.' It seemed as if very few, if any, of the sinners then present were unmoved.

Mon. 28. I inquired into the state of the work of God which was so remarkable two years ago. It is not yet at an end; but there has been a grievous decay, owing to several causes: 1. The Preachers that followed Thomas Tattershall were neither so zealous nor so diligent as he had been. 2. The two Leaders to whom the young men and lads were committed, went up and down to preach, and so left them in a great measure to themselves; or, rather, to the world and the devil. 3. The two women who were the most useful of all others, forsook them; the one leaving town, and the other leaving God. 4. The factories which employed so many of the children failed, so that all of them were scattered abroad. 5. The meetings of the children by the Preachers were discontinued; so their love soon grew cold; and as they rose into men and women, foolish desires entered, and destroyed all the grace they had left. Nevertheless great part of them stood firm, especially the young maidens, and still adorn their profession. This day I met the children myself, and found some of them still alive to God. And I do not doubt, but if the Preachers are zealous and active, they will recover most of those that have been scattered.

To-day I entered on my eighty-second year, and found myself just as strong to labour, and as fit for any exercise of body or mind, as I was forty years ago. I do not impute this to second causes, but to the Sovereign Lord of all. It is He who bids the sun of life stand still, so long as it pleaseth him.

I am as strong at eighty-one, as I was at twenty-one; but abundantly more healthy, being a stranger to the head-ache, tooth-ache, and other bodily disorders which attended me in my youth. We can only say, 'The Lord reigneth!' While we live, let us live to him . . .

Tuesday, July 13. I went to Burnley, a place which had been tried for many years, but without effect. It seems, the time was now come. High and low, rich and poor, now flocked together from all quarters; and all were eager to hear, except one man, who was the Town-crier. He began to bawl amain, till his wife ran to him, and literally stopped his noise: She seized him with one hand, and clapped the other upon his mouth, so that he could not get out one word. God then began a work, which, I am persuaded, will not soon come to an end . . .

Tuesday, August 31 [Bristol]. Dr. Coke, Mr. Whatcoat, and Mr. Vasey, came down from London, in order to embark for America.

Wednesday, September 1. Being now clear in my own mind, I took a step which I had long weighed in my mind, and appointed Mr.

Whatcoat and Mr. Vasey to go and serve the desolate sheep in America. *Thursday, 2*. I added to them three more; which, I verily believe, will be much to the glory of God . . .[65]

Sunday, September 12. Dr. Coke read Prayers, and I preached, in the new Room. Afterward I hastened to Kingswood, and preached under the shade of that double row of trees which I planted about forty years ago. How little did any one then think that they would answer such an intention! The sun shone as hot as it used to do even in Georgia; but his rays could not pierce our canopy; and our Lord, meantime, shone upon many souls, and refreshed them that were weary . . .

Thur. 30. I had a long conversation with John McGeary, one of our American Preachers, just come to England. He gave a pleasing account of the work of God there continually increasing, and vehemently importuned me to pay one more visit to America before I die. Nay, I shall pay no more visits to new worlds, till I go to the world of spirits . . .

Saturday, November 6. I was an hour or two in conversation with that truly great man, Pascal Paoli; who is a tall, well-made, graceful man, about sixty years of age; but he does not look to be above forty. He appears to have a real regard for the public good, and much of the fear of God. He has a strong understanding, and seemed to be acquainted with every branch of polite literature. On my saying he had met with much the same treatment with that of an ancient lover of his country, Hannibal, he immediately answered, 'But I have never yet met with a King of Bithynia.' . . .[66]

Monday, December 20. I went to Hinxworth, where I had the satisfaction of meeting Mr. Simeon, Fellow of King's College, in Cambridge. He has spent some time with Mr. Fletcher, at Madeley; two kindred souls; much resembling each other, both in fervour of spirit, and in the earnestness of their address. He gave me the pleasing information, that there are three parish churches in Cambridge, wherein true scriptural religion is preached; and several young gentlemen who are happy partakers of it . . .

Tuesday, January 25, 1785. I spent two or three hours in the House of Lords. I had frequently heard that this was the most venerable assembly in England. But how was I disappointed! What is a Lord, but a sinner, born to die! . . .

Thursday, March 24. I was now considering how strangely the grain of mustard-seed, planted about fifty years ago, has grown up. It has spread through all Great Britain and Ireland; the Isle of Wight, and the Isle of Man; then to America, from the Leeward Islands, through the whole continent, into Canada and Newfoundland. And the societies, in all these parts, walk by one rule, knowing religion is holy tempers; and striving to worship God, not in form only, but likewise 'in spirit and in truth'. ...

[Wesley visited Ireland between 10 April and 11 July.]

Wednesday, June 8. After preaching in the morning, I left many of the loving people in tears, and went on to Ballymoney; where I preached in the Court-House, to a very civil, and a very dull, congregation. From hence we went to Ballymena. In the afternoon I walked over to Gracehill, the Moravian settlement. Beside many little houses for them that are married, they have three large buildings; ... having the chapel in the middle, the house for the single men on the left hand, that for the single women on the right. We spent one or two agreeable hours in seeing the several rooms. Nothing can exceed the neatness of the rooms, or the courtesy of the inhabitants: But if they have most courtesy, we have more love. We do not suffer a stranger, especially a Christian brother, to visit us, without asking him either 'to bite or sup'. 'But it is their way.' I am sorry to say, so it is. When I called on Bishop Antone, in Holland, an old acquaintance, whom I had not seen for six-and-forty-years, till both he and I were grown grey-headed, he did not ask me so much as to wet my lips. Is not this a shameful way? A way, contrary not only to Christianity, but to common humanity? Is it not a way that a Jew, a Mahometan, yea, an honest Heathen, would be ashamed of? ...

Monday, December 5 [London]. And so the whole week, I spent every hour I could spare, in the unpleasing but necessary work of going through the town, and begging for the poor men who had been employed in finishing the new chapel. It is true, I am not obliged to do this; but if I do it not, nobody else will ...

Wednesday, June 21, 1786 ... Having now given a second reading to 'Fingal', rendered into heroic verse, I was thoroughly convinced it is one of the finest Epic Poems in the English language. Many of the lines are worthy of Mr. Pope; many of the incidents are deeply pathetic; and the character of Fingal exceeds any in Homer, yea, and Virgil too. No such speech comes out of his mouth as,

Sum pius Æneas, famâ super æthera notus:

[I am devout Aeneas, my reputation has reached the heavens above.]

No such thing in his conduct as the whole affair of Dido is in the Trojan Hero. Meantime, who is Ewen Cameron? Is it not Doctor Blair? And is not one great part of this publication to aggrandize the character of the old Highlanders, as brave, hospitable, generous men?

In the evening I preached to a large congregation at Gainsborough, in Sir Nevil Hickman's yard. But Sir Nevil is no more, and has left no son; so the very name of that ancient family is lost! And how changed is the house since I was young, and good Sir Willoughby Hickman lived here! One of the towers is said to have been built in the reign of King Stephen, above six hundred years ago. But it matters not; yet a little while, and the earth itself, with all the works of it, will be burned up . . . *Tuesday, 27.* At one in the afternoon I preached at Belton. While I was preaching, three little children, the eldest six years old, the youngest two and a half, whom their mother had left at dinner, straggled out, and got to the side of a well, which was near the house. The youngest, leaning over, fell in: The others striving to pull it out, the board gave way; in consequence of which, they all fell in together. The young one fell under the bucket, and stirred no more; the others held for a while by the side of the well, and then sunk into the water, where it was supposed they lay half an hour. One coming to tell me, I advised, immediately to rub them with salt, and to breathe strongly into their mouths. They did so, but the young one was past help; the others in two or three hours were as well as ever.

Wed. 28. I entered into the eighty-third year of my age. I am a wonder to myself. It is now twelve years since I have felt any such sensation as weariness. I am never tired (such is the goodness of God!), either with writing, preaching, or travelling. One natural cause undoubtedly is, my continual exercise and change of air.

How the latter contributes to health I know not; but certainly it does.

This morning, Abigail Pilsworth, aged fourteen, was born into the world of spirits. I talked with her the evening before, and found her ready for the Bridegroom. A few hours after, she quietly fell asleep. When we went into the room where her remains lay, we were surprised. A more beautiful corpse I never saw: We all sung,

> Ah, lovely appearance of death!
>   What sight upon earth is so fair?
> Not all the gay pageants that breathe
>   Can with a dead body compare![67]

All the company were in tears; and in all, except her mother, who sorrowed (but not as one without hope), they were tears of joy. 'O Death, where is thy sting?'

Tuesday, July 4 [Sheffield]. I met the select society, most of them walking in glorious liberty. Afterwards I went to Wentworth-House, the splendid seat of the late Marquis of Rockingham. He lately had forty thousand a year in England, and fifteen or twenty thousand in Ireland. And what has he now? Six foot of earth.

> A heap of dust is all remains of thee!
> 'Tis all thou art, and all the proud shall be.[68]

The situation of the house is very fine. It commands a large and beautiful prospect. Before the house is an open view; behind, a few acres of wood; but not laid out with any taste. The green-houses are large; but I did not observe anything curious in them. The front of the house is large and magnificent, but not yet finished. The entrance is noble, the saloon exceeding grand, and so are several of the apartments. Few of the pictures are striking: I think none of them to be compared with some in Fonmon Castle. The most extraordinary thing I saw was the stables: A Square, fit for a royal palace, all built of fine stone, and near as large as the old Quadrangle at Christ-Church in Oxford. But for what use were these built? To show that the owner had near three-score thousand pounds a year! O how much treasure might he have laid up in heaven, with all this mammon of unrighteousness! About one I preached at Thorpe, to three or four times as many as the preaching-house would have contained; and in the evening to the well-instructed and well-behaved congregation at Sheffield. O what has God wrought in this town! The leopard now lies down with the kid.

Wed. 5. Notice was given, without my knowledge, of my preaching at Belper, seven miles short of Derby. I was nothing glad of this, as it obliged me to quit the turnpike-road, to hobble over a miserable common. The people, gathered from all parts, were waiting. So I went immediately to the market-place; and, standing under a large tree, testified, 'This is life eternal, to know thee, the only true God, and Jesus Christ, whom thou hast sent.' The House at Derby was throughly filled in the evening. As many of the better sort (so called) were there, I explained (what seemed to be more adapted to their circumstances and experience), 'This only have I found, that God made man upright; but they have found out many inventions.'

Thur. 6. In going to Ilston we were again entangled in miserable roads. We got thither, however, about eleven. Though the church is large, it was sufficiently crowded. The Vicar read Prayers with great earnestness and propriety: I preached on, 'Her ways are ways of pleasantness'; and the people seemed all ear. Surely good will be done in this place; though it is strongly opposed both by the Calvinists and Socinians.

We went on in a lovely afternoon, and through a lovely country, to Nottingham. I preached to a numerous and well-behaved congregation. I love this people: There is something wonderfully pleasing, both in their spirit and their behaviour.

Fri. 7. The congregation at five was very large, and convinced me of the earnestness of the people. They are greatly increased in wealth and grace, and continue increasing daily. *Saturday, 8.* I walked through the General Hospital. I never saw one so well ordered. Neatness, decency, and common sense, shine through the whole. I do not wonder that many of the patients recover. I prayed with two of them. One of them, a notorious sinner, seemed to be cut to the heart. The case of the other was quite peculiar: Both her breasts have been cut off, and many pins taken out of them, as well as out of her flesh in various parts. 'Twelve', the Apothecary said, 'were taken out of her yesterday, and five more to-day.' And the physicians potently believe, she swallowed them all; though nobody can tell when or how! Which is the greater credulity? To believe this is purely *natural*? Or to ascribe it to preternatural agency? . . .

Tues. 25 [Bristol]. Our Conference began: About eighty Preachers attended. We met every day at six and nine in the morning, and at two in the afternoon. On *Tuesday* and on *Wednesday* morning the characters of the Preachers were considered, whether already admitted or not. On *Thursday* in the afternoon we permitted any of the society to be present, and weighed what was said about separating from the Church: But we all determined to continue therein, without one dissenting voice; and I doubt not but this determination will stand, at least till I am removed into a better world . . .

Monday, September 25. We took coach in the afternoon; and on *Tuesday* morning reached London. I now applied myself in earnest to the writing of Mr. Fletcher's Life, having procured the best materials I could. To this I dedicated all the time I could spare, till November, from five in the morning till eight at night. These are my studying hours; I cannot write longer in a day without hurting my eyes . . .

Thursday, October 19. I returned to London. In this journey I had a full sight of Lord Salisbury's seat, at Hatfield. The park is delightful. Both the fronts of the house are very handsome, though antique. The hall, the assembly-room, and the gallery, are grand and beautiful. The chapel is extremely pretty; but the furniture in general (excepting the pictures, many of which are originals) is just such as I should expect in a gentleman's house of five hundred a year.

Sun. 22. I preached at West-Street, morning and afternoon, and at Allhallows church in the evening. It was much crowded; and God gave us so remarkable a blessing, as I scarce ever found at that church. *Tuesday, 24.* I met the classes at Deptford, and was vehemently importuned to order the Sunday service in our Room at the same time with that of the church. It is easy to see that this would be a formal separation from the Church. We fixed both our morning and evening service, all over England, at such hours as not to interfere with the Church; with this very design—that those of the Church, if they chose it, might attend both the one and the other. But to fix it at the same hour, is obliging them to separate either from the Church or us; and this I judge to be not only inexpedient, but totally unlawful for me to do . . .[69]

Tuesday, December 5. In the afternoon I took coach again and returned to London at eight on *Wednesday* morning. All the time I could save to the end of the week I spent in transcribing the society; a dull, but necessary, work, which I have taken upon myself once a year for near these fifty years . . .

Friday, March 2, 1787 . . . In the afternoon I went over to Plymouth, and drank tea at Mr. Hawker's, the Minister of the new church. He seems to be a man of an excellent spirit, and is a pattern to all the Clergy round about. It rained all the evening; but that did not hinder the House from being thoroughly filled with people that heard as for life. This congregation likewise seemed to be, 'all but their attention, dead'. The like has hardly been seen here before. What! is God about to work in Plymouth also? . . .

Wed. 28 . . . In the evening I opened the new House at Wolverhampton, nearly as large as that at Newcastle-upon-Tyne. It would not near contain the people, though they were wedged together as close as possible. I believe such a congregation was never seen in Wolverhampton before; not only so serious, but so well-behaved. I hope this is a token for good.

Thur. 29. About twelve I preached at Lane-End. It being too cold to stand abroad, the greater part of the earnest congregation squeezed into the preaching-house. Here we entered into the country which seems to be all on fire—that which borders on Burslem on every side: Preachers and people provoking one another to love and good works, in such a manner as was never seen before. In the evening I preached at Burslem. Observing the people flocking together, I began half an hour before the appointed time. But, notwithstanding this, the House would not contain one half of the congregation: So, while I was preaching in the House to all that could get in, John Broadbent preached in a yard to the rest. The love-feast followed; but such a one as I have not known for many years. While the two or three first spoke, the power of God so fell upon all that were present, some praying, and others giving thanks, that their voices could scarce be heard: And two or three were speaking at a time, till I gently advised them to speak one at a time; and they did so, with amazing energy. Some of them had found peace a year ago, some within a month or a week, some within a day or two; and one of them, a potter's boy, told us, 'At the prayer-meeting I found myself dropping into hell; and I cried to the Lord, and he showed me he loved me. But Satan came immediately, and offered me a bag of money, as long as my arm; but I said, "Get thee behind me, Satan." ' Several also testified that the blood of Christ had cleansed them from all sin. Two declared, after bitter cries, that they knew their sins were just then blotted out by the blood of the Lamb; and I doubt not but it will be found, upon inquiry, that several more were either justified or sanctified. Indeed there has been, for some time, such an outpouring of the Spirit here, as has not been in any other part of the kingdom; particularly in the meetings for prayer. Fifteen or twenty have been justified in a day. Some of them had been the most notorious, abandoned sinners, in all the country; and people flock into the society on every side; six, eight, or ten, in an evening.

Fri. 30. I had appointed to preach at five in the morning; but soon after four I was saluted by a concert of music, both vocal and instrumental, at our gate, making the air ring with a hymn to the tune of Judas Maccabeus: It was a good prelude. So I began almost half an hour before five; yet the House was crowded both above and below. I strongly, but very tenderly, enforced that caution, 'Let him that standeth take heed lest he fall.' And is not God able to make them stand? Yea, and he will do it, if they walk humbly with God.

In the evening I preached at Congleton to a serious and well-established people. Here I found my coeval, Mr. [Troutbeck], two months (I think) younger than me, just as a lamp going out for want of oil, gently sliding into a better world: He sleeps always, only waking now and then just long enough to say, 'I am happy.'

Sat. 31. I went on to Macclesfield, and found a people still alive to God, in spite of swiftly increasing riches. If they continue so, it will be the only instance I have known, in above half a century. I warned them in the strongest terms I could, and believe some of them had ears to hear . . .

[Wesley visited Ireland between 7 April and 11 July.]

Wednesday, April 25. I once more visited my old friends at Tullamore. Have all the balloons in Europe done so much good as can counterbalance the harm which one of them did here a year or two ago? It took fire in its flight, and dropped it down on one and another of the thatched houses so fast that it was not possible to quench it till most of the town was burned down . . .

Saturday, May 12. A gentleman invited me to breakfast, with my old antagonist, Father O'Leary. I was not at all displeased at being disappointed. He is not the stiff, queer man that I expected; but of an easy, genteel carriage, and seems not to be wanting either in sense or learning. In the afternoon, by appointment, I waited on the Mayor—an upright, sensible man, who is diligently employed, from morning to night, in doing all the good he can. He has already prevailed upon the Corporation to make it a fixed rule, that the two hundred a year, which was spent in two entertainments, should for the future be employed in relieving indigent freemen, with their wives and children. He has carefully regulated the House of Industry, and has instituted a Humane Society for the relief of persons seemingly drowned; and he is unwearied in removing abuses of every kind. When will our English Mayors copy after the Mayor of Cork? He led me through the Mayoralty-House—a very noble and beautiful structure. The dining-room and the ball-room are magnificent, and shame the Mansion-House in London by their situation; commanding the whole river, the fruitful hills on every side, and the meadows running between them. He was then so good as to walk with me quite through the city to the House of Industry, and to go with me through all the apartments; which are quite sweet and commodious. An hundred and ninety-two poor are now lodged therein; and the master (a pious man, and a member of our society) watches over them, reads with them, and prays with them, as if they were his own children . . .

Wednesday, June 13. Being informed we had only six-and-twenty miles to go, we did not set out till between six and seven. The country was uncommonly pleasant, running between two high ridges of mountains. But it was up hill and down, all the way; so that we did not reach Rathfriland till near noon. Mr. Barber, the Presbyterian Minister (a princely personage, I believe six feet and a half high), offering me his new spacious preaching-house, the congregation quickly gathered together. I began without delay to open and enforce, 'Now God commandeth all men everywhere to repent.' I took chaise the instant I had done; but the road being still up hill and down, we were two hours going what they called six miles. I then quitted the chaise, and rode forward. But even then four miles, so called, took an hour and a half riding; so that I did not reach Dr. Lesley's, at Tanderagee, till half an hour past four. About six I stood upon the steps, at Mr. Godly's door, and preached on, 'This is not your rest,' to a larger congregation, by a third, than even that at Downpatrick. I scarce remember to have seen a larger, unless in London, Yorkshire, or Cornwall.

Thur. 14. Mr. Broadbent and I walked round Dr. Lesley's domain. I have not seen anything of the size in England that is equal to it. The house stands in the midst of a fruitful hill, which is part beneath, and part above it. In approaching it, you see no walls, nothing but green trees and shrubs of various kinds. Enter the court-yard and gate, and you still see no stone walls; but on either hand,

> The verdurous wall of Paradise upsprings;[70]

and that summer and winter; consisting wholly of ever-greens, that bloom all the year round. On the upper side of the house, the gently rising hill yields the loveliest scene that can be conceived; such a mixture of shady walks, and lawns sprinkled with trees; at the top of which is a natural rock, under which you may sit and command a most beautiful and extensive prospect: And all this variety has arisen from a rough, furzy heath, by the industry of Dr. Lesley, in thirty years ...

Tues. 19. We went on through horrible roads to Newry. I wonder any should be so stupid as to prefer the Irish roads to the English. The huge unbroken stones, of which they are generally made, are enough to break any carriage in pieces. No, there is nothing equal to good English gravel, both for horses, carriages, and travellers ...

Tuesday, August 14. Sailing on [from Swanage], with a fair wind, we fully expected to reach Guernsey in the afternoon; but the wind turning contrary, and blowing hard, we found it would be impossible. We then judged it best to put in at the Isle of Alderney; but we were very near being shipwrecked in the bay. When we were in the middle of the rocks, with the sea rippling all round us, the wind totally failed. Had this continued, we must have struck upon one or other of the rocks: So we went to prayer, and the wind sprung up instantly. About sunset we landed; and, though we had five beds in the same room, slept in peace.

About eight I went down to a convenient spot on the beach, and began giving out a hymn. A woman and two little children joined us immediately. Before the hymn was ended, we had a tolerable congregation; all of whom behaved well: Part, indeed, continued at forty or fifty yards' distance; but they were all quiet and attentive.

It happened (to speak in the vulgar phrase) that three or four who sailed with us from England, a gentleman with his wife and sister, were near relations of the Governor. He came to us this morning, and, when I went into the room, behaved with the utmost courtesy. This little circumstance may remove prejudice, and make a more open way for the Gospel.

Soon after we set sail, and, after a very pleasant passage, through little islands on either hand, we came to the venerable Castle, standing on a rock, about a quarter of a mile from Guernsey. The isle itself makes a beautiful appearance, spreading as a crescent to the right and left; about seven miles long, and five broad; part high land, and part low. The town itself is boldly situated, rising higher and higher from the water. The first thing I observed in it was, very narrow streets, and exceeding high houses. But we quickly went on to Mr. De Jersey's, hardly a mile from the town. Here I found a most cordial welcome, both from the master of the house, and all his family. I preached at seven in a large room, to as deeply serious a congregation as I ever saw, on, 'Jesus Christ, of God made unto us wisdom, righteousness, sanctification, and redemption.'

Thur. 16. I had a very serious congregation at five, in a large room of Mr. De Jersey's house. His gardens and orchards are of a vast extent, and wonderfully pleasant; and I know no Nobleman in Great Britian that has such variety of the most excellent fruit; which he is every year increasing, either from France, or other parts of the Continent. What quantity of fruit he has, you may conjecture from one sort only: This summer he gathered fifty pounds of strawberries daily, for six weeks together.

In the evening I preached at the other end of the town, in our own preaching-house. So many people squeezed in (though not near all who came), that it was as hot as a stove. But this none seemed to regard; for the word of God was sharper than a two-edged sword . . .

Sat. 25. Having now leisure, I finished a sermon on discerning the 'Signs of the Times'. This morning I had a particular conversation (as I had once or twice before) with Jeannie Bisson of this town; such a young woman as I have hardly seen elsewhere. She seems to be wholly devoted to God, and to have constant communion with him. She has a clear and strong understanding; and I cannot perceive the least tincture of enthusiasm. I am afraid she will not live long. I am amazed at the grace of God which is in her: I think she is far beyond Madame Guion, in deep communion with God;[71] and I doubt whether I have found her fellow in England. Precious as my time is, it would have been worth my while to come to Jersey, had it been only to see this prodigy of grace . . .

Sunday, December 9 [London]. I went down at half-hour past five, but found no Preacher in the chapel, though we had three or four in the house: So I preached myself. Afterwards, inquiring why none of my family attended the morning preaching, they said, it was because they sat up too late. I resolved to put a stop to this; and therefore ordered, that, 1. Every one under my roof should go to bed at nine; that, 2. Every one might attend the morning preaching: And so they have done ever since.

Mon. 10. I was desired to see the celebrated wax-work at the Museum in Spring-Gardens: It exhibits most of the crowned heads in Europe, and shows their characters in their countenance. Sense and majesty appear in the King of Spain; dulness and sottishness in the King of France; infernal subtlety in the late King of Prussia (as well as in the skeleton Voltaire); calmness and humanity in the Emperor, and King of Portugal; exquisite stupidity in the Prince of Orange; and amazing coarseness, with everything that is unamiable, in the Czarina ...

Tues. 18. I retired to Newington, and hid myself for almost three days. *Friday 21.* The Committee proposed to me, 1. That families of men and women should sit together in both chapels: 2. That every one who took a pew should have it as his own: Thus overthrowing, at one blow, the discipline which I have been establishing for fifty years!

Sat. 22. I yielded to the importunity of a painter, and sat an hour and a half, in all, for my picture.[72] I think it was the best that ever was taken; but what is the picture of a man above fourscore?

Mon. 24. We had another meeting of the Committee; who after a calm and loving consultation, judged it best, 1. That the men and women should sit separate still; and, 2. That none should claim any pew as his own, either in the new chapel, or in West-Street ...

Monday, March 3, 1788. I went on to Bristol, and having two or three quiet days, finished my sermon upon Conscience. On *Tuesday* I gave notice of my design to preach on Thursday evening, upon (what is now the general topic) Slavery. In consequence of this, on *Thursday*, the House from end to end was filled with high and low, rich and poor. I preached on that ancient prophecy, 'God shall enlarge Japhet. And he shall dwell in the tents of Shem; and Canaan shall be his servant.' About the middle of the discourse, while there was on every side attention still as night, a vehement noise arose, none could tell why, and shot like lightning through the whole congregation. The terror and confusion were inexpressible. You might have imagined it was a city taken by storm. The people rushed upon each other with the utmost violence; the benches were broke in pieces; and nine-tenths of the congregation appeared to be struck with the same panic. In about six minutes the storm ceased, almost as suddenly as it rose; and, all being calm, I went on without the least interruption.

It was the strangest incident of the kind I ever remember; and I believe none can account for it, without supposing some preter-natural influence. Satan fought, lest his kingdom should be delivered up. We set *Friday* apart as a day of fasting and prayer, that God would remember those poor outcasts of men; and (what seems impossible with men, considering the wealth and power of their oppressors) make a way for them to escape, and break their chains in sunder . . .

Saturday, April 19. We went on to Bolton, where I preached in the evening in one of the most elegant Houses in the kingdom, and to one of the liveliest congregations. And this I must avow, there is not such a set of singers in any of the Methodist congregations in the three kingdoms. There cannot be; for we have near a hundred such trebles, boys and girls, selected out of our Sunday-schools, and accurately taught, as are not found together in any chapel, cathedral, or music-room within the four seas. Besides, the spirit with which they all sing, and the beauty of many of them, so suits the melody, that I defy any to exceed it; except the singing of angels in our Father's house.

Sun. 20. At eight, and at one, the House was throughly filled. About three, I met between nine hundred and a thousand of the children belonging to our Sunday-schools. I never saw such a sight before. They were all exactly clean, as well as plain, in their apparel. All were serious and well-behaved. Many, both boys and girls, had as beautiful faces as, I believe, England or Europe can afford. When they all sung together, and none of them out of tune, the melody was beyond that of any theatre; and, what is best of all, many of them truly fear God, and some rejoice in his salvation. These are a pattern to all the town. Their usual diversion is to visit the poor that are sick (sometimes six, or eight, or ten together), to exhort, comfort, and pray with them. Frequently ten or more of them get together to sing and pray by themselves; sometimes thirty or forty; and are so earnestly engaged, alternately singing, praying, and crying, that they know not how to part. You children that hear this, why should not you go and do likewise? Is not God here as well as at Bolton? Let God arise and maintain his own cause, even 'out of the mouths of babes and sucklings'! . . .

Sunday, May 18 [Glasgow]. I preached at eleven on the parable of the Sower; at half-past two on Psalm 1. 23; and in the evening on, 'Now abideth faith, hope, love; these three.' I subjoined a short account of Methodism, particularly insisting on the circumstances—There is no other religious society under heaven which requires nothing of men in order to their admission into it, but a desire to save their souls. Look all round you, you cannot be admitted into the Church, or society of the Presbyterians, Anabaptists, Quakers, or any others, unless you hold the same opinions with them, and adhere to the same mode of worship.

The Methodists alone do not insist on your holding this or that opinion; but they think and let think. Neither do they impose any particular mode of worship; but you may continue to worship in your former manner, be it what it may. Now, I do not know any other religious society, either ancient or modern, wherein such liberty of conscience is now allowed, or has been allowed, since the age of the Apostles. Here is our glorying; and a glorying peculiar to us. What society shares it with us? . . .

Tuesday, June 10. We went through one of the pleasantest countries I ever saw, to Darlington. Before I left Newcastle, I was desired to read a strange account of a young woman, late of Darlington. But I told the person who brought it, 'I can form no judgment till I talk with Margaret Barlow herself.' This morning she came to me, and again in the afternoon; and I asked her abundance of questions. I was soon convinced, that she was not only sincere, but deep in grace; and therefore incapable of deceit. I was convinced, likewise, that she had frequent intercourse with a spirit that appeared in the form of an angel. I know not how to judge of the rest. Her account was: 'For above a year, I have seen this angel, whose face is exceeding beautiful; her raiment', so she speaks, 'white as snow, and glistering like silver; her voice unspeakably soft and musical. She tells me many things before they come to pass. She foretold, I should be ill at such a time, in such a manner, and well at such an hour; and it was so exactly. She has said, such a person shall die at such a time; and he did so. Above two months ago, she told me, your brother was dead (I did not know you had a brother); and that he was in heaven. And some time since she told me, you will die in less than a year. But what she has most earnestly and frequently told me, is, that God will in a short time be avenged of obstinate sinners, and will destroy them with fire from heaven.' Whether this will be so or no, I cannot tell; but when we were alone, there was a wonderful power in her words; and, as the Indian said to David Brainerd, 'They did good to my heart.'

It is above a year since this girl was first visited in this manner, being then between fourteen and fifteen years old. But she was then quite a womanish girl, and of unblamable behaviour.

Suppose that which appeared to her was really an angel; yet from the face, the voice, and the apparel, she might easily mistake him for a female; and this mistake is of little consequence.

Much good has already resulted from this odd event; and is likely to ensue; provided those who believe, and those who disbelieve, her report, have but patience with each other.

We had a love-feast in the evening, at which several spoke deep experience in a plain, artless manner; and many were greatly comforted, and stirred up more intensely to hunger and thirst after righteousness.

Wed. 11. About noon I preached at Stockton; but the House would not contain the congregation; nor indeed at Yarm, in the evening. Here I heard what was quite new to me, namely, that it is now the custom, in all *good* company, to give obscene healths, even though Clergymen be present; one of whom, lately refusing to drink such a health, was put out of the room; and one of the forwardest, in this *worthy* company, was a Bishop's steward ...

Sat. 28. I this day enter on my eighty-fifth year: And what cause have I to praise God, as for a thousand spiritual blessings, so for bodily blessings also! How little have I suffered yet by 'the rush of numerous years'! It is true, I am not so agile as I was in times past. I do not run or walk so fast as I did; my sight is a little decayed; my left eye is grown dim, and hardly serves me to read; I have daily some pain in the ball of my right eye, as also in my right temple (occasioned by a blow received some months since), and in my right shoulder and arm, which I impute partly to a sprain, and partly to the rheumatism. I find likewise some decay in my memory, with regard to names and things lately passed; but not at all with regard to what I have read or heard, twenty, forty, or sixty years ago; neither do I find any decay in my hearing, smell, taste, or appetite (though I want but a third part of the food I did once); nor do I feel any such thing as weariness, either in travelling or preaching: And I am not conscious of any decay in writing sermons; which I do as readily, and I believe as correctly, as ever.

To what cause can I impute this, that I am as I am? First,

doubtless, to the power of God, fitting me for the work to which I am called, as long as He pleases to continue me therein; and, next, subordinately to this, to the prayers of his children.

May we not impute it, as inferior means,

1. To my constant exercise and change of air?

2. To my never having lost a night's sleep, sick or well, at land or at sea, since I was born?

3. To my having sleep at command; so that whenever I feel myself almost worn out, I call it, and it comes, day or night?

4. To my having constantly, for above sixty years, risen at four in the morning?

5. To my constant preaching at five in the morning, for above fifty years?

6. To my having had so little pain in my life; and so little sorrow, or anxious care?

Even now, though I find pain daily in my eye, or temple, or arm; yet it is never violent, and seldom lasts many minutes at a time.

Whether or not this is sent to give me warning that I am shortly to quit this tabernacle, I do not know; but be it one way or the other, I have only to say,

> My remnant of days
> I spend to his praise
> Who died the whole world to redeem:
> Be they many or few,
> My days are his due,
> And they all are devoted to Him![73]

I preached in the morning on Psalm xc. 12; in the evening on Acts xiii. 40, 41; and endeavoured to improve the hours between to the best advantage.

Sun. 29. At eight I preached at Misterton, as usual; about one to a numerous congregation at Newby, near Haxey, and about four at my old stand in Epworth market-place, to the great congregation. Here there used to be a few mockers; but there were none now: All appeared serious as death, while I applied those solemn words, 'When the breath of man goeth forth,' &c. We concluded with a love-feast, at which many declared, with an excellent spirit, the wonderful works of God.

Mon. 30. About eight I preached in Scotter; and found it good to be there. About eleven I preached in Scowby, two miles from Brigg, to a very numerous and serious congregation. In the afternoon, going just by that curious building, Mr. Pelham's Mausoleum, I alighted, and took a view of it within and without. The like, I suppose, is not to be found in England. It is exactly round, fifty-two feet in diameter, and will be sixty-five feet high. The lower part contains, I believe, near a hundred places for the bodies of the Pelham family. (O what a comfort to the departed spirits, that their carcases shall rot above ground!) Over this is to be a chapel. It is computed the whole building will cost sixty thousand pounds . . .

Saturday, September 6 [Kingswood]. I walked over to Mr. Henderson's, at Hannam, and thence to Bristol. But my friends, more kind than wise, would scarce suffer it. It seemed so sad a thing to walk five or six miles! I am ashamed, that a Methodist Preacher, in tolerable health, should make any difficulty of this . . .

Monday, December 15. This week I dedicated to the reading over my brother's works. They are short poems on the Psalms, the four Gospels, and the Acts of the Apostles. Some are bad; some mean; some most excellently good: They give the true sense of Scripture, always in good English, generally in good verse; many of them are equal to most, if not to any, he ever wrote; but some still savour of that poisonous mysticism, with which we were both not a little tainted before we went to America. This gave a gloomy cast, first to his mind, and then to many of his verses: This made him frequently describe religion as a melancholy thing: This so often sounded in his ears, 'To the desert'; and strongly persuaded in favour of solitude . . .

Sunday, March 29, 1789. Came safe to Dublin quay.

I went straight up to the new Room. We had a numerous congregation, and as serious as if we had been at West-Street. I preached on the sickness and recovery of King Hezekiah and King George; and great was our rejoicing.[74] I really took knowledge of the change which God has wrought in this congregation within a few years. A great part of them were light and airy; now almost all appear as serious as death. *Monday, 30.* I began preaching at five in the morning; and the congregation, both then and the following mornings, was far larger in proportion than those at London. Meantime, I had letter upon letter concerning the Sunday service; but I could not give any answer till I had made a full inquiry both into the occasion and the effects of it. The occasion was this: About two years ago it was complained, that few of our society attended the church on Sunday; most of them either sitting at home, or going on Sunday morning to some Dissenting meeting. Hereby many of them were hurt, and inclined to separate from the Church. To prevent this, it was proposed to have service at the Room; which I consented to, on condition that they would attend St. Patrick's every first Sunday in the month. The effect was, 1. That they went no more to the meetings. 2. That three times more went to St. Patrick's (perhaps six times) in six or twelve months, than had done for ten or twenty years before. Observe! This is done not to *prepare for*, but to *prevent*, a separation from the Church . . .

April 12. (Being *Easter-Day*) We had a solemn assembly indeed; many hundred communicants in the morning; and in the afternoon far more hearers than our Room would contain; though it is now considerably enlarged. Afterwards I met the society, and explained to them at large the original design of the Methodists, viz., not to be a distinct party, but to stir up all parties, Christians or Heathens, to worship God in spirit and in truth; but the Church of England in particular; to which they belonged from the beginning. With this view, I have uniformly gone on for fifty years, never varying from the doctrine of the Church at all; nor from her discipline, of choice, but of necessity: So, in a course of years, necessity was laid upon me (as I have proved elsewhere), 1. To preach in the open air. 2. To pray extempore. 3. To form societies. 4. To accept of the assistance of Lay Preachers: And, in a few other instances, to use such means as occurred, to prevent or remove evils that we either felt or feared . . .

Sunday, July 12. About two we left Dublin, and hastened down to the ship; the Princess Royal, of Parkgate; the neatest and most elegant packet I ever saw. But the wind failing, we did not get out of the bay till about twelve. We had exceeding agreeable company; and I slept as well as if I had been in my own bed. *Monday,*

13. The sea being smooth, I shut myself up in my chaise, and read over the life of the famous Mr. George F——, one of the most extraordinary men (if we may call him a man) that has lived for many centuries. I never heard before of so cool, deliberate, relentless a murderer! And yet from the breaking of the rope at his execution, which gave him two hours of vehement prayer, there is room to hope he found mercy at last . . .[75]

Saturday, August 8 [London]. I settled all my temporal business, and, in particular, chose a new person to prepare the Arminian Magazine; being obliged, however unwillingly, to drop Mr. O[livers], for only these two reasons: 1. The errata are unsufferable; I have borne them for these twelve years, but can bear them no longer. 2. Several pieces are inserted without my knowledge, both in prose and verse. I must try whether these things cannot be amended for the short residue of my life . . .

Monday, December 28. I retired to Peckham; and at leisure hours read part of a very pretty trifle—the Life of Mrs. Bellamy. Surely never did any, since John Dryden, study more

> To make vice pleasing, and damnation shine,[76]

than this lively and elegant writer. She has a fine imagination; a strong understanding; an easy style, improved by much reading; a fine, benevolent temper; and every qualification that could consist with a total ignorance of God. But God was not in all her thoughts. Abundance of anecdotes she inserts, which may be true or false. One of them, concerning Mr. Garrick, is curious. She says, 'When he was taking ship for England, a lady presented him with a parcel, which she desired him not to open till he was at sea. When he did he found Wesley's Hymns, which he immediately threw overboard.' I cannot believe it. I think Mr. G. had more sense. He knew my brother well; and he knew him to be not only far superior in learning, but in poetry, to Mr. Thomson, and all his theatrical writers put together: None of them can equal him, either in strong, nervous sense, or purity and elegance of language. The musical compositions of his sons are not more excellent than the poetical ones of their father . . .

Monday, March 1, 1790. I left Brentford early in the morning, and in the evening preached at Newbury. The congregation was

large, and most of them attentive; but a few were wild as colts
untamed. We had none such at Bath the following evening, but all
were serious as death. Indeed, the work of God seems to flourish
here, deepening as well as widening. *Wednesday, 3.* I took a view of
the new buildings. There are at present none like them in England.
They have not only added a second Crescent, with two beautiful
rows of houses, near Ludstown, but a whole town on the other side
of the city, which is swiftly increasing every day.[77] And must all
these fine buildings be burned up? Yea,

> Earth and heaven destroy'd,
> Nor left even one in the mighty void! . . .[78]

Sunday, 14 [Bristol], was a comfortable day. In the morning I
met the Strangers' Society, instituted wholly for the relief, not of
our society, but for poor, sick, friendless strangers. I do not know
that I ever heard or read of such an institution till within a few
years ago. So this also is one of the fruits of Methodism . . .

Tuesday, June 8. I wrote a form for settling the preaching-houses,
without any superfluous words, which shall be used for the time to
come, verbatim, for all the Houses to which I contribute anything.
I will no more encourage that villanous tautology of lawyers,
which is the scandal of our nation. In the evening I preached to
the children of our Sunday-school; six or seven hundred of whom
were present. N.B. None of our masters or mistresses teach for pay:
They seek a reward that man cannot give . . .

Mon. 14. In the evening I preached to as many as the Town-Hall
would contain at Hartlepool. *Tuesday, 15.* I received a farther
account of Mrs. B., from two that had lived with her a year and a
quarter; and was thoroughly convinced, that she is a woman of
strong sense, and a lively imagination; but that she is given up to a
strong delusion (whether natural or diabolical I know not), to
believe a lie. One proof may suffice: Some time since, she told the
community, as from God, that the day of judgment would begin
that evening. But how could she come off when the event did not
answer? Easily enough. 'Moses', said she, 'could not see the face of
God, till he had fasted forty days and forty nights. We must all do
the same.' So for three weeks they took no sustenance, but three
gills of water per day; and three weeks more, they took each three

gills of water-gruel per day. What a mercy that half of them did not die in making the experiment!

Sunday, August 29 [Bristol]. Mr. Baddiley being gone to the north, and Mr. Collins being engaged elsewhere, I had none to assist in the service, and could not read the Prayers myself; so I was obliged to shorten the service, which brought the Prayers, sermon, and Lord's supper, within the compass of three hours. I preached in the afternoon near King's Square; and the hearts of the people bowed down before the Lord ... *Tuesday, 31.* William Kingston, the man born without arms, came to see me of his own accord. Some time since he received a clear sense of the favour of God; but after some months he was persuaded by some of his old companions to join in a favourite diversion, whereby he lost sight of God, and gave up all he had gained: But God now touched his heart again, and he is once more in earnest to save his soul. He is of a middling height and size, has a pleasing look and voice, and an easy, agreeable behaviour. At breakfast he shook off his shoes, which are made on purpose, took the tea-cup between his toes, and the toast with his other foot. He likewise writes a fair hand, and does most things with his feet which we do with our hands ...

Thursday, September 16 [London]. I was desired to see a monster properly speaking. He was as large as the largest lion in the tower; but covered with rough hair, of a brown colour; has the head of a swine, and feet like a mole. It is plain to me, it was begotten between a bear and a wild boar. He lives on fruit and bread, chiefly the latter. The keeper handles him as he pleases, putting his hand in his mouth, and taking hold of his tongue; but he has a horrible roar, between that of a lion and of a bull.

At the same time I saw a pelican. Is it not strange that we have no true account or picture of this bird? It is one of the most beautiful in nature; being indeed a large swan, almost twice as big as a tame one; snow-white and elegantly shaped. Only its neck is three quarters of a yard long, and capable of being so distended as to contain two gallons of liquid or solid. She builds her nest in some wood, not far from a river; from which she daily brings a quantity of fish to her young: This she carries in her neck (the only pouch which she has), and then divides it among her young; and hence is fabricated the idle tale of her feeding with her blood . . .

*   *   *

[The *Journal* ends abruptly on Sunday 24 October 1790. Wesley continued making entries in his Diary until a week before his death on Wednesday 2 March 1791.]

APPENDIX A

Mr. Wesley's Last Will and Testament

In the name of God, Amen.

I, JOHN WESLEY, Clerk, some time Fellow of Lincoln College, Oxford, revoking all others, appoint this to be my last Will and Testament.

I give all my books, now on sale, and the copies of them (only subject to a rent-charge of eighty-five pounds a year, to the widow and children of my brother), to my faithful friends, John Horton, Merchant; George Wolff, Merchant; and William Marriott, Stock-Broker, all of London, in trust, for the general Fund of the Methodist Conference, in carrying on the work of God, by Itinerant Preachers; on condition that they permit the following Committee, Thomas Coke, James Creighton, Peard Dickenson, Thomas Rankin, George Whitfield, and the London Assistant, for the time being, still to superintend the printing-press, and to employ Hannah Paramore and George Paramore, as heretofore; unless four of the Committee judge a change to be needful.

I give the books, furniture, and whatever else belongs to me in the three houses at Kingswood, in trust, to Thomas Coke, Alexander Mather, and Henry Moore, to be still employed in teaching and maintaining the children of poor Travelling Preachers.

I give to Thomas Coke, Doctor John Whitehead, and Henry Moore, all the books which are in my study and bed-chamber at London, and in my studies elsewhere, in trust, for the use of the Preachers who shall labour there from time to time.

I give the coins, and whatever else is found in the drawer of my bureau at London, to my dear grand-daughters, Mary and Jane Smith.

I give all my manuscripts to Thomas Coke, Doctor Whitehead, and Henry Moore, to be burned or published as they see good.

I give whatever money remains in my bureau and pockets, at

my decease, to be equally divided between Thomas Briscoe, William Collins, John Easton, and Isaac Brown.

I desire my gowns, cassocks, sashes, and bands, may remain in the chapel for the use of the Clergymen attending there.

I desire the London Assistant, for the time being, to divide the rest of my wearing apparel between those four of the Travelling Preachers that want it most; only my pelisse I give to the Rev. Mr. Creighton; my watch to my friend Joseph Bradford; my gold seal to Elizabeth Ritchie.

I give my chaise and horses to James Ward and Charles Wheeler, in trust, to be sold, and the money to be divided, one half to Hannah Abbott, and the other to the members of the select society.

Out of the first money which arises from the sale of books, I bequeath to my dear sister, Martha Hall (if alive), forty pounds; to Mr. Creighton aforesaid, forty pounds; and to the Rev. Mr. Heath, sixty pounds.

And whereas I am empowered, by a late Deed, to name the persons who are to preach in the new chapel, at London (the Clergymen for a continuance), and by another Deed, to name a Committee for appointing Preachers, in the new chapel, at Bath, I do hereby appoint John Richardson, Thomas Coke, James Creighton, Peard Dickenson, Clerks; Alexander Mather, William Thompson, Henry Moore, Andrew Blair, John Valton, Joseph Bradford, James Rogers, and William Myles, to preach in the new chapel at London and to be the Committee for appointing Preachers in the new chapel at Bath.

I likewise appoint Henry Brooke, Painter; Arthur Keene, Gent.; and William Whitestone, Stationer, all of Dublin, to receive the annuity of five pounds (English), left to Kingswood School, by the late Roger Shiel, Esq.

I give six pounds to be divided among the six poor men, named by the Assistant, who shall carry my body to the grave; for I particularly desire there may be no hearse, no coach, no escutcheon, no pomp, except the tears of them that loved me, and are following me to Abraham's bosom. I solemnly adjure my Executors, in the name of God, punctually to observe this.

Lastly, I give to each of those Travelling Preachers who shall remain in the Connexion six months after my decease, as a little token of my love, the eight volumes of sermons.

I appoint John Horton, George Wolff, and William Marriott, aforesaid, to be Executors of this my last Will and Testament; for which trouble they will receive no recompence till the resurrection of the just.

Witness my hand and seal, the 20th day of February, 1789.

JOHN WESLEY (Seal.)

Signed, sealed, and delivered, by the said Testator, as and for his last Will and Testament, in the presence of us,

　　WILLIAM CLULOW
　　ELIZABETH CLULOW

Should there be any part of my personal estate undisposed of by this my last Will, I give the same unto my two nieces, E. Ellison, and S. Collet, equally.

JOHN WESLEY

　　WILLIAM CLULOW
　　ELIZABETH CLULOW

Feb. 25, 1789

I give my types, printing-presses, and every thing pertaining thereto, to Mr. Thomas Rankin, and Mr. George Whitfield, in trust, for the use of the Conference.

JOHN WESLEY

APPENDIX B
Miss Sophia Hopkey

The section of the *Journal* recording Wesley's friendship with Sophia Hopkey was first published by Nehemiah Curnock in 1909 (*Journals*, Standard Edition, vol. I). From the tidy state of the MS, significantly prefaced by the words 'SNATCHED AS A BRAND OUT OF THE FIRE', Curnock surmised that Wesley drafted the final version two years later back in Oxford, possibly with the intention of showing it to his mother.

Wesley first met Sophia in Savannah on 13 March 1736. In the ensuing months he became her religious instructor, meeting her almost daily. That autumn she went to stay with friends in Frederica where Wesley visited her. Before leaving Savannah he called on her uncle to ask 'what commands he had to Miss Sophy'. Mr Causton replied, 'I give her up to you. Do what you will with her. Take her into your own hands. Promise her what you will. I will make it good.' In Frederica Wesley persuaded Sophia to return to Savannah rather than to leave the colony for England.

*   *   *

Monday, October 25. I asked Mr. Oglethorpe in what boat she should go. He said, 'She can go in none but yours, and indeed there is none so proper.' I saw the danger to myself, but yet had a good hope I should be delivered out of it, (1) because it was not my choice which brought me into it; (2) because I still felt in myself the same desire and design to live a single life; and (3) because I was persuaded should my desire and design be changed, yet her resolution to live single would continue.

We set out about noon. The afternoon, and so the greater part of the following days, we spent partly in using Bishop Patrick's *Prayers*, and partly in reading the first volume of Fleury's *History of the Church*, a book I chose for her sake chiefly, as setting before her such glorious examples of truth and patience, in the sufferings of those ancient worthies, 'who resisted unto blood, striving against sin'.

In the evening we landed on an uninhabited island, made a fire, supped, went to prayers together, and then spread our sail over us on four stakes, to keep off the night dews. Under this on one side were Miss Sophy, myself, and one of our boys who came with me from Savannah; on the other, our boat's crew. The north-east wind was high and piercingly cold, and it was the first night she had ever spent in such a lodging. But she complained of nothing, appearing as satisfied as if she had been warm upon a bed of down.

The next morning, as we crossed Doboy Sound, the wind being high and the sea rough, I asked her, 'Miss Sophy, are you not afraid to die?' She answered calmly, 'No, I don't desire to live any longer. Oh that God would let me go now! Then I should be at rest. In the world I expect nothing but misery.'

In the evening, the wind being contrary, we landed on the south end of St. Katherine's Island. And here we were obliged to stay till Friday; so that I had time to observe her behaviour more nearly. And the more I observed, the more I was amazed. Nothing was ever improper or ill-timed. All she said and did was equally tinctured with seriousness and sweetness. She was often in pain, which she could not hide; but it never betrayed her into impatience. She gave herself up to God, owning she suffered far less than she deserved.

Wed. 27. In the afternoon we fell into a conversation on 'Lying in order to do good.' She owned she used to think there was no harm in it, and that she had herself sometimes done it to me; but added, 'she was now convinced no lying was lawful, and would therefore watch against all kinds of it for the future'.

Thur. 28. In the afternoon, after walking some time, we sat down in a little thicket by the side of a spring. Here we entered upon a close conversation on Christian holiness. The openness with which she owned her ignorance of it, and the earnest desire she showed for fresh instruction, as it much endeared her to me, so it made me hope she would one day prove an eminent pattern of it.

Fri. 29. We ventured to set out, though the wind was very high. The waves dashed over the boat every moment, and the cold was extremely piercing. She showed no concern, nor made any complaint, but appeared quite cheerful and satisfied.

It was not without some difficulty that in the afternoon we

landed on St. Katherine's again. Observing in the night, the fire
we lay by burning bright, that Miss Sophy was broad awake, I
asked her, 'Miss Sophy, how far are you engaged to Mr. Melli-
champ?' She answered, 'I have promised him either to marry him
or to marry no one at all.' I said (which indeed was the expression
of a sudden wish, not of any formed design), 'Miss Sophy, I should
think myself happy if I was to spend my life with you.' She burst
out into tears and said, 'I am every way unhappy. I won't have
Tommy; for he is a bad man. And I can have none else.' She
added, 'Sir, you don't know the danger you are in. I beg you
would speak no word more on this head.' And after a while, 'When
others have spoken to me on the subject, I felt an aversion to them.
But I don't feel any to you. We may converse on other subjects as
freely as ever.' Both my judgment and will acquiesced in what she
said, and we ended our conversation with a psalm.

Sat 30. In the afternoon we landed on Bear Island, and walked
together for near two hours. Here again Miss Sophy expressed the
strongest uneasiness, and an utter aversion to living at Mr.
Causton's, saying, with many tears, 'I can't live in that house: I
can't bear the shocks I meet with there.' I said, 'Don't be uneasy,
Miss Sophy, on that account. If you don't care to be at Mr.
Causton's, you are welcome to a room in our house; or, which I
think would be best of all, and your aunt once proposed it, you
may live in the house with the Germans.' She made little reply . . .

*　　*　　*

Wesley then secured her uncle's agreement that she would not be
forced to meet anyone she did not wish to in his house, that her
ne'er-do-well suitor Mellichamps (Tommy) would not be mentioned and that she might spend her days at Wesley's house.

*　　*　　*

My desire and design still was to live single; but how long it would
continue I knew not. I therefore consulted my friends whether it
was not best to break off all intercourse with her immediately.
They expressed themselves so ambiguously that I understood them
to mean that I ought not to break it off. And accordingly she came
to me (as had been agreed) every morning and evening.

The time she was at my house was spent thus. Immediately after breakfast we all joined in Hickes's *Devotions*. She was then alone till eight. I taught her French between eight and nine, and at nine we joined in prayer again. She then read or wrote French till ten. In the evening I read to her and some others select parts of Ephrem Syrus, and afterwards Dean Young's and Mr. Reeve's *Sermons*. We always concluded with a psalm.

This I began with a single eye. But it was not long before I found it a task too hard for me to preserve the same intention with which I began, in such intimacy of conversation as ours was …

Thursday, February 3, 1737. I was now in a great strait. I still thought it best for me to live single. And this was still my design; but I felt the foundations of it shaken more and more every day. Insomuch that I again hinted at a desire of marriage, though I made no direct proposal. For indeed it was only a sudden thought, which had not the consent of my own mind. Yet I firmly believe, had she (Miss Sophy) closed with me at that time, my judgment would have made but a faint resistance. But she said, 'she thought it was best for clergymen not to be encumbered with worldly cares, and that it was best for her, too, to live single, and she was accordingly resolved never to marry'. I used no argument to induce her to alter her resolution.

Upon reflection, I thought this a very narrow escape; and after much consideration, I went to Mr. Töltschig, the pastor of the Moravians, and desired his advice, whether I had not best, while it was yet in my power, break off so dangerous an acquaintance. He asked, 'What do you think would be the consequence if you should?' I said, 'I fear her soul would be lost, being surrounded with dangers, and having no other person to warn her of and arm her against them.' He added, 'And what do you think would be the consequence if you should not break it off? I said, 'I fear I should marry her.' He replied short, 'I don't see why you should not.'

I went home amazed to the last degree; and it was now first that I had the least doubt whether it was best for me to marry or not, which I never before thought would bear a question. I immediately related what had occurred to Mr. Ingham and Dela-motte. They utterly disapproved of Mr. Töltschig's judgment, and in the evening went, as I desired they would, and talked largely with him and Antone (the Moravian Bishop Seifart) about it. It was midnight when I went to them; but even then they did not seem to be fully assured. Mr. Ingham still insisted I had not sufficient proof of her sincerity and religion, since the appearance of it might be owing partly to an excellent natural temper, partly to her desire of marrying me. I asked, 'How he could reconcile such a desire with what she had said on Thursday.' He said, 'Very well; she would soon recall those words, if I made a direct proposal.' He added that I could not judge coolly of these things while I saw her every day, and therefore advised me 'to go out of town for a few days'. I clearly saw the wisdom of this advice, and accordingly went to Irene the next day, four miles from Savannah. But first I writ two or three lines which I desired Miss Bovey to give Miss Sophy. They were, I think, in these words: '*Feb. 6.* I find, Miss Sophy, I can't take fire into my bosom, and not be burnt. I am therefore retiring for a while to desire the direction of God. Join with me, my friend, in fervent prayer, that He would show me what is best to be done.'

When I came to Irene, I did not care to ask counsel of God immediately, being 'a man of so unclean lips'. I therefore set aside *Monday the 7th* for self-examination; adding only that general prayer, whenever thoughts arose in my heart concerning the issue of things, 'Lord, Thou knowest! If it be best, let nothing be allowed to hinder; if not, let nothing be allowed to affect it.' And this exercise I continued for several hours with some measure of cheerfulness. But towards evening God hid His face, and I was troubled. My heart sank in me like a stone. I felt how bitter a thing it is for a spirit of an unbounded appetite to be left a prey to its own desires. But it was not long. For I no sooner stretched forth my hands to Heaven and bewailed my having departed from Him, than God sent me help from His holy place, and my soul received comfort.

Tue. 8. The next morning I was obliged to go down to Savannah. There I stayed about an hour; and there again I felt, and groaned under the weight of, an unholy desire. My heart was with Miss Sophy all the time. I longed to see her, were it but for a moment. And when I was called to take boat, it was as the sentence of death; but believing it was the call of God, I obeyed. I walked awhile to and fro on the edge of the water, heavy laden and pierced through with many sorrows. There One came to me and said, 'You are still in doubt what is best to be done. First, then, cry to God, that you may be wholly resigned, whatever shall appear to be His will.' I instantly cried to God for resignation. And I found that and peace together. I said, 'Sure it is a dream.' I was in a new world. The change was as from death to life. I went back to Irene wondering and rejoicing; but withal exceeding fearful, lest my want of thankfulness for this blessing, or of care to improve it, might occasion its being taken away.

I was now more clear in my judgement every day. Beside that I believed her resolve, never to marry, I was convinced it was not expedient for me, for two weighty reasons: (1) because it would probably obstruct the design of my coming into America, the going among the Indians; and (2) because I was not strong enough to bear the complicated temptations of a married state.

Sat. 12. Of this I informed my friends at my return to Savannah.

Mon. 14. About seven in the morning, I told her in my own garden, 'I am resolved, Miss Sophy, if I marry at all, not to do it till I have been among the Indians.'

Tues. 15. The next morning she told me, 'People wonder what I can do so long at your house; I am resolved not to breakfast with you any more. And I won't come to you any more alone.'

Wed. 16. She said, 'I don't think it signifies for me to learn French any longer.' But she added, 'My uncle and aunt, as well as I, will be glad of your coming to our house as often as you please.' I answered, 'You know, Miss Sophy, I don't love a crowd, and there is always one there.' She said, 'But we needn't be in it.' . . .

When, on *Thursday the 24th*, I mentioned to Miss Sophy that either Mr. Ingham or I must go to England, she fixed her eyes upon me all the time I spoke, changed colour several times, and then broke out 'What, are you going to England? Then I have no tie to America left.' Mrs. Causton said, 'Indeed I think I must go too. Phiky, will you go with me?' Miss Sophy answered, 'Yes, with all my heart.' Mrs. Causton added, 'Last night you said you would not.' She said, 'True; but now all the world is alike to me.'

Walking home with her from my house in the evening, I asked

her, 'Miss Sophy, what did you mean this afternoon by saying if I went to England, you had no tie to America left?' She answered with tears, 'You are the best friend I ever had in the world. You showed yourself a friend indeed at a time when no one else would have afforded me any more than common pity.' I said, 'You would hardly confess this if the Trustees should be set against me, and take away all I have here.' She replied with much earnestness, 'Indeed I would; and you or your friends can never want while I have anything.'

Calling at Mrs. Causton's (*Saturday 26th*), she was there alone. This was indeed an hour of trial. Her words, her eyes, her air, her every motion and gesture, were full of such a softness and sweetness! I know not what might have been the consequence had I then but touched her hand. And how I avoided it I know not. Surely God is over all!

Sun. 27. After all the company but Miss Sophy was gone, Mr. Delamotte went out and left us alone again. Finding her still the same, my resolution failed. At the end of a very serious conversation, I took her by the hand, and, perceiving she was not displeased, I was so utterly disarmed, that that hour I should have engaged myself for life, had it not been for the full persuasion I had of her entire sincerity, and in consequence of which I doubted not but she was resolved as she had said) 'never to marry while she lived'.

A moment's reflection when she was gone convinced me that I had done foolishly. And I once more resolved by God's help to be more wary for the future. Accordingly, though I saw her every day in the following week, I touched her not. Yet on Thursday evening (*March 3*), after we came from her, Mr. Delamotte was deeply concerned. I had never seen him in such uneasiness before. He said, with many tears, 'He found we must part, for he could not live in that house when I was married to Miss Sophy.' I told him, 'I had no intention to marry her.' He said, 'I did not know my own heart; but he saw clearly it would come to that very soon, unless I broke off all intercourse with her.' I told him, 'This was a point of great importance, and therefore not to be determined suddenly.' He said, 'I ought to determine as soon as possible; for I was losing ground daily.' I felt what he said to be true, and therefore easily consented to set aside the next day for that purpose.

Friday, March 4. Having both of us sought God by deep consideration, fasting and prayer, in the afternoon we conferred together, but could not come to any decision. We both apprehended Mr. Ingham's objection to be the strongest, the doubt whether she was what she appeared. But this doubt was too hard for us to solve. At length we agreed to appeal to the Searcher of hearts. I accordingly made three lots. In one was writ 'Marry'; in the second, 'Think not of it this year.' After we had prayed to God to 'give a perfect lot', Mr. Delamotte drew the third in which were these words, 'Think of it no more.' Instead of the agony I had reason to expect, I was enabled to say cheerfully, 'Thy will be done.' We cast lots again to know whether I ought to converse with her any more; and the direction I received from God was, 'Only in the presence of Mr. Delamotte.'

I saw and adored the goodness of God, though what He required of me was a costly sacrifice. It was indeed the giving up at once whatever this world affords of agreeable—not only honour, fortune, power (which indeed were nothing to me, who despised them as the clay in the streets), but all the truly desirable conveniences of life—a pleasant house, a delightful garden, on the brow of a hill at a small distance from the town; another house and garden in the town; and a third a few miles off, with a large tract of fruitful land adjoining to it. And above all, what to me made all things else vile and utterly beneath a thought, such a companion as I never expected to find again, should I live one thousand years twice told. So that I could not but cry out: *O Lord God, Thou God of my fathers, plenteous in mercy and truth, behold I give Thee, not thousands of rams or ten thousands of rivers of oil, but the desire of my eyes, the joy of my heart, the one thing upon earth which I longed for! O give me Wisdom, which sitteth by Thy throne, and reject me not from among Thy children! . . .*

*   *   *

For the next few days Wesley strove, not always successfully, to keep to his decision of not seeing Miss Sophy alone. Meanwhile on Tuesday 8 March Sophy engaged herself provisionally to Mr Williamson. Wesley 'full of perplexity' asked to see her.

Wed. 9. Mr. Williamson and she were together. She began with her usual sweetness, 'Why would you put yourself to the trouble of sending? What need of that ceremony between us? You know your company is always welcome to me.' Then silence ensued, which Mr. Williamson broke thus: 'I suppose, sir, you know what was agreed on last night between Miss Sophy and me.' I answered, 'I have heard something; but I could not believe it, unless I should hear it from Miss Sophy herself.' She replied, 'Sir, I have given Mr. Williamson my consent—unless you have anything to object.' It started into my mind, 'What if she means, unless you will marry me?' But I checked the thought with, 'Miss Sophy is so sincere: if she meant so, she would say so'; and replied, 'If you have given your consent, the time is past; I have nothing to object.' Mr. Williamson desired me, if I had, to speak, and then left her and me together. 'Tis hard to describe the complication of passions and tumult of thought which I then felt: fear of her approaching misery, and tender pity; grief for my own loss; love shooting through all the recesses of my soul, and sharpening every thought and passion. Underneath there was a faint desire to do and suffer the will of God, which, joined to a doubt whether that proposal would be accepted, was just strong enough to prevent my saying plainly (what I wonder to this hour I did not say), 'Miss Sophy will you marry me?' As soon as I could speak, I reminded her of her resolution, 'If she married at all, to marry none but a religious man,' and desired her to consider whether Mr. Williamson was such. She said, 'She had no proof to the contrary.' I told her, 'That was not enough. Before she staked so much upon it, she ought to have full, positive proof that he was religious.' She said again, 'I no otherwise consented, than if you had nothing to object.' Little more was said, tears in both supplying the place of words. More than an hour was spent thus. About two Mr. Williamson came again. I think it was just as he came she said, 'I hope I shall always have your friendship.' I answered, 'I can still be your friend, though I should not stay in America.' She said, 'But I hope you won't leave us.' I said, 'I can't at all judge how God will dispose of me.' She added, 'However, you will let me have your correspondence?' I replied, 'I doubt it cannot be.' I then exhorted them both to 'assist each other in serving God with all their strength'; and her in particular 'to remember the many instructions and advices I had given her'. I kissed them both, and took my leave of her as one I was to see no more.

I came home and went into my garden. I walked up and down, seeking rest but finding none. From the beginning of my life to this hour I had not known one such as this. God let loose my inordinate affection upon me, and the poison thereof drank up my spirit. I was as stupid as if half awake, and yet in the sharpest pain I ever felt. To see her no more: that thought was as the piercings of a sword; it was not to be borne, nor shaken off. I was weary of the world, of light, of life. Yet one way remained, to seek to God—a very present help in time of trouble. And I did seek after God, but I found Him not. I forsook Him before: now He forsook me. I could not pray. Then indeed the snares of death were about me; the pains of hell overtook me. Yet I struggled for life; and though I had neither words nor thoughts, I lifted up my eyes to the Prince that is highly exalted, and supplied the place of them as I could: and about four o'clock He so far took the cup from me that I drank so deeply of it no more . . .

*   *   *

On 12 March, a year after first meeting Wesley, Sophy hurriedly married Mr Williamson, without publishing the banns of marriage. After her marriage Wesley repeatedly taxed her with her 'insincerity' to him in the preceding months. Unsurprisingly Mr Williamson tried to dissuade her from seeing Wesley alone on the grounds that it upset her and made her too strict in religious observances. Wesley, on the other hand, had reason to believe that she had desisted from the fasting and prayers he deemed indispensable for admission to Holy Communion

*   *   *

Saturday, June 4. I related this to Mr. Delamotte, and at his instance consented still to admit her to the Holy Communion. But a new hindrance now occurred. She would not admit herself. Looking over the Register, I found she had absented herself five times in April and May only; and in this month, June, four times more, viz. the 11th, 12th, 24th and 29th. To clear up all difficulties at once, I determined to speak to her yet again . . .

Tues. 7. I writ to my sister Kezzy and made her an offer of living with me here. But upon reflection, I was in doubt whether I had done well, considering the slippery ground on which I stand. However, I leave the whole matter in God's hands. Let him order what is best!

*   *   *

In July Wesley both spoke and wrote to Mrs Williamson about 'what I dislike in your past and present behaviour'. The events which followed Wesley's refusal, on 7 August, to admit her to Communion are recorded in the main body of the published journal.

APPENDIX C
Sister Grace Murray

This account of John Wesley's relationship with Grace Murray is taken from J. A. Leger, *John Wesley's Last Love* (1910), in which a diary of John Wesley 'copied by an amanuensis' is reproduced. Grace Murray, converted in London whilst her master-mariner husband was at sea, became one of the band leaders at the Foundery in London. After her husband's death she became housekeeper of the Newcastle Orphan House where she at various times nursed both her suitors, the itinerant Methodist preachers, John Wesley and John Bennet.

*   *   *

What Thou dost, I know not now
but I shall know hereafter!

In June 1748, we had a Conference in London. Several of our Brethren then objected to the Thoughts upon Marriage, & in a full & friendly debate convinced me That a Believer might marry, without suffering Loss in his Soul.

In August following, I was taken ill at Newcastle. Grace Murray attended me continually. I observ'd her more narrowly than ever before, both as to her Temper, Sense, & Behaviour. I esteem'd & lov'd her more & more. And, when I was a little recover'd, I told her, sliding into it I know not how, 'If ever I marry, I think you will be ye Person.' After some time I spoke to her more directly. She seem'd utterly amaz'd, & said, 'This is too great a Blessing for me: I can't tell how to believe it. This is all I cou'd have wish'd for under Heaven, if I had dar'd to wish for it.'

From that time I convers'd wth her as my own. The Night before I left Newcastle, I told her, 'I am convinc'd God has call'd you to be my Fellow-labourer in ye Gospel. I will take you wth me to Ireland in Spring. Now we must part for a time. But, if we meet again, I trust we shall part no more.' She beg'd we might not part so soon, saying, 'It was more than she c^d bear.' Upon wch I took her wth me thro' Yorkshire & Derbyshire, where she was unspeakably usefull both to me & to ye Societies. I left her in Cheshire wth Jn. Bennett, & went on my way rejoicing.

Not long after I rec^d a Letter from J. B^t & another from Her. He desired my Consent to marry her. She said, 'She believ'd it was the Will of God.' Hence I date her Fall: Here was ye First False Step: wch GOD permitted indeed, but not approved. I was utterly amazed: But wrote a mild Answer to both, supposing they were married already. She replied in so affectionate a Manner, y^t I thought the whole Design was at an end.

John Bennet afterwards told me, That on ye very night after he had engag'd to G. M., just after he lay down in Bed, & before he had slept at all, he 'saw her sitting in deep Distress. Mr. W. came to her wth an Air of Tenderness, & said, 'I love thee as well as I did, on ye day when I took Thee first.' But she put him away from her wth her Hand. In ye Morn^g, instead of writing to me, He ask'd her, 'Is there not a Contract between you & Mr. W.?' Partly out of love to him, partly out of Fear of exposing me, she replied, 'There is not.' This was doubtless another False Step. He y^t standeth, let him take heed lest he fall!

She felt ye Effects of this all ye Winter, being under racking Uncertainty of Mind. When she rec^d a Letter from me, she resolv'd to live & die wth me, & wrote to me just what she felt. When she heard from him, her Affection for him reviv'd, & she wrote to him in the tenderest manner. In February particularly she sent him Word, 'That if he loved her He sh^d meet her at Sheffield: For she was sent for to Ireland: And if he did not come now, she c^d not answer for what might follow.'

One cannot excuse her Behaviour in all this time: Doubtless she sh^d have renounc'd One or ye Other. But those who know Human Nature will pity her much, at least as much as they will blame her.

J. B. determin'd to meet her at Sheffield. But, just as he was taking Horse, one brought him word, 'He must come away directly; for his Brother in law was dead.' So, G. M., seeing nothing of him, came on to Bristol. There I talk'd wth her at large. She told me what had past between her & J. B., & seem'd to think that Contract was binding. But she was quite convinc'd, It was not, when I reminded her of what had past before, between her and me: Adding y^t 'till now all this had seem'd to her as a Dream, nor c^d she possibly think, what I propos'd w^d ever come to pass: And y^t ye Difficulty was ye greater, because she c^d not consult wth any living Soul, for fear of betraying or displeasing me.'

We past several Months together in Ireland [18 April–20 July, 1749]. I saw the Work of God prosper in her Hands. She lightned my Burthen more than can be exprest. She examin'd all ye Women in ye smaller Societies & ye Believers in every Place. She settled all ye Women-Bands; visited ye Sick; pray'd wth ye Mourners; more & more of whom receiv'd remission of Sins, during her Conversation or Prayer. Mean time she was to me both a Servant & Friend, as well as a Fellow-labourer in ye Gospel. She provided everything I wanted. She told me with all Faithfulness & Freedom, if she thought anything amiss in my Behaviour. And (what I never saw in any other to this Day) she knew to reconcile ye utmost Plainness of Speech, wth such deep Esteem & Respect, as I often trembled at, not thinking it was due to any Creature: And to join wth ye most exquisite Modesty, a Tenderness not to be exprest.

The more we convers'd together, ye more I lov'd her; &, before I return'd from Ireland, we contracted by a Contract *de praesenti*: All this while she neither wrote to J. B. nor he to Her: So that ye Affair between *them* was as if it had never been.

We return'd together to Bristol. It was there, or at Kingswood, y^t she heard some idle Tales concerning me & Molly Francis. They were so plausibly related y^t she believ'd them: And in a sudden vehement Fit of Jealousy writ a loving Letter to J. B. Of this she told me the next day in great Agony of Mind: but it was too late. His Passion reviv'd: And he wrote her Word, 'He w^d meet her when she came into the North.'

[Sat. Aug. 12] We came to London. Talking wth an intimate Acquaintance there, she hinted at a distance, 'that Mr. W. loved her.' E. M^d replied, 'Sister M., never think of it. I know you thro'ly. It will never do. The People here w^d never suffer you. And your Spirit w^d not bear their Behaviour. You have not Humility enough, or Meekness, or Patience: You w^d be miserable all y^r Life. And that w^d make him miserable too. So y^t, instead of strengthening, you w^d weaken his Hands. If you love yourself, or if you love him, never think of it more.'

This sunk deep, and yᵉ more, because she durst not tell me of it. Soon after we set out for yᵉ North. [30 Aug.] At Epworth in Lancashire [Lincolnshire] J. B. met us. I was beginning to speak to him freely. But when he told me, 'She had sent him all my Letters': with several other Circumstances of yᵉ same kind, all wᶜʰ I then believ'd to be true, I stopt & said no more. I saw, if these things were so, he had yᵉ best right to her. So I thought it better to bear yᵉ blame, then to lessen his Affection for her. I judg'd it right, yᵗ they shᵈ marry without delay, & wrote her Word in yᵉ Morning, 'I thought it was not proper yᵗ she and I shᵈ converse any more together.'

She ran to me in an Agony of Tears, & beg'd me, 'not to talk so, unless I design'd to kill her.' She utter'd many other tender Expressions. I was distrest exceedingly. Before I was recover'd, J. B. came in. He claim'd her as his right. I was stunn'd & knew not what to say, still thinking, 'She loves him best. And why shᵈ I speak, to lay a ground of future uneasiness betwⁿ yᵐ?' Compassion likewise, and Love to her sway'd me much, observing she was sorrowful almost to Death; & fearing, 'If each insist on his Claim, it will be cutting her in sunder. She can never survive it: She will die in yᵉ Contest.' So I again determin'd to give her up.

In this purpose I went home. I felt no Anger, no murmuring, or repining; but deep Anguish of Spirit from a piercing Conviction of yᵉ irreparable Loss I had sustain'd. I had no design to converse with her any more. But about Two, one brought me word, 'S. Murray is exceeding ill: She is obliged to keep her Bed.' I then believ'd it right to visit her. When I came, she told me in terms, 'My Dear Sir, How can you possibly think I love any other better than you? I love you a thousand times better than ever I loved J. B. in my Life. But I know not what to do. I am afraid, if I don't marry him, he will run mad.' She shew'd me a Letter he had just sent her, wᶜʰ confirm'd that Fear. In the Evening he came himself. And then, he on one Side, & David Trathen on yᵉ other, continued urging her, (telling her, they wᵈ not go all Night unless they had an Answer) till at length she said, 'I *will* marry J. Bᵗ.'

The next Morning, She told me wᵗ had past. I was more perplext than ever. As I now knew she loved me, & as she was contracted to me before, I knew not whether I ought to let her go?

For several Days I was utterly unresolv'd: Till on Wedn. Septr 6, I put it home to herself, 'W^{ch} will you chuse?' and she declar'd again & again, 'I am determin'd by Conscience, as well as Inclination, To live & die wth *you*.' . . .

Friday, Septr 8, we set out for Berwick, visiting all ye intermediate Societies. Every hour gave me fresh proof of her Usefulness on ye one hand, & her Affection on ye other. Yet I c^d not consent to her repeated Request, To marry immediately. I told her 'before this c^d be done, it w^d be needful, 1. To satisfy J. B., 2. To procure my Brother's Consent, &, 3. To send an Acc^t of ye Reasons on wch I proceeded, to every Helper, & every Society in England, at the same time desiring their Prayers.' She said she sh^d not be willing to stay above a Year. I replied, 'Perhaps less time will suffice.' . . .

On Monday & Tuesday, [18–19 Sept., Newcastle] that I might be able to form a clearer Judgm^t of her real Character, I talk'd at large with all those who were disgusted at her, & inquir'd into their Reasons for it. I found none of them new, except Sister Lyddel's, 'That she had ye impudence to ride into ye Town wth Mr. W.' (wch was accidentally true; Mr. P. & Ja^s Kirshaw having rode away from us). Mr. Williams accus'd her 'Of not lending his Wife her Saddle' (being just going to take horse herself). Mrs. Williams, of buying a Holland Shift (wch was not true). Nancy & Peggy Watson, of buying a Joseph before she wanted it: Ann Mattison, of being proud & insolent: And Betty Graham, of buying an Apron worth ten Shillings' (wch indeed was not bought at all). I plainly perceiv'd Jealousy & Envy were ye real ground of most of these Accusations: And idle, senseless Prejudice, of ye rest. Offence taken, but not given. So that after all, her Character appear'd untouch'd, & for any thing they c^d prove, She had done all things well . . .

Thurs. 21. At her request, we renew'd the Contract made in Dublin. . . . An hour after I took horse for Whitehaven, leaving her to examine & settle ye Women-Bands in Allandale. She stood looking after me, till I was up ye Hill. I had not one uneasy Thought, believing God w^d give us to meet again, at ye time when he saw good.

Yet from ye time I came to Whitehaven, there was something hanging on my Mind, which I knew not how to explain . . .

As soon as I had finisht my Letter to J. B. on ye 7th [Sept.] Instant, I had sent a Copy of it to my Brother at Bristol. The Thought of my *marrying* at all, but especially of my marrying a *Servant*, & one so *low-born*, appear'd above measure shocking to him. Thence he infer'd, That it wou'd appear so to all Mankind: & consequently, that it w^d break up all our Societies, & put a stop to ye whole Work of GOD.

Full of this, instead of writing to me (who would have met him any where at ye first Summons) he hurried up from Bristol to Leeds. There he met with Robt Swindells, & Willm Shent; Who inform'd him (wch he had heard slightly mention'd before) 'That G. M. was engaged to J.B.' This was adding Oil to ye Flame: So he posted to Newcastle, taking wth him Willm Shent, not many degrees cooler than himself.

Here he met wth Jane Keith, a woman of strong Sense & exquisite Subtlety. She had long been prejudiced ag^st G. M., wch had broke out more than once. She gave him just such an Acc^t as he wish'd to hear, & at his Request, set it down in writing. The Sum of it was, '1. That Mr. W. was in love wth G. M. beyond all sense & reason: 2. That he had shewn this in ye most publick manner, & had avow'd it to all ye Society, and, 3. That all ye Town was in an uproar, & all ye Societies ready to fly in pieces.'

My Brother, believing all this, flew on for Whitehaven, concluding G. M. & I were there together. He reach'd it (with W. Shent) on Monday. I was not at all surpriz'd when I saw him. He urg'd, 'All our Preachers w^d leave us, all our Societies disperse, if I married so mean a woman.' He then objected, That she was engag'd to J. B. As I knew she was pre-engaged to me, as I regarded not her Birth, but her Qualifications, & as I believ'd those Consequences might be prevented, I c^d see no valid Objection yet. However I did not insist on my own Judgm^t; but desired ye whole might be prefer'd to Mr. Per^t wch he readily consented to.

As soon as I was alone, I began to consider with myself, Whether I was *in my Senses*, or no? Whether Love had *put out my Eyes* (as my Brother affirm'd) or I had ye use of y^m still? I weigh'd ye Steps I had taken, yet again, & ye grounds on wch I had proceeded. A short Acc^t of these I wrote down simply, in the following terms . . .

* * *

Here, Wesley reviews the reasons he used to have against marriage, which varied from the unlikelihood of finding 'such a Woman as my Father had' to convictions based upon his reading of Scripture, the Early Fathers, and mystical writers. These objections he overcame, but,

*   *   *

The two other Objections weigh'd with me still, Increase of Expence & Hindering ye Gospel. But wth regard to ye former, I now clearly perceive, That my Marriage w^d bring little Expence, if I married one I maintain now, who w^d afterw^d desire nothing more than she had before: And w^d chearfully consent, That our Children (if any) sh^d be wholly brought up at Kingswood.

As to ye latter, I have ye strongest Assurance, wch ye nature of the Thing will allow, y^t ye person proposed w^d not hinder, but exceedingly further me in ye Work of ye Gospel. For, from a close Observation of several Years (three of which she spent under my own roof) I am persuaded she is in every Capacity an Help meet for me.

First, As a Housekeeper, She has every qualification I desire. She understands all I want to have done. She is remarkably neat in person, in cloaths, in all things. She is nicely frugal, yet not sordid. She has much Common Sense: Contrives every thing for ye best; makes every thing go as far as it can go: Foresees what is wanting & provides it in time; does all things quick & yet without hurry: She is a good Workwoman; able to do ye finest, ready to do ye coarsest Work: Observes my Rules, when I am absent as well as when I am present: And takes care, that those about her observe y^m, yet seldom disobliges any of them.

As a Nurse, (which my poor, shatter'd infeebled Carcase now frequently stands in need of) She is careful to ye last degree, indefatigably patient, & inexpressibly tender. She is quick, cleanly, skilfull, & understands my Constitution better than most Physicians.

As a Companion, She has Good Sense, & some Knowledge both of books & men. She is of an engaging Behaviour, & of a mild, sprightly, chearful, & yet serious Temper.

As a Friend, She has been long tried & found faithfull. She watches over me both in Body & Soul; understanding all my Weaknesses, sympathizing with me & helpfull to me in all: Never ashamed, never afraid: Having a continual Presence of mind, in all Difficulties & Dangers: In all enabled to cover my head & strengthen my hands in GOD.

Lastly, as a Fellow Labourer in the Gospel of X^t (the light wherein my Wife is to be chiefly consider'd) She had in a measure wch I never found in any other both Grace & Gifts & Fruit. With regard to ye first; She is crucified to ye world, desiring nothing but GOD, dead to ye Desire of ye Flesh, ye Desire of ye Eye, ye Pride of Life: Exemplarily chast, modest, temperate; yet without any Affectation. She is teachable & reprovable; Gentle & longsuffering: Eminently compassionate, weeping with those that weep, bearing both my Burthens, those of ye Preachers, & those of ye People: Zealous of Good Works, longing to spend & be spent for ye Glory of GOD and ye Good of Men.

As to her Gifts, She has a clear Apprehension & a deep Knowledge of the things of GOD: A quick Discernment of Spirits, & no small Insight into ye Devices of Satan. She has been train'd up, more especially for these ten years, in ye word of truth: Having constantly attended both ye Morning & Evening Preaching, without despising ye Meanest of our Preachers. She is well acquainted with, & exercised in, our Method of leading Souls; having gone thro' all our little Offices, & discharg'd them all entirely well. She has a ready utterance, a Spirit of convincing as well as of persuasive Speech: A winning Address, an agreeable Carriage, in whatever Company she is engaged. By means of all which she is exceedingly beloved, almost wherever she comes, & is dear, in an uncommon degree, to great numbers of ye People.

And as to ye Fruits of her Labours, I never yet heard or read of any woman so own'd of GOD: So many have been convinc'd of Sin by her private Conversation: And so many have rec^d Remission of Sins in her Bands or Classes or under her Prayers. I particularly insist upon this. If ever I have a Wife, she ought to be the most usefull Woman in ye Kingdom: Not barely one, who probably *may* be so, (I c^d not be content to run such a hazard) but one that undeniably is so. Now, shew me ye Woman in England, Wales, or

Ireland, who has already done so much Good as G. M. I will say more. Shew me one in all ye English Annals, whom GOD has employ'd in so high degree? I might say, In all ye History of the Church, from ye Death of our Lord to this day. This is no Hyperbole, but plain, demonstrable fact. And, if it be, who is so proper to be my Wife?

I cannot doubt but such a person being constantly with me (for she is both willing & able to accompany me in all my Journeys. Another Circumstance which is absolutely necessary in such an Helper as I want) w^d be so far from being a Hindrance to my Work, y^t she w^d remove many Hindrances out of ye way. She w^d, in great measure, either prevent or remove, those bodily Weaknesses & Disorders, which now increase fast upon me. By caring for me, she w^d free me from a thousand cares, & enable me to serve GOD wth less Distraction. She is & w^d be a continual Defence (und^r GOD) agst unholy Desires & inordinate Affections: Which I never did entirely conquer, for six Months together, before my intercourse w^{ith} her. Now y^t 'tis 'κρεῖττον μᾶλλον γαμεῖν ἢ πυρουσ-θαι'[better to marry than to burn] is own'd. And Marriage being suppos'd, point out a properer Person.

But she w^d not only remove Hindrances. Such a Friend & Fellow-labour^r (I do not say probably w^d, but actually does) greatly assists & furthers me in my Work; inlivening my dull & dead Affections, composing & calming my hurried thoughts, sweetning my Spirits, wh^n I am rough & harsh, & convincing me of what is true, or persuading me to what is right, when perhaps no other cou'd. At ye same time, loosening my Soul from all below, & raising it up to GOD.

She w^d likewise remove many Hindrances from others, from Women in particular. She w^d guard many from inordinate Affection for me, to which they w^d be far less expos'd, both because they w^d have far less Hope of Success, & because I sh^d converse far more sparingly with y^m. Perhaps not in private with any Young Women at all; at least not wth any Member of our own Societies . . .

*   *   *

Wesley then examines other people's objections to his proposed marriage. He dismisses in turn the arguments that marrying his servant and travelling companion will cause scandalous conjecture as to their previous relationship, that her promise to John Bennet overrides all else, and that he has publicly stated his intention never to marry.

* * *

The next Morning [Tues., 26 Sept.] my Brother spoke more warmly, till I left him & W. Shent together. I came back about One, & found they had both taken horse some hours before. I had appointed to preach ye next night at Hineely hill. About Two I set out . . .

Hannah Broadwood (at whose House I left S[ister M[urray] met me at a little distance from it, & said, 'Mr. Charles left us two hours since, & carried S. M. behind him.' I said, 'The Lord gave, & ye Lord hath taken away! Blessed be ye name of ye Lord!' Soon after Ja^s Broadwood came in. He look'd at me, & burst into tears. I said, 'I must go on to Newcastle.' James said, 'No, I will go, & wth GOD's leave bring her back.' In a quarter of an hour, he took horse, & I calmly committed ye Cause to GOD! . . .

Thursday, ye 28, was a Day which I set apart for seeking GOD by Fasting & Prayer. John Brown & B. Hopper were with me. It was a day never to be forgotten. I was calm, tho' sad, looking for Help from Him only, to whom all things are possible. We had all free Access to ye Throne of Grace, & a sure Trust, That, 'GOD w^d do all things well.'

I now closely examin'd myself touching what was so confidently laid to my charge, viz. Inordinate affection. And this I clearly perceiv'd. That I had never before had so strong an Affection for any Person under Heaven. W^{ch} I c^d easily account for, by ye Concurrence of so many little Streams in one. Gratitude for Blessings of various kinds wch God had given me by Her, Esteem upon many Accounts, Regard for my own Health both of Soul & Body; & Desire of inlarging ye Work of GOD, all conspired wth a Conviction of her intire Love to me, to confirm & increase my Affection. But yet I cou'd not perceive it was inordinate by any of ye Marks wch use to attend such an Affection. For, 1. Inordinate affection leads from GOD. But this continually led me to him. 2. Inord. Affec.

makes us less desirous of doing ye Works of GOD, less zealous to pray, preach, or do Good in any kind. But this increas'd my Desire of doing Good in every kind, & my Zeal to do all ye Works of GOD. 3. Inord. Aff. makes us cold & dead, in preaching, praying, or any other Office of Religion. But this made me more alive in all: More Sensible of ye Power & Presence of GOD. 4. Inord. Aff. creates Jealousy tow^d Rivals & Resentment tow^d them that oppose it. But I never felt a Minute's Jealousy, even of J. B., nor a minute's Resentment tow^d those who tore her from me. 5. Inord. Aff. necessarily creates Uneasiness in the Absence of ye Object of it. Whereas I never was uneasy, neither *in* parting, nor *after* it; no more than if she had been a Common Person. For all these Reasons (& I might mention several more) I c^d not conceive, That mine was an Inord. Affec. Unless it was *such* an Inord. Affection, as never was before from ye beginning of the World.

I need add no more, then that if I had had more Regard for her I loved, than for ye Work of God, I sh^d now have gone strait to Newcastle, & not back to Whitehaven. I knew this was giving up all: But I knew GOD call'd: And therefore, on Frid. 29, set out.

In ye^e Evening [Sun., 1 Oct.] my Heaviness return'd but wth much of ye Spirit of Prayer. It seem'd to me, that I ought not to linger here; & yet I knew not whither to go: Till Mr. P. [Charles Perronet] ask'd, Will you go to Leeds on Tuesd.? Immediatly my mind was easy. I had sent notice of being there on Wedn. Evening, but it was gone out of my thoughts. I determin'd to go. Only I was concern'd, to leave Whitehaven without a Preacher.

We then pour'd out our Hearts before GOD. And I was led, I know not how to ask, That if he saw good, he w^d shew me what w^d be ye end of these things, in dreams or visions of ye night. I dream'd I saw a Man bring out G. M., who told her, she was condemn'd to die: And that all things were now in readiness, for the Execution of that Sentence. She spoke not one word, nor shew'd any Reluctance, but walk'd up wth him to ye place. The Sentence was executed, without her stirring either hand or foot. I look'd at her, till I saw her face turn black. Then I c^d not bear it, but went away. But I return'd quickly, & desir'd she might be cut down. She was then laid upon a bed. I sat by mourning over her. She came to herself & began to speak, & I awaked . . .

Tuesday 3rd, we rode to Old-hutton, & ab^t 9 the next night reach'd Leeds. Here I found, not my Brother, but Mr. Whitefield. I lay down by him on ye bed. He told me, 'My Brother w^d not come, till J. B. & G. M. were married.' I was troubled. He perceived it. He wept & pray'd over me. But I c^d not shed a Tear. He said all that was in his power to comfort me: But it was in vain. He told me, 'It was his Judgm^t y^t she was MY Wife, & that he had said so to J. B.: That he w^d fain have persuad^d them to wait, & not to marry till they had seen me: But that my Brother's Impetuosity prevail'd & bore down all before it.'

I felt no murmuring thought, but deep Distress. I accepted ye just Punishm^t of my manifold Unfaithfulness & Unfruitfulness, & therefore c^d not complain. But I felt ye Loss both to me & ye People, wch I did not expect c^d ever be repair'd. I tried to sleep: but I tried in vain; for Sleep was fled from my Eyes. I was in a burning Fever, & more & more Thoughts still crouding into my Mind, I perceiv'd, if this continued long, it w^d affect my Senses. But GOD took that matter into his Hand; giving me on a sudden, sound & quiet sleep.

Thurs. 5. about 8. One came in from Newcastle, & told us, 'They were married on Tuesday'. My brother came an hour after. I felt no Anger. Yet I did not desire to see him. But Mr. Wh[itefield] constrain'd me. After a few Words had past, He accosted me with, 'I renounce all intercourse with you, but what I w^d have wth an heathen man or a publican'. I felt little Emotion. It was only adding a drop of water to a drowning man.

*   *   *

When Wesley subsequently discovered the deception and emotional blackmail that his brother had practised by delivering to Grace Murray a letter in which John was purported to have renounced her, he commented sadly, 'She must have been more than Human, if this Letter deliver'd with such Circumstances, had not wrought ye desir'd Effect'.

NOTES

1. Wesley's opposition to the slave trade probably provoked the animosity and allegations of the slave-trader and settler from Georgia.

2. The letter was to Richard Morgan, a Dublin lawyer, whose son, William, had been a founding member of the Holy Club and had initiated the group's practical Christian work in the community. His illness and disturbed mental state prior to his death that August had given rise to the rumour that fanatical 'methodist asceticism' had caused his death. William's father was wholly satisfied by this letter and, as a proof of his confidence, sent his only surviving son, Richard, to Lincoln as Wesley's pupil. Richard's initial aspirations of leading the worldly life of a gentleman-commoner made him resentful of Wesley's over-solicitous spiritual supervision. Slowly he was 'overborne' by Wesley and became a member of the Holy Club.

3. Trio.

4. The Revd Joseph Hoole of Haxey, near Epworth.

5. John Clayton, fellow of Brasenose, whose efforts to restore sacramental worship at the heart of Anglicanism won Wesley's respect.

6. Those who do more than is commanded.

7. Ingham was an undergraduate at Queen's College when he first met John Wesley in 1733. He adopted the Methodist pattern of living and, after his ordination in 1735, sailed to Georgia with the Wesley brothers. He returned home in 1737 to find further recruits for Georgia. Like Wesley, Ingham had become interested in the Moravians and together they visited their headquarters at Herrnhutt. Ingham then worked as a Moravian missionary in England, concentrating his activities in Yorkshire, Lancashire, and the midlands. In 1741 Ingham married Lady Margaret Hastings, sister of the Countess of Huntingdon (see n. 41 below). In 1742 Ingham transferred the societies he had established to the Moravians, for whom he worked for the next twelve years. Becoming dissatisfied with their arrogance Ingham and his eighty-odd societies separated themselves in 1754. An attempt to amalgamate with the Methodists came to nothing and his congregations retained an independent existence acknowledging Ingham as their leader. Ingham's adoption, in 1760, of Sandemanian views (see n. 33 below) led to schism amongst his followers, many of whom seceded to join other sects, chiefly the Methodists.

8. The Indians' descriptive phrase for priests.

9. For the events leading up to this see Appendix A.

10. Re-reading this account at a later date Wesley qualified several remarks, and against this statement wrote 'I am not sure of this'.

11. Out-of-the-way house.

12. Count Zinzendorf (1700–60) founded two settlements which formed the administrative centre for the Moravian Brethren. Wesley had already been much impressed by the primitive Christian discipline and the faith of the Moravian missionaries he had encountered and he had translated some of the hymns which played so large a part in their liturgical life. For the substance of Wesley's subsequent doctrinal disagreement with the Moravians see *Journal* entry for 31 December 1739.

13. Beau Nash, dandy and gambler. He had become the master of ceremonies and arbiter of fashion in Bath, which had recently achieved a new prominence as a fashionable resort.

14. Philip Henry Molther was currently the leading Moravian in Britain. His quietist teaching has unsettled some and convinced other members of the London religious societies that they did not as yet have true faith.

15. For an explanation of 'justification' see n. 35 below.

16. Jakob Boehme (1575–1624) claimed to write only what he had learned by Divine illumination. His mystical writings had achieved a wider audience in England through the work of William Law, a former inspiration to, friend, and defender of Wesley. Wesley's ultimate rejection of mysticism stemmed from his distrust of the individualism and quietism it fostered in contradistinction to the life of Christian discipline and responsibility for others that Wesley taught.

17. Madame Guyon (1648–1717), the French Quietist, taught a complete spiritual abandonment to God which included an indifference to personal salvation.

18. *De Officiis* (On Duties), Cicero's last work, written in 44 BC, taught a socially concerned ethic.

19. A sect founded by David Culey (d. 1725?). Culey joined a fellowship of itinerant evangelists preaching in Northamptonshire, Bedfordshire, Huntingdonshire, and Cambridgeshire in 1691. By 1693 he had become leader of a separate congregation at Guyhirm which survived accusations levelled at him for unorthodoxy and sexual misconduct. 'Culimite' became a pejorative used to describe all dissenters in this area. Two congregations of Culimites survived until the mid-1840s.

20. John Wesley, *An Earnest Appeal to Men of Reason and Religion* (1743).

21. The court of Chancery, under the Lord High Chancellor, dealt with matters of equity, providing redress for grievances which had no remedy in the courts of common law. The excessive technicalities and the number of lawyers its working required had made it a by-word for the law's delay.

22. From a poem by John Wesley's older brother, Samuel.

23. The Pretender had proclaimed his father king at Derby.

24. Daniel Neal, *The History of the Puritans* (4 vols., 1732–8).

25. *A Short View of the Difference between the Moravian brethren . . . and . . . John and Charles Wesley*, revised edn. (1741).

26. Westley Hall (1711–76) had been Wesley's pupil at Lincoln College, Oxford and was ordained priest preparatory to accompanying Wesley to Georgia. At the last moment he withdrew, preferring that his relations should obtain him a living in England. In 1734 Wesley's older sister, Martha, had been secretly engaged to Hall, who, on a subsequent visit to Epworth Rectory, transferred his affections to Kezia, the youngest of Wesley's sisters, and was accepted by the family as her suitor. Thereupon Martha declared their former engagement and Hall threw over Kezia, who, according to Wesley, never recovered from this blow, and married Martha. In 1739 Hall, together with his wife and mother-in-law, joined Wesley in London and became an active member of Wesley's Methodist society. From entering the dispute with the Moravians on Wesley's side, Hall, by 1742, had become a Moravian and attempted to sabotage the London-based Methodist organization during the absence of the Wesley brothers. In 1743 Hall seceded from the Church of England and quarrelled with the Wesleys, including his wife, for not doing likewise. He next became a deist preacher. In 1750 and 1751 he created disturbances at Charles Wesley's prayer meetings in Bristol. Alienated from his family, Hall went on to preach polygamy and emigrated to the West Indies, accompanied by a mistress. When she died, Hall returned to England. The *Journal* entry for 2 January 1776 shows Wesley hoping that at the last Hall had made his peace with God.

27. A story taken from the *Turkish Tales*, retold by Steele in *The Guardian*, no. 148, 31 Aug. 1718. A hermit of one hundred years old was asked to save the life of the King's daughter. The Devil, seizing his chance, inflamed the old man with lust. The Devil promised the hermit that no one would believe the Princess's tale of seduction, but she became pregnant. Acting again on the Devil's suggestion, the hermit mur-

dered her, but the Devil disclosed his deed. As the hermit was about to be hanged the Devil promised him his life in exchange for his soul. When the hermit submitted the Devil instantly left him to his fate, spitting in the hermit's face and declaring his triumph over goodness, thus proving that the Devil takes an especial delight in the fall of a good man and that the Devil's promises are not to be trusted.

28. Howell Harris (1714–73), the Welsh Calvinist preacher, had spent only one term at Oxford. Harris led the evangelical revival in Wales and in 1752 founded a community, known as the 'family' at his home in Trevecca.

29. Sir James Lowther, 4th Baronet, (c.1673–1755), was MP for Carlisle (1694–1755) and a very wealthy local landowner with a reputation for miserliness. In September 1749 he had quelled anti-Methodist rioting in his capacity as magistrate for Whitehaven and it was perhaps this act that led Wesley to pay the dying man a pastoral visit.

30. Jonathan Edwards (1703–58), the American Calvinist whose preaching had played a leading part in the American revival in the 1740s. He had been a Congregationalist minister until his wish to exclude all the unconverted from the Communion led to his removal in 1749.

31. To be valid, gifts to public charities had to be made in the form of a deed at least twelve months before the donor's death.

32. Isaac Watts (1674–1748), an Independent minister and author of the immensely popular *Divine and Moral Songs*.

33. Robert Sandeman (1718–71) became the leader of a sect in England of which his father-in-law, John Glas (1697–1773) had been the Scottish founder. Glas had doubted the Scriptural basis for a national church. It is likely that Wesley is referring to the sect's practices, such as celebrating the Agapé with broth, or members washing one another's feet, rather than their views on the relation between state and church.

34. On 14 March 1757 Admiral Byng had been shot after a court martial had found him guilty of gross negligence in his defence of Minorca against the French.

35. John Newton (1725–1807), or 'the old African blasphemer' as he described himself, had worked on slave-trading ships. Converted during a storm at sea, he had taken a job ashore in 1755. He responded enthusiastically to Whitefield's teaching. Almost entirely self-taught, he had been refused ordination by the Archbishop of York in 1758. In 1764 he was ordained under Evangelical patronage and attained fame in his subsequent ministry at Olney, where William Cowper was one of his parishioners.

36. A French smuggler, whom the French King had licensed to lead a raid on the Irish coast.

37. Thomas Arne's *Judith*, first performed in 1761.

38. This letter provides an interesting summary of Wesley's doctrinal differences with the Calvinists. The Calvinist tenets of Particular Election and Final Perseverance claimed that all men were fore-ordained to salvation or damnation and that those who had been predestined to salvation would finally achieve this whatever their apparent lapses on earth, in accordance with the promise of John 10: 28, 'And I give unto them eternal life; and they shall never perish, neither shall any man pluck them out of my hand'. Wesley's position was based upon the Arminian premise that salvation was open to all, not merely the elect, and depended upon man's grasping hold of the Justification promised by God. God had pronounced man 'just' or righteous by virtue of Christ's atoning sacrifice. To rely upon Particular Election or Final Perseverance seemed to Wesley to limit the value of Christ's sacrifice and to diminish man's moral responsibi-lity to produce those good works which were a proof of Justification. Wesley saw life after conversion as a period of probation in which, whilst total backsliding remained a possibility, one might aim at the goal of Perfection or entire Sanctification. If Sanctification implied the renewal of man to God's likeness by the continuous action of the Holy Ghost, Perfection, as taught by Wesley, seemed to Calvinists and even some Arminians too positive an interpretation of biblical promises. Final victory or perseverance might be assured, but Perfec-tion could only remain an aim never to be achieved, even by a Christian, on an earth permanently vitiated by the Fall. The doc-trinal consistency claimed in this letter is more fully expounded in Wesley's book of the following year, *A Plain Account of Christian Perfection as Believed and Taught by the Rev. Mr. John Wesley from the Year 1725 to 1765* (Bristol 1766).

39. From a poem by John Wesley's older brother, Samuel.

40. William Mompesson had been instrumental in the imprisonment of a vagrant carrying a forged pass as a military drummer and further-more impounded the man's drum until such time as he should prove himself entitled to it. Soon Mompesson's house was visited by a poltergeist whose presence was signalled by a drumming noise. The imprisoned drummer was said to have obtained his revenge by means of witchcraft. Wesley's interest in such phenomena dated from his schooldays when the family home had been visited by Old Jeffery. Wesley recounted the activities of both poltergeists in the *Arminian Magazine* in 1784 and 1785, basing the Tedworth story upon the

'Narrative of the Demon of Tedworth' found in Joseph Glanvill, *Saducismus Triumphatus* (1688). Wesley's acceptance of such manifestations prompted Hogarth's cartoon, 'Credulity, Superstition, and Fanaticism: A Medley' in which a column beside the pulpit is formed of a thermometer resting on a base of Wesley's *Sermons* on top of Glanvill's *Witches* and topped by the figure of the Tedworth Drummer.

41. Selina Hastings, Countess of Huntingdon (1707–91), was a member of the first Methodist society in Fetter Lane. She subsequently made Whitefield her chaplain, and, after an attempt to heal the breach between him and the Wesleys, espoused his cause. By exercising her right as a peeress to appoint chaplains she protected many Anglican clergy suspected of Methodism, but after a court case in 1779 her chapels had to be registered as dissenting places of worship and those chaplains without benefices were forced to take the oath of allegiance as dissenting ministers. Her seminary at Trevecca for the training of ministers either for the Church of England or for other Protestant denominations had been opened the previous year by Whitefield.

42. From a poem by John Wesley's father.

43. George Cheyne (1671–1743), a physician whose most popular works were *The Essay of Health and Long Life* (1724), highly praised by Samuel Johnson, and *The Natural Method of Curing the Diseases of The Body, and the Disorders of the Mind* (1742). Since at one stage in his life he weighed thirty-two stone it is perhaps not surprising that he advocated a 'moderate diet' of milk and vegetables.

44. From a hymn by Charles Wesley.

45. William Augustus, Duke of Cumberland (1721–65), third son of George II, was popularly known as 'butcher Cumberland' for his ruthless efficiency in stamping out the clan system in the Scottish Highlands after the defeat of Charles Edward Stuart in 1745. From 1748 he lived when in England chiefly at Windsor where he took a great interest in improving the park. Although he resigned his role as military leader in 1757 there is little evidence to support Wesley's pious speculations as to his new religious interests.

46. By Laurence Sterne, published in 1768.

47. This brief vignette of Adam Oldham's household grown wealthy through zealous pursuit of his feltmaking business is the type of case-history appealed to by those who claim that Methodism encouraged those virtues which enabled its followers to rise to the middle classes.

48. Henry Home, Lord Kames (1696–1782), was a Scottish judge who wrote philosophical as well as legal treatises. The *Essays* to which

Wesley alludes were intended to combat Hume's views but attracted an unsuccessful charge of heresy.

49. These Welsh Calvinistic Methodists received their nickname from the practice Wesley describes of 'leaping for joy' at their meetings.

50. An unacknowledged abridgement of Samuel Johnson's pamphlet, *Taxation no Tyranny* (1775).

51. Augustus Toplady (1740–78) was an ultra-Calvinist who never missed an opportunity for a polemical onslaught on Wesley. *An Old Fox Feathered and Tarred* was one of the most virulent attacks provoked by Wesley's political pamphlet.

52. Richard Price (1723–71) was a nonconformist minister who wrote on moral, economic, and political questions. He wrote three papers concerned with demographical calculations.

53. Henry Hoare, owner of Stourhead House, Wiltshire, sought to model his gardens upon the Claudian landscapes found amongst his extensive picture collection. Henry Flitcroft was employed to reproduce a Pantheon of Claudian proportions to be seen across the lake. Lord Weymouth's property, Longleat, and the Duke of Somerset's home were both to be found within six miles of Stourhead.

54. Probably a reference to Lord Dartmouth, an Evangelical peer, described by William Cowper as 'one who wears a coronet and prays', who was Secretary of State for the Colonies from 1772 to 1775.

55. Probably Raphael's.

56. Vicesimus Knox, *Essays Moral and Literary* (1778).

57. By Henry Home. See n. 43 above.

58. John Toland (1670–1722), the deist philosopher. *Nazarenus* (1718) was a speculative work on ecclesiastical history.

59. John Hawkesworth (1715?–73). In 1773 *An Account of the Voyages undertaken by order of his present Majesty for making Discoveries in the Southern Hemisphere* ... (3 vols.) appeared and was much criticized for its refusal to attribute any of the escapes from danger it recorded 'to the particular interposition of providence'.

60. See *Journal* entry for 20 July 1736.

61. By an American painter of great contemporary popularity, Benjamin West (1738–1820).

62. A horse-drawn canal boat.

63. Pasquale de Paoli (1725–1807), the Corsican patriot, was exiled with his father in 1739. He returned to Corsica and in 1755 became Commander in Chief of the forces attempting to repel the Genoese.

In 1768 the Genoese sold Corsica to the French and in 1769, after the defeat of his forces, Paoli escaped to England. With the French Revolution Paoli became Governor of Corsica, but subsequently organized an insurrection against the French in favour of a union between Corsica and England. He returned to England again in 1796.

64. James Macpherson (1736–90) had produced *Fingal, an ancient epic poem in six books* (1762), purporting to be the translation of a Gaelic poet named Ossian. Samuel Johnson and others had challenged the authenticity of this work and Macpherson had been forced to fabricate his sources. *Fingal* and a subsequent epic, *Temora* (1763), appear to have been a liberal translation of traditional Gaelic poems smattered with Macpherson's own contributions. Hugh Blair published a defence of the authenticity of these poems.

65. Behind these three bare entries concerning the embarkation of Methodist missionaries to America lies a decision of great significance for the future of the Methodist movement. Wesley had come to the conclusion, partly because of the pressure of contemporary circumstances and partly from theological conviction, that he was entitled as a 'presbyter' to ordain ministers. He therefore ordained Thomas Coke as a 'superintendent' and Richard Whatcoat and Thomas Vasey to act as elders licensed to baptize and administer the Sacraments in America. The number of Methodists in America was fast increasing and they often found themselves without access to an ordained minister who could administer the Sacraments. Moreover, since the War of Independence had ended in 1783, the Church of England in America, discredited by its loyalist allegiance, no longer exerted the paramount claims which the Wesley brothers had always insisted upon to their English followers. Wesley's reading led him to believe that he would be following the practice of the Early Church in assuming that presbyters were equally entitled with bishops to the right of ordination. Unfortunately, although Wesley had the aid of another presbyter in the ceremony of the laying on of hands, he had, as was his wont, acted on his own judgement and authority in a matter which effectively challenged the entire nature and structure of the Church of England. Furthermore, it was not precisely clear what he had created in declaring Coke a 'superintendent', an order unknown to Anglicanism, and Coke assumed himself to have been made a bishop, promptly arrogating to himself episcopal authority on his arrival in America. Despite his own frequently declared continuing allegiance to the Church of which he was an ordained minister, Wesley had by this act and the subsequent ordination of twenty-five other ministers, chosen a path which was bound to lead to the

separation of his organization from that of the Established Church in England.

66. Wesley was clearly charmed by Paoli's ability to respond to his own classical allusion (with which he was obviously much taken, see *Journal* entry for 19 Feb. 1784). Hannibal took refuge at the Bithynian court, but the King agreed to hand him over to the Romans so that Hannibal was obliged to commit suicide to escape their vengeance.

67. From a hymn by Charles Wesley.

68. A misquotation from Pope's *Elegy; To the Memory of an Unfortunate Lady*, l. 73.

69. For Wesley's forceful quelling of this potential rebellion see Introduction, p. xxiv.

70. Adapted from Milton's *Paradise Lost*, iv, l. 143.

71. See n. 15 above.

72. The comment probably refers to William Hamilton's painting reproduced on the cover of this book.

73. From a hymn by Charles Wesley.

74. In November 1788 George III had suffered an attack of violent insanity and political warfare had broken out between those, like Pitt, who enjoyed George III's patronage and those, led by Fox, who urged that full powers be given to the dissolute Prince of Wales as Regent. On 19 February 1789 the King recovered his sanity and on 10 March resumed his authority.

75. Wesley's interest in the execution of this notorious Anglo-Irish nobleman, George Robert Fitzgerald, sprang partly from the fact of his mother, Lady Mary Hervey, being a staunch Methodist. Curnock suggests, in his edition of the *Journal*, that Wesley would have deleted the lengthy account of Fitzgerald's vindictive violence and treacherous murders (19 May 1789) had he edited the last extract from the *Journals* before its publication.

76. From a poem by John Wesley's father.

77. Presumably a reference to Lansdown Crescent, constructed between 1788 and 1793.

78. Adapted from lines by Young, *The Last Day*, Book I, ll. 67–8.

INDEX OF MAJOR NAMES

This selective index contains major place names and the names of persons who receive more than one entry or are otherwise noteworthy. Places outside mainland Britain are subsumed under an entry for the relevant country.